**Association for
Computing Machinery**

Advancing Computing as a Science & Profession

UIST'15

Adjunct Publication of the 28th Annual ACM Symposium on

User Interface Software and Technology

Sponsored by:

ACM SIGCHI & ACM SIGGRAPH

Supported by:

AutoDesk, Microsoft, Synaptics, FXPal, SMART Technologies, UNC Charlotte, Adobe, Google, NVIDA, WaCom

**Association for
Computing Machinery**

Advancing Computing as a Science & Profession

ISBN: 978-1-4503-3780-9 (Digital)

ISBN: 978-1-4503-4105-9 (Print)

Additional copies may be ordered prepaid from:

ACM Order Department
PO Box 30777
New York, NY 10087-0777, USA

Phone: 1-800-342-6626 (USA and Canada)
+1-212-626-0500 (Global)
Fax: +1-212-944-1318
E-mail: acmhelp@acm.org
Hours of Operation: 8:30 am – 4:30 pm ET

Printed in the USA

Chairs' Welcome

We are very excited to welcome you to the 28th Annual ACM Symposium on User Interface Software and Technology (UIST), held from November 8-11th 2015, in Charlotte, North Carolina, USA.

UIST is the premier forum for the presentation of research innovations in the software and technology of human-computer interfaces. Sponsored by ACM's special interest groups on computer-human interaction (SIGCHI) and computer graphics (SIGGRAPH), UIST brings together researchers and practitioners from diverse areas including graphical & web user interfaces, tangible & ubiquitous computing, virtual & augmented reality, multimedia, new input & output devices, fabrication, wearable computing and CSCW.

UIST 2015 received 297 technical paper submissions. After a thorough review process, the 39-member program committee accepted 70 papers (23.6%). Each anonymous submission that entered the full review process was first reviewed by three external reviewers, and a meta-review was provided by a program committee member. If, after these four reviews, the submission was deemed to pass a rebuttal threshold, we asked the authors to submit a short rebuttal addressing the reviewers' concerns. A second member of the program committee was then asked to examine the paper, rebuttal, and reviews, and to provide their own meta-review. The program committee met in person in Berkeley, California, USA on June 25th and 26th, 2015, to select which papers to invite for the program. Submissions were accepted only after the authors provided a final revision addressing the committee's comments.

In addition to papers, our program includes two papers from the ACM Transactions on Computer-Human Interaction journal (TOCHI), as well as 22 posters, 45 demonstrations, and 8 student presentations in the eleventh annual Doctoral Symposium. Our program also features the seventh annual Student Innovation Contest. Teams from all over the world will compete in this year's contest, which focuses on blurring the lines between art and engineering and creating tools for robotic storytelling. UIST 2015 will feature two keynote presentations. The opening keynote will be given by Ramesh Raskar (MIT Media Lab) on extreme computational imaging. Blaise Aguera Y Arcas from Google will deliver the closing keynote on machine intelligence.

We welcome you to Charlotte, a city full of southern hospitality. We hope that you will find the technical program interesting and thought-provoking. We also hope that UIST 2015 will provide you with enjoyable opportunities to engage with fellow researchers from both industry and academia, from institutions around the world.

Celine Latulipe	**Bjoern Hartmann**	**Tovi Grossman**
UIST '15 General Chair	UIST '15 Program Co-Chair	UIST '15 Program Co-Chair
UNC Charlotte, USA	*UC Berkeley, USA*	*Autodesk Research, Canada*

Table of Contents

Doctoral Symposium

Demonstrations

Posters

Trygve Cossette *(RATH Workshop)*, Dilrukshi Gamage *(University of Moratuwa)*,
Angela Richmond-Fuller *(University of Reading)*, Ryo Suzuki *(University of Colorado, Boulder)*,
Jeerel Herrejón *(UNAM)*, Kevin Le *(University of California, Santa Cruz)*,
Claudia Flores-Saviaga *(Carnegie Mellon University)*, Haritha Thilakarathne *(Rajarata University)*,
Kajal Gupta *(JSS Academy Of Technical Education)*, William Dai *(Troy High School)*,
Ankita Sastry *(SAP Labs India)*, Shirish Goyal *(Interaktiviti)*, Thejan Rajapakshe *(Rajarata University)*,
Niki Abolhassani *(University of Western Ontario)*, Angela Xie *(University of Texas Austin)*,
Abigail Reyes *(University of California, Santa Cruz)*, Surabhi Ingle *(Vellore Institute of Technology)*,
Verónica Jaramillo, Martin Godínez, Walter Ángel, Carlos Toxtli, Juan Flores *(UNAM)*,
Asmita Gupta *(Fidelity Investments)*, Vineet Sethia *(Sardar Vallabhbhai National Institute of Technology)*,
Diana Padilla *(UNAM)*, Kristy Milland *(Ryerson University)*, Kristiono Setyadi *(The Jakarta Post Digital)*,
Nuwan Wajirasena *(University of Moratuwa)*, Muthitha Batagoda *(Middlesex University)*,
Rolando Cruz *(San Marin High School)*, James Damon *(Harvard-Smithsonian Center for Astrophysics)*,
Divya Nekkanti *(Notre Dame High School)*, Tejas Sarma *(Mumbai University)*,
Mohamed Saleh *(Independent researcher)*, Gabriela Gongora-Svartzman *(Stevens Institute of Technology)*,
Soroosh Bateni *(University of Texas at Dallas)*, Gema Toledo Barrera *(UNAM)*,
Alex Peña *(Abraham Lincoln High School)*, Ryan Compton *(University of California Santa Cruz)*,
Deen Aariff *(University of Texas at Austin)*, Luis Palacios *(The GovLab, New York University)*,
Manuela Paula Ritter *(University of Osnabrück)*, Nisha K.K. *(Intuit India)*,
Alan Kay *(Sardar Vallabhbhai National Institute of Technology)*, Jana Uhrmeister *(University of Copenhagen)*,
Srivalli Nistala *(Independent Researcher)*, Milad Esfahani *(IUT)*,
Elsa Bakiu, Christopher Diemert *(Pentland Firth Software GmbH)*, Luca Matsumoto *(Adrian Wilcox High School)*,
Manik Singh *(Thapar University, Patiala)*, Krupa Patel *(Milpitas High School)*,
Ranjay Krishna, Geza Kovacs *(Stanford University)*, Rajan Vaish *(University of California Santa Cruz)*,
Michael Bernstein *(Stanford University)*

UIST 2015 Symposium Organization

General Chair: Celine Latulipe *(UNC Charlotte, USA)*

Program Chairs: Bjoern Hartmann *(UC Berkeley, USA)*
Tovi Grossman *(Autodesk Research, Canada)*

Sponsorship Chair: Jeff Nichols *(Google, USA)*

Demos Chairs: Chris Harrison *(Carnegie Mellon University, USA)*
Nicolai Marquardt *(University College London, UK)*

Posters Chairs: Daniel Vogel *(University of Waterloo, Canada)*
Juho Kim *(Massachusetts Institute of Technology, USA)*

Local Arrangements Chair: David Wilson *(UNC Charlotte, USA)*

Doctoral Symposium Chair: Patrick Baudisch *(Hasso Plattner Institut, Germany)*

Doctoral Symposium Panelists: Eric Paulos *(UC Berkeley, USA)*
Dan Ashbrook *(Rochester Institute of Technology, USA)*

Student Innovation Contest Chairs: Valkyrie Savage *(UC Berkeley, USA)*
Stefanie Mueller *(Hasso Plattner Institut, Germany)*

Video Previews Chairs: Stéphan Huot *(Inria, France)*
Justin Matejka *(Autodesk Research, Canada)*

Registration Chairs: Siddharth Khullar *(Quanttus, Inc., USA)*
Jessica Cauchard *(Stanford, USA)*

Keynotes Chair: Aaron Quigley *(University of St. Andrews, Scotland)*

Proceedings Chair: Joe Tullio *(Google, USA)*

Publicity Chair: Sean Follmer *(Stanford University, USA)*

Lasting Impact Award Chair: Ken Hinckley *(Microsoft Research, USA)*

Student Volunteer Chairs: Christian Rendl *(University of Applied Sciences, Upper Austria)*
Berto Gonzalez *(UNC Charlotte, USA)*

Web and Social Media Chair: Stephen MacNeil *(UNC Charlotte, USA)*

UIST 2015 Reviewers

Fadel Adib	Amy Bruckman	Richard Davis	Elena Glassman
Daniel Afergan	Duncan Brumby	Alexander De Luca	Michael Glueck
Maneesh Agrawala	Leah Buechley	Luigi De Russis	Mayank Goel
Salman Ahmad	Erin Buehler	Cagatay Demiralp	Alix Goguey
Tanja Aitamurto	Andreas Bulling	Tony DeRose	Jorge Goncalves
Marc Alexa	Margaret Burnett	Anind Dey	Raphael Grasset
Jason Alexander	Varun Perumal C	Nicholas Diakopoulos	Erin Griffiths
Daniel Aliaga	Michael Cafarella	Paul Dietz	Cindy Grimm
M. Ercan Altinsoy	Tim Campbell	Morgan Dixon	Mark Gross
Saleema Amershi	Robert Capra	Mira Dontcheva	Jens Grubert
Christoph Amma	Baptiste Caramiaux	Julie Dorsey	Anselm Grundhöfer
Erik Andersen	Sheelagh Carpendale	Steven Dow	Tiago Guerreiro
Fraser Anderson	Scott Carter	Pierre Dragicevic	François Guimbretière
Michelle Annett	Jessica Cauchard	George Drettakis	Sumit Gulwani
Caroline Appert	Daniel Cernea	Steven Drucker	Philip Guo
Bruno Araujo	Liwei Chan	Ruofei Du	Sidhant Gupta
Ferran Argelaguet Sanz	Remco Chang	Andrew Duchowski	Cathal Gurrin
Ahmed Arif	Kerry Chang	Cody Dunne	Carl Gutwin
Rosa Arriaga	Olivier Chapuis	Lucy Dunne	Martin Hachet
Chieko Asakawa	Siddhartha Chaudhuri	Darren Edge	Michael Haller
Ignacio Avellino	Hsiang-Ting Chen	Serge Egelman	Raffay Hamid
Shiri Azenkot	Nicholas Chen	David Engel	Mark Hancock
Seok-Hyung Bae	Ke-Yu Chen	Barrett Ens	Sudheendra Hangal
Nilanjan Banerjee	Xiang 'Anthony' Chen	Anna Feit	Vicki Hanson
Nikola Banovic	Lung-Pan Cheng	Denzil Ferreira	Kotaro Hara
Scott Bateman	Justin Cheng	Rebecca Fiebrink	John Hardy
Olivier Bau	Fanny Chevalier	Leah Findlater	Chris Harrison
Jared Bauer	Pei-Yu Chi	Danyel Fisher	Eiji Hayashi
Derek Bean	Francesco Chinello	George Fitzmaurice	Vincent Hayward
Hrvoje Benko	Eun Kyoung Choe	David Flatla	Brent Hecht
Anastasia Bezerianos	Seungmoon Choi	Cédric Fleury	Jeffrey Heer
Xiaojun Bi	David Chu	James Fogarty	Florian Heller
Bernd Bickel	Jason Chuang	Angus Forbes	Niels Henze
Mark Billinghurst	Haeyong Chung	Clifton Forlines	Aaron Hertzmann
Renaud Blanch	Andy Cockburn	Adam Fourney	Keita Higuchi
Kellogg Booth	Daniel Cohen-Or	Dustin Freeman	Otmar Hilliges
Cati Boulanger	Gabe Cohn	Wai-Tat Fu	Ken Hinckley
Doug Bowman	Christopher Collins	Hongbo Fu	Matthew Hirsch
Andrew Bragdon	Matthew Cooper	Susan Fussell	Steve Hodges
Joel Brandt	Cory Cornelius	Roberto García	Guy Hoffman
Anke Brock	Stelian Coros	Steffen Gauglitz	Kenneth Holmqvist
Eric Brockmeyer	James Coughlan	Sven Gehring	Christian Holz
Christopher Brooks	Mary Czerwinski	Hans Gellersen	Sungsoo (Ray) Hong
Carrie Bruce	Florian Daiber	Elizabeth Gerber	Michael Horn

Kasper Hornbæk
Takayuki Hoshi
Steven Houben
Gary Hsieh
Jeff Huang
Matt Huenerfauth
Stephane Huot
Masahiko Inami
Shamsi Iqbal
Pourang Irani
Yoshio Ishiguro
Poika Isokoski
Ali Israr
Shahram Izadi
Jennifer Jacobs
Mads Møller Jensen
Brett Jones
Michael Jones
Joaquim Jorge
Ricardo Jota
Wendy Ju
Antti Jylhä
Sanjay Kairam
Adam Kalai
Karrie Karahalios
Abhijit Karnik
Kasun Karunanayaka
Shunichi Kasahara
Jun Kato
Keiko Katsuragawa
Yoshihiro Kawahara
Matthew Kay
Brian Keegan
Mohammadreza
Khalilbeigi
Azam Khan
Wolf Kienzle
Johan Kildal
Jin Ryong Kim
Vladimir Kim
Juho Kim
Aniket Kittur
Kiyoshi Kiyokawa
Predrag Klasnja
Clemens Klokmose
Andrew Ko
Nicolas Kokkalis

Adriana Kovashka
Sven Kratz
Per Ola Kristensson
Kyriakos Kritikos
Antonio Krüger
Todd Kulesza
Chinmay Kulkarni
Raja Kushalnagar
Richard Ladner
Benjamin Lafreniere
Anthony LaMarca
Cliff Lampe
Joel Lanir
Edward Lank
Edward Lank
Eric Larson
Walter Lasecki
Celine Latulipe
Manfred Lau
Joseph LaViola Jr.
Edith Law
Seungyon "Claire" Lee
Geehyuk Lee
Bongshin Lee
Sylvain Lefebvre
Darren Leigh
Daniel Leithinger
Catherine Letondal
Yin Li
Wilmot Li
Rong-Hao Liang
Henry Lieberman
Can Liu
Zhicheng Liu
Pedro Lopes
Hao Lu
Kris Luyten
Kent Lyons
Scott MacKenzie
Steven Maesen
Andrew Maimone
Carmel Majidi
Sylvain Malacria
Alexander Mariakakis
Gloria Mark
Anders Markussen
Nicolai Marquardt

Diego Martinez Plasencia
Toshiyuki Masui
Justin Matejka
Nolwenn Maudet
James McCann
Kathleen Mccoy
James McCrae
Daniel McDuff
Mark McGill
David McGookin
Michael McGuffin
Paul Merrell
Jussi Mikkonen
Andrew Miller
Robert Miller
Jun Mitani
Niloy Mitra
Karyn Moffatt
David Molyneaux
Andres Monroy-
Hernandez
Neema Moraveji
Carlos Morimoto
Dan Morris
Tomer Moscovich
Philippa Mothersill
Stefanie Mueller
Adiyan Mujibiya
Jörg Müller
Sean Munson
Roderick Murray-Smith
Brad Myers
Miguel Nacenta
Lennart Nacke
Mathieu Nancel
Abhishek Narula
Vidhya Navalpakkam
Matei Negulescu
Mark Newman
David Nguyen
Jeffrey Nichols
Ryuma Niiyama
Peter O'Donovan
Ian Oakley
Yoichi Ochiai
Ohan Oda
Simon Olberding

Patrick Olivier
Alex Olwal
Stephen Oney
Jifei Ou
Antti Oulasvirta
Joseph Paradiso
Pablo Paredes
Sylvain Paris
Matt Parker
Fabio Paternò
Sameer Patil
Fabrizio Pece
Thomas Pederson
Simon Perrault
Simon Peter
Ken Pfeuffer
Emmanuel Pietriga
Thomas Pietrzak
Matthew Pike
Henning Pohl
Ivan Poupyrev
Bodhi Priyantha
Halley Profita
Zhan Fan Quek
Alexander Quinn
Pernilla Qvarfordt
Kari-Jouko Räihä
Raf Ramakers
Gonzalo Ramos
Jussi Rantala
Adrian Reetz
Derek Reilly
Jun Rekimoto
Karen Renaud
Christian Rendl
Paul Resnick
Matthew Reynolds
Christoph Rhemann
Kathryn Ringland
Michael Rohs
Anne Roudaut
Thijs Roumen
Nicolas Roussel
Steve Rubin
Jaime Ruiz
Enrico Rukzio
Jeffrey Rzeszotarski

Daniel Saakes
Niloufar Salehi
Alanson Sample
Munehiko Sato
Arvind Satyanarayan
Valkyrie Savage
Florian Schaub
Bernt Schiele
Chris Schmandt
Albrecht Schmidt
Dominik Schmidt
Ryan Schmidt
Johannes Schöning
m.c. schraefel
James Scott
Stacey Scott
Kent Seamons
Hartmut Seichter
Marcos Serrano
Vidya Setlur
Orit Shaer
Ariel Shamir
Corey Shemelya
Roy Shilkrot
Hiroyuki Shinoda
Mike Sinclair
Brian Smith
Jeffrey Snyder
Rajinder Sodhi
Timothy Sohn
Erin Solovey
Hyunyoung Song
Caleb Southern
Daniel Spelmezan
Robert St. Amant
Frank Steinicke
Sophie Stellmach
Daniel Strazzulla
Wolfgang Stuerzlinger
Mengu Sukan
Aurélien Tabard
Ana Tajadura-Jiménez
Justin Talbot
Jerry Talton
Jiaqi Tan
Hong Tan
Hao Tang
Craig Tashman
Michael Terry
Bruce Thomas
Feng Tian
Christian Tominski
Long Tran-Thanh
Khai Truong
Theophanis Tsandilas
Nobuyuki Umetani
Rajan Vaish
Kristof Van Laerhoven
Jean Vanderdonckt
Marynel Vázquez
Eduardo Veas
Gina Venolia
Jo Vermeulen
Roel Vertegaal
Nicolas Villar
Stephen Voida
Chat Wacharamanotham
Julie Wagner
James Wallace
Wei Wang
Jingtao Wang
Christian Weichel
Daryl Weir
Sean White
Emily Whiting
Mary Whitton
Wesley Willett
Joseph Williams
Michele Williams
Julie Williamson
John Williamson
Karl Willis
Graham Wilson
Raphael Wimmer
Holger Winnemoeller
Jacob Wobbrock
Katrin Wolf
Krist Wongsuphasawat
Woontack Woo
Robert Xiao
Anbang Xu
Ying-Qing Xu
Ruigang Yang
Jishuo Yang
Xing-Dong Yang
Lining Yao
Yi-Ting Yeh
Tom Yeh
Sai-Kit Yeung
James Young
Chen-Hsiang Yu
Neng-Hao Yu
Yisong Yue
Thorsten Zander
Pei Zhang
Haimo Zhang
Nan Zhao
Jian Zhao
Shengdong Zhao
Amit Zoran

UIST 2015 Sponsors & Supporters

UIST 2015 gratefully acknowledges our sponsoring SIGs and the support of the following organizations:

Sponsors

Platinum Supporters

Gold Supporters

Silver Supporters

Bronze Supporters

Adobe

Google

NVIDIA.

wacom

Responsive Facilitation of Experiential Learning Through Access to Attentional State

Scott W. Greenwald
MIT Media Lab
Cambridge, MA, USA
scottgwald@media.mit.edu

ABSTRACT

The planned thesis presents a vision of the future of learning, where learners explore environments, physical and virtual, in a curiosity-driven or intrinsically motivated way, and receive contextual information from a companion facilitator or teacher. Learners are instrumented with sensors that convey their cognitive and attentional state to the companion, who can then accurately judge what is interesting or relevant, and when is a good moment to jump in. I provide a broad definition of the possible types of sensor input as well as the modalities of intervention, and then present a specific proof-of-concept system that uses gaze behavior as a means of communication between the learner and a human companion.

ACM Classification Keywords

H.5.1 Information Interfaces and Presentation (e.g., HCI): Multimedia Information Systems—*artificial, augmented, and virtual realities*; K.3.1 Computers and Education: Computer Uses in Education—*collaborative learning, distance learning*; H.4.3 Information Systems Applications: Communications Applications; H.5.3: Group and Organization Interfaces—*computer-supported cooperative work, synchronous interaction.*

Author Keywords

Experiential Learning; Eye Gaze Interaction; Contextual Information; Remote Collaboration

INTRODUCTION

I consider wearable systems that allow a learner to be remotely accompanied by a facilitator or teacher, that is aware of both what she is attending to and what her level of engagement with that object is. The companion is able to view the environment in such a way that he can direct the attention of the learner to new objects that she is not currently aware of or attending to. The concept is both to mimic and to go beyond the learning experience of being guided through a new environment by an expert, who provides relevant information along the way – as one might be guided through a jungle and warned of various dangerous plants or animals along the way. Consider the fact that it is not always obvious when someone is confused or losing focus, especially when they seek to make an impression of intelligence or prowess. That is, an in-person guide has indirect and incomplete knowledge of the learner's attentional state. In contrast, a remote "wearable companion," with access to sensor-based attentional state data that is able to create a better experience by seeing and reacting to this more direct and complete information source. In this way the learning process can be accelerated by giving the expert companion access to sensor-based information on the learner's attentional and cognitive state.

This paper is structured as follows: First I provide a specific definition of the class of interactions to be considered, and pose corresponding research questions. Then a section on background and related work introduces three relevant bodies of work in HCI. Next I present prior work with a prototype system, TagAlong, including results from formative trials. The following section presents a preliminary list of design dimensions for the systems in question. Finally, I discuss ongoing and future work on a version of TagAlong with eye gaze interaction that will form the core of my thesis.

LEARNING INTERACTION AND RESEARCH QUESTIONS

The basic learning interaction I propose, which will be referred to as *experiential learning with a remote companion*, is one where the learner explores an environment in such a way that the focus of his attention is shifted through his own volition, and the companion facilitator provides information or feedback that is relevant to the current focus. The companion has access to data on the internal and external state of the learner, which helps her to judge what input to provide, and at what point in time. I propose the following research questions that pertain to systems that facilitate experiential learning with a remote companion:

I. How can giving the companion facilitator access to the internal context (attentional state) of the learner improve the learning interaction?

II. What is the right amount and kind of environmental and internal contextual information for a companion facilitator, given that viewing large amounts of data carries an attentional burden?

UIST '15 Adjunct, November 08-11, 2015, Charlotte, NC, USA
ACM 978-1-4503-3780-9/15/11.
http://dx.doi.org/10.1145/2815585.2815586

This concept and its corresponding research questions are informed and inspired by trials related to mobile telepresence, learning, and collaboration that will be described in the section *Prototype System and Preliminary Results*.

BACKGROUND AND RELATED WORK

I build on prior work in the areas of learning companions, telepresence, and interruptibility. Learning companions and work on interruptibility can inform the design of ideal learner interactions, while work on telepresence can help us to understand how to design companion interactions with the remote environment. These areas are described below, along with their implications for responsive facilitation of experiential learning through access to attentional state.

Learning Companions

The concept of an automatic "learning companion" was made popular by two 2001 publications [8, 9], which suggested that there might be measurable phases of learning that necessarily involve positive and negative affect, as well as constructing knowledge and eliminating misconceptions. The vision was a system that would continuously respond by intervening in a way that was tailored to the learner's momentary affective state. I observe that efforts to quantify the *affective* state of a learner in learning-companion research efforts generally require a great amount of structure and specificity within the learning activity. To first order, this is incommensurable with a learning environment where the learner controls the focus of attention. That is, from a practical standpoint, in an experiential learning setting, we cannot know enough about the learning activity to make detailed inferences about affective state. I propose trading off precision for generality by incorporating sensors whose data can be intuitively interpreted by a human companion. Gaze tracking, for instance, can help the companion identify the focus of attention without the system needing to possess semantic knowledge about what that object is. In this way, the planned thesis builds on the idea of quantifying the attentional state of the learner and incorporating it into an instructional feedback loop. In contrast, however, a human teacher is incorporated into that loop as well.

Interruption

Addressing the question of when and how tasks can be interrupted without disruption, there is a substantial body of work in HCI which looks in particular at computer-based tasks with a known structure [3]. It shows that the disruptiveness of an interruption depends on both the particular place one is at in the primary task as well as the relevance of the interrupting information to the current task [4, 11]. While it is currently not feasible to predict the structure of a learners explorations in-the-wild in the same way as, e.g., multi-part data entry tasks, these results on interruptibility give us insight into the kinds of cognitive boundaries a companion facilitator should ultimately accommodate. The ideal system would characterize the learner's cognitive state and provide assistance to the facilitator in choosing wisely when to interrupt.

Telepresence

Next we seek insight into the question of how to give the remote companion effective awareness and capabilities for expression in the remote environment. I'll give several examples of prior work that highlight different perspectives on telepresence. *Telepresence* tends to refer to interaction using systems that involve physical actuators, e.g. acting as robotic limbs for a remote person [12, 2, 7]. Telerobotic surgery, first commercialized around 2000, was designed to be a superior instrument for laproscopic surgery for a surgeon on site with the patient. It offered the advantage that the robot could hold both the camera and the surgical instruments more steadily than a human. The fact that the surgeon could be remote was incidental. Similarly it was then noted that telementoring was a trivial extension of the technology – giving the ability of a remote expert or *mentor* to comment but not intervene. Steve Mann's Telepointer [10] took telepresence mobile with a self-contained device that would stream video to a remote party, and allow that remote party to point at objects, mediated by a laser pointer in the Telepointer device. The TeleAdvisor [6] extends this concept by give the remote party not just a laser dot but a full-color projected image with which to give feedback to the user of the system. Finally the ShowMe system [1] uses a head-mounted camera and display-based system to immerse the remote user, and capture his hand-gestures. These gestures are then projected back into the visual field of the primary user as a form of guidance.

These examples illustrate that telepresence can be used to convey various kinds of information. Although any of them could be used for experiential learning with a remote companion, I'll focus on a technique that is well-adapted to the conveyance of spatial and factual information. The ShowMe approach of displaying annotations using a head-mounted display is advantageous over something like TeleAdvisor, since it eliminates a physical calibration problem (providing a consistent projection when the projector or object may move) by shifting it to a computational one – where computer vision and graphics hardware may be employed to provide apparent stabilization of annotations on a video stream.

PROTOTYPE SYSTEM AND PRELIMINARY RESULTS

I describe the TagAlong system and formative trials we performed with it, and then summarize the results that are most relevant to experiential learning with a remote companion, as well as the future work proposed in the sections that follow.

TagAlong System

The goal of the TagAlong system was to create a collaborative system for situated learning that could be worn continuously and with minimal burden to its wearer. This system should be truly mobile to enable us to do trials in the wild. As there are always performance tradeoffs related to bandwidth, latency, battery life, and so on, we would compare the fully mobile system to some less flexible alternatives in controlled settings.

The TagAlong system is a mobile context-sharing system that runs on Google Glass and a mobile phone or tablet. The user can send still images on-demand to a remote companion, who can then reply by annotating the source material and sending it back.

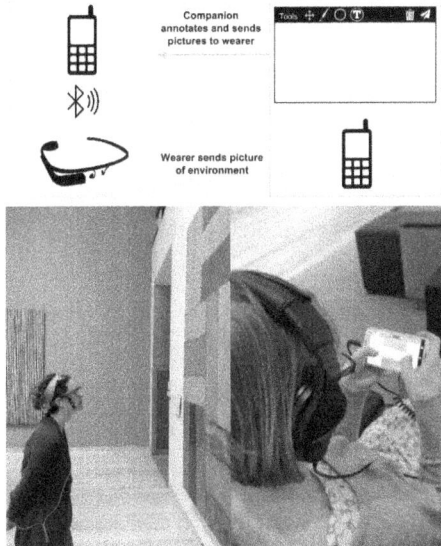

Figure 1. TagAlong System

Informal Learning Trial Setup

We sought to investigate the qualitative difference between still-image versus streaming video sharing and in-person versus remote learning. In this trial, a remote art expert conveyed knowledge about a work of art to a non-expert wearer, who was in the presence of the original work of art, as depicted in Figure 1. There was a dialog between the remote art expert and non-expert wearer during which information is conveyed and further clarifications are requested. As such, we were able to investigate the effectiveness of the TagAlong system for facilitating a discourse-based remote teaching and learning scenario in which reference must be made to specific visual subjects.

Trial Results: Still Images vs. Streaming Video

Still images from TagAlong provided a clear advantage over streaming video as a vehicle for detailed, persistent annotations by the companion. The companion could circle, underline, outline, and label with text specific visual elements. In the video streaming condition, companions needed to use verbal cues and descriptions to draw the wearer's attention to particular subject matter in order to explicate it. Once a subject was identified, a verbal description was needed to make detailed comments. As a corollary, the ability to freeze the subject matter allowed the dialog to be more focused.

A disadvantage of still images in our implementation was that the companion was limited to annotate only the most recent image taken by the wearer. When this was a close-up, she no longer had an effective way of suggesting the next subject of focus. One way of addressing this limitation would be to allow the companion to refer back to previous (less close-up) images to suggest the next focal point (e.g. as shown by Greenwald, et al. [5]).

Trial Results: In-Person vs Telepresent

Our wearer-participants noted that using mobile devices to interact remotely allowed them to focus more exclusively on the work of art than than they could with in-person dialog. We concluded this was due to the fact that a face-to-face interaction carries with it the burden of proxemics– the ensemble of body and facial gestures and eye contact that must be constantly maintained during co-present social interaction. Eliminating that burden liberates the learner's attention to focus only on the subject matter.

Trial Conclusion: Targeted Emulation of Co-Presence

We can cast both of these conclusions in relation to in-person interaction in the following way. In-person, the facilitator always has the ability to point at a fixed object, independent of whether the learner looks away. Our experts had complained that they weren't able to do this using the TagAlong interface. Hence this is a feature of in-person interaction that a system for experiential learning with a remote companion needs to emulate. On the other hand, we saw that the attentional burden of in-person interaction can distract the learner from the subject matter. Hence the requirements of social gestures like nodding, and making eye contact need not be emulated. In the next section we'll see how this consideration fits into the overall design space of the proposed class of systems for experiential learning with a remote companion.

DESIGN SPACE

A comprehensive taxonomy of the design dimensions of these systems will be a contribution of my thesis. As a starting point, I have identified four core design dimensions, which are described briefly below.

Physical Design. This dimension defines physical affordances and ergonomics associated with system usage. It determines what modalities of input and output are available to the learner and companion.

Sensing Design. This defines the forms of awareness that the companion has of the remote environment and learner. Understanding of and attention to the learner's cognitive and affective state can greatly improve learning, and the incorporation of appropriate sensing in the system determines to what degree this is possible. What knowledge does the companion have of the learner's cognitive state? Can the companion see objects that are not the learner's current focus?

Presence Design. This determines how the participants perceive and interact with one another, in terms of awareness as well as how interactions are initiated. This dimension also encompasses the question of where interactions lie on the synchronous-asynchronous spectrum.

Intervention Design. Interrupting a learner's primary activity in the wrong way or at the wrong time can be detrimental to both learning and the positive perception of the system user experience. Interventions can be more or less subtle, as appropriate for the activity and context.

EYE GAZE INTERACTION FOR EXPERIENTIAL LEARNING

In order to explore the research questions mentioned above, I plan to build a version of the TagAlong system that uses eye gaze as an input method for both companion and learner. The components of this system are shown in Figures 2 and 3.

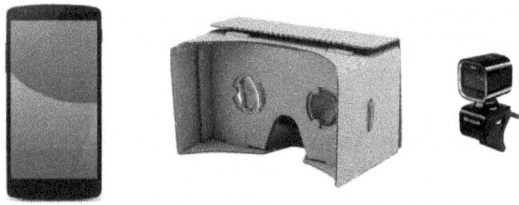

Figure 2. GazeGuide Learner platform technologies: Android phone, Google Cardboard enclosure, external webcam

Figure 3. GazeGuide Companion platform technologies: Microsoft Surface, Tobii EyeX, Nod ring

Eye gaze is more effortless and sometimes faster than a hand- or head-operated 2D pointing device, if the mechanism for switching between active and passive input modes is carefully designed. Eye gaze can also give information about cognitive state, particularly when the level of ambient illumination is known. Hence it will both decrease the attentional load associated with using the system, and serve as a good basis for addressing the question of how the learning experience can be improved by making attentional state information available to the companion (Question I).

In order to investigate Question II, I'll experiment with providing different levels of detail and bandwidth in the signals conveyed to the companion – e.g. still images vs streaming video, blurring all but the area of focus, momentary versus averaged eye gaze information, and so on.

ACKNOWLEDGEMENTS
Thanks to my committee, Pattie Maes, Chris Schmandt, and Albrecht Schmidt, for their feedback and support, and to Selene Mota for her valuable feedback. Thanks to Mina Khan, Cory Kinberger, and Christian Vazquez for their contributions to TagAlong. This work is supported by a Google Faculty Research Award and a gift from Pearson Education.

REFERENCES
1. Judith Amores, Xavier Benavides, and Pattie Maes. 2015. ShowMe. (apr 2015), 1343–1348.

2. Garth H Ballantyne. 2002. Robotic surgery, telerobotic surgery, telepresence, and telementoring. *Surgical Endoscopy and Other Interventional Techniques* 16, 10 (2002), 1389–1402.

3. Mary Czerwinski, Edward Cutrell, and Eric Horvitz. 2000. Instant messaging and interruption: Influence of task type on performance. In *OZCHI 2000 conference proceedings*, Vol. 356. 361–367.

4. Sandy J. J. Gould, Duncan P. Brumby, and Anna L. Cox. 2013. What does it mean for an interruption to be relevant? An investigation of relevance as a memory effect. *Proceedings of the Human Factors and Ergonomics Society Annual Meeting* 57, 1 (2013), 149–153.

5. Scott Greenwald, Mina Khan, and Pattie Maes. 2015. Enabling Human Micro-Presence Through Small-Screen Head-Up Display Devices. In *CHI '15 Extended Abstracts on Human Factors in Computing Systems (CHI EA '15)*. ACM, New York, NY, USA.

6. Pavel Gurevich, Joel Lanir, Benjamin Cohen, and Ran Stone. 2012. TeleAdvisor: A Versatile Augmented Reality Tool for Remote Assistance. In *Proceedings of the SIGCHI Conference on Human Factors in Computing Systems (CHI '12)*. ACM, New York, NY, USA, 619–622.

7. Richard Held. 1992. Telepresence. *The Journal of the Acoustical Society of America* 92, 4 (1992).

8. Ashish Kapoor, Selene Mota, and Rosalind Picard. 2001. Towards a learning companion that recognizes affect. *AAAI Fall Symposium* (2001).

9. B. Kort, R. Reilly, and R.W. Picard. 2001. An affective model of interplay between emotions and learning: reengineering educational pedagogy-building a learning companion. (jan 2001), 43–46.

10. S. Mann. 2000. Telepointer: Hands-free completely self-contained wearable visual augmented reality without headwear and without any infrastructural reliance. (2000).

11. Gloria Mark, Daniela Gudith, and Ulrich Klocke. 2008. The Cost of Interrupted Work: More Speed and Stress. In *Proceedings of the SIGCHI Conference on Human Factors in Computing Systems (CHI '08)*. ACM, New York, NY, USA, 107–110.

12. Marvin Minsky. 1980. Telepresence. (1980).

Reconfiguring and Fabricating Special-Purpose Tangible Controls

Raf Ramakers

Hasselt University - tUL - iMinds
Expertise Centre for Digital Media
Diepenbeek, Belgium
raf.ramakers@uhasselt.be

ABSTRACT
Unlike regular interfaces on touch screens or desktop computers, tangible user interfaces allow for more physically rich interactions that better uses the capacity of our motor system. On the flipside, the physicality of tangibles comes with rigidity. This makes it hard to (1) use tangibles on systems that require a variety of controls and interaction styles, and (2) make changes to physical interfaces once manufactured. In my research, I explore techniques that allow users to reconfigure and fabricate tangible interfaces in order to mitigate these issues.

ACM Classification Keywords: H.5.2 [Information interfaces and presentation]: User Interfaces

Author Keywords: Tangible Interfaces, Deformable devices, End-User Fabrication, Actuator Mechanisms

INTRODUCTION
Until the rise of the micro-controller in the eighties, products were mechanical or electro-mechanical. Due to the rapid flood of digital technologies, many physical artifacts have disappeared and replaced with the most general of appliances: computing devices. Key to the success of devices, such as mobile devices and desktop computers is their flexibility to scale to a variety of application domains and their adaptability to changing user needs. On the flipside, the majority of digital devices support pointing interactions with a mouse or touch screen as sole input technique, using only a small portion of motor skills of the human body [6]. When manipulating physical objects in the real world however, a wide variety of tactile sensations and precise grasping interactions are used [4].

Tangible User Interfaces [2, 3] retain the richness of physical controls in computing devices by perceptually coupling physical artifact to their digital counterpart. These systems are known to provide great affordances [12], stimulate bimanualism [2] and reduce the cognitive load for some tasks [13].

UIST'15 Adjunct, November 8–11, 2015, Charlotte, NC, USA.
ACM 978-1-4503-3780-9/15/11.
http://dx.doi.org/10.1145/2815585.2815587

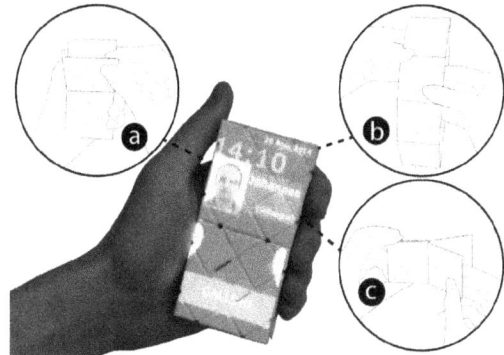

Figure 1. Paddle supports several physical controls, including (a) peeking, (b) scrolling, (c) leafing.

Despite these benefits, the physicality of these controls often comes with rigidity, making it hard to (1) use tangibles in systems that support a wide variety of controls, and (2) make changes to the physical interface over time. As such, over the past few years, many physical controls in systems, such as mobile devices, game consoles, and electrical appliances have been replaced by touch controls or even gesture-based interfaces.

My PhD work focuses on how advancements in technology allow us to combine the flexibility of computing devices with the qualities that we get from real world controls. I therefore investigate how to address two important challenges in tangible interfaces, raised above, in two parts of my research. In the first part, I explore how to reconfigure physical properties of a single tangible controls at run-time in order to support different interaction styles in the same device. In the second part of my research, I explore how end-users can create and (re-)define tangible interactions styles themselves using personal fabrication techniques.

RECONFIGURABLE TANGIBLE SYSTEMS
Unlike controls in virtual user interfaces, physical controls are mostly static and always behave according to the laws of physics. On the one hand, this makes it inconvenient to deploy tangibles in general-purpose systems that support applications with a variety of controls. Especially for those situations where one does not want to take care of an arsenal of physical artifacts, such as in mobile settings. On the other hand, the static and real world nature of tangibles makes it

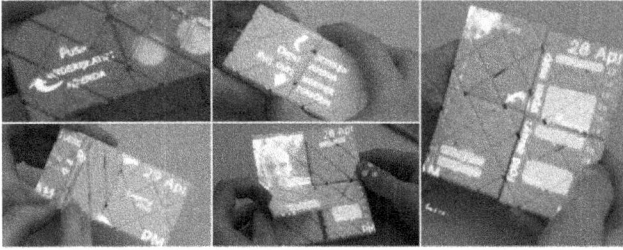

Figure 2. An example interaction that demonstrates how Paddle is used during a call.

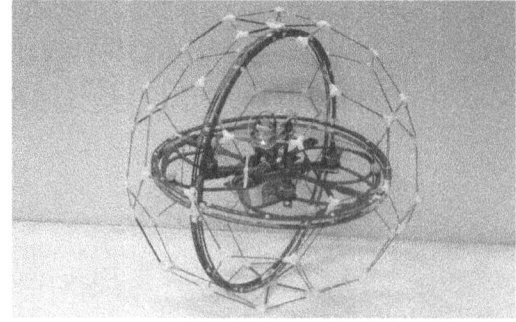

Figure 3. Our prototyped actuated ball uses an integrated quadcopter.

hard to use tangibles in situations where a non-realistic behavior is desired, such as digital sports platforms. As such, there has been a major trend towards "non-tangible" interfaces in both of these settings, i.e. touch screens for mobile devices and gestural interfaces for digital sports platforms, such as the Nintendo Wii and Microsoft Kinect.

In this first part of my research, I trade the space-multiplexed input nature of traditional tangible interfaces [2] for flexibility by investigating how a single physical artifact can dynamically reconfigure to embody a variety of physical controls with different properties.

Paddle: Reconfigurable Tangible Controls for Mobile Devices (CHI 2014)

Paddle [9] is a deformable mobile device that is based on engineering principles used in creating 3D puzzles, more specifically the Rubik's Magic design. Paddle shows how to bring tangibles to mobile devices by transforming the device itself to different physical controls, including a window to peek at content (Figure 1-a), a ring to scroll through lists (Figure 1-b), and a book-like form factor to leaf through pages (Figure 1-c).

Figure 2 shows an example interaction that illustrates how Paddle can be used during a phone call. The system in this scenario uses a prototyped setup that consists of an optical tracking system to track the topology of Paddle and a projector to provide visual output. Tiny infrared reflective markers are attached on both sides of every tile of the Rubik's Magic Puzzle. This provides the system with precise information on how to distort every region of the projected user interface. Similar infrared reflective markers are also attached to the user's fingers to allow for touch interactions.

In contrast to paper-like devices [7, 5] that use origami transformation principles, Paddle uses an extension of the Jacobs Ladder folk toy transformation principle which enables transformations to completely different shapes in only a few steps. So instead of using paper-like devices that traditionally map bending [7] and folding [5] gestures to actions in an interface, Paddle can be transformed quickly to more closely resemble different real world controls, thus keeping up with the tangible interaction paradigm. As a side-effect of being highly transformable, Paddle also bridges the gab between differently-sized mobile devices, such as phones, phablets and tablets.

We conducted two studies to gain a deeper understanding of the differences between the physical controls, supported by

Paddle, and regular touch interactions. Our results show that even tough physical interactions tax our motor system a lot more as compared to touch, there are still fundamental benefits that we get from physical controls, including more efficient access to spatial memory (for scrolling) and better recall of spatial structure and content (for leafing). See [9] for more details.

Actuated Ball Sports: Reconfigurable Tangible Controls for Digital Sports

Unlike traditional virtual games, popular exertion game platforms, such as the Microsoft Kinect and Nintendo Wii, require investing physical effort by tracking full-body gestures. To preserve the dexterity and skills players develop while interacting with physical attributes in sports, such as a ball, researchers introduced game aspects to real life sports [8]. Similar to traditional tangible user interfaces, these systems are often hard to use across different sports and restrict interactions to whats physically possible (e.g. no adjustments to gravity, balls bouncing off invisible objects or computational changes to the trajectory of a ball).

In this part of my research, we introduce *Actuated Ball Sports*: digital sports that are played using a physical ball with an integrated actuator mechanism that introduces non-realistic game aspects in the real world. Figure 3 shows a prototyped ball controller that integrates a quadcopter to allow for control in all 6 degrees of freedom. An integrated three-gimbal mechanism ensures that the quadcopter, located inside the ball, always remains stable. Other mechanisms, such as a flywheel[1] can be used when actuation in 2D is sufficient. Even tough the actuated ball prototype consist of materials that have specific properties, the actuation mechanism allows to adapt a variety of parameters, such as the bounciness, weight, and inertia. Thus making it possible to introduce non-realistic game aspects and use a single tangible controller over different ball sports that traditionally require balls with different properties.

Our prototyped actuated ball sports platform uses an optical tracking system and passive infrared reflective markers attached to the quadcopter and the hull. A control-loop mechanism uses the precise tracking information of the quadcopter to correct its movement every few milliseconds. Orientation

---

[1]http://www.sphero.com

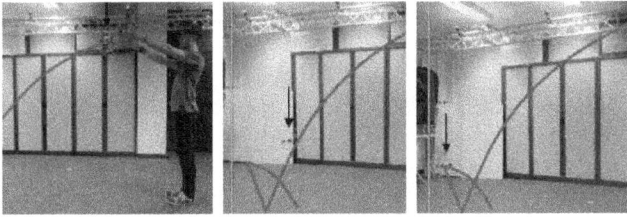

Figure 4. Actuated ball sports can change the behavior of tangible ball controllers.

information of hull is used to predict the external forces applied to the ball using inverse kinematics.

Figure 4 shows an example interaction in which a user throws an actuated ball, that then bounces off the floor and a virtual wall. During the example interaction, the system went through the following steps to change the trajectory in time: (1) The system estimates the external forces that were applied, based on the trajectory during the first 50 milliseconds, starting when the user released the actuated ball. (2) The estimated external forces are then applied to a virtual ball in a physics simulator in which all virtual as well as real world objects (e.g. floor) are present. The physics simulation is speed-up by a factor of 10 to predict the trajectory of the actuated ball in time. (3) If desired, the game logic can decide to change the trajectory of the ball further (e.g. handicaps for specific players). (4) The control-loop mechanisms that correct the movements of the actuated ball are then updated using the computed trajectory.

In contrast to exertion games (e.g. Microsoft Kinect) that map gestural interactions to virtual objects, actuated ball sports preserve the tangible interaction paradigm by computing the users manipulations on the actuated ball using inverse kinematics. This makes it possible for actuated ball sports to capture very dexterous manipulations, such as applying torque to a ball. In gesture-based interfaces, in contrast, it is often hard to capture and map these kind of subtle hand manipulations.

Using the actuated ball sports platform, we implemented a variety of sports, including actuated basketball, volleyball and bowling. The system supports two alternative types of feedback to update players on the game logic: spatial augmented feedback using the RoomAliveToolkit[2] and audio feedback similar to [1].

END-USER FABRICATION OF TANGIBLE SYSTEMS

In contrast to adapting the physical form and behavior of tangible controls at run-time, this part of my research explores fabrication techniques that allows end-users to create and (re-)define tangible systems.

PaperPulse: End-User Fabrication of Paper Tangibles (CHI 2015)

PaperPulse [10], is a design and fabrication approach that enables designers without a background in programming or electronics to produce standalone tangible paper artifacts by augmenting them with electronics.

[2]http://research.microsoft.com/en-us/projects/roomalivetoolkit

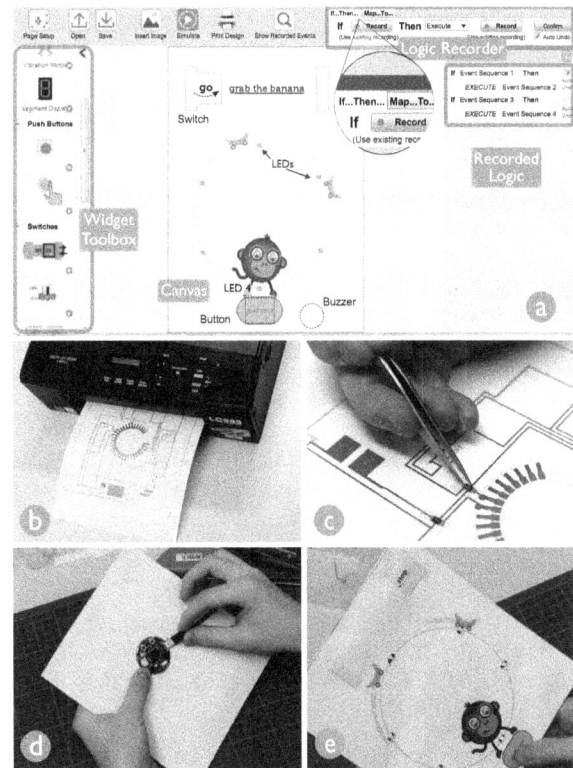

Figure 5. The workflow of PaperPulse to design and fabricate paper tangibles.

Figure 5 shows how PaperPulse streamlines the design and fabrication process of tangible paper artifacts: (a) The user adds interactive elements (e.g. push buttons, sliders, LEDs, microphones) to the visual design and specifies the logic between components by demonstration. (b) PaperPulse generates different layers, consisting of visual elements and electronic circuits printed using an inkjet printer filled with conductive ink. (c) By following step-by-step instructions, the user assembles the different parts. (d) Next, PaperPulse generates code that can directly be uploaded to the microcontroller attached to the paper. (e) The final standalone tangible artifact is powered with a battery.

To provide designers with appropriate widgets, suitable for their paper designs, we contributed three families of standard widgets that each support basic controls such as push buttons, switches, sliders, and radio buttons: (a) off-the-shelf widgets, (b) paper-membrane widgets, and (c) pull-chain widgets. Every family is unique in its own way and differs in terms of its assembly time, how well they blend in the paper design, and how much tangibility they provide.

We also contributed a logic specification approach, Pulsation, that allows end-users without any programming background to define interaction logic using a recording and demonstration approach. The key idea behind Pulsation is that the system records all input and output actions that designers simply demonstrate on top of their design in the canvas. After the user specifies the type of functional relationship between these demonstrated actions (i.e. if–then or map–to), the system automatically generate code for the microcontroller.

FUTURE RESEARCH PLANS

Until now most of my PhD research took on an engineering perspective. In the remaining time of my PhD, I plan to gain a deeper understanding of the novel interaction styles that are allowed by the systems discussed in this paper. One of the main premises of tangible interfaces is that users can utilize the motor skills that they learned over a lifetime to interact with computing devices. However, most of the systems discussed in this work also support tangible interactions that are be unknown to first time users, such as the transformation model of *Paddle* and the non-realistic behaviors of *Actuated Ball Sports*. I therefore want to investigate how these novel interfaces can assist users in learning and mastering new motor skills. Once mastered, our motor memory takes over. From that moment, these interactions do not require any conscious effort anymore and we tend to experience them as "intuitive".

In a similar vein, I plan to study how the novel personal fabrication techniques presented in this work, allow users to fabricate tangible interfaces that better match their individual motor skills and abilities.

The overarching vision behind the research in my PhD is to realize user interfaces that make better use of the capacity of our motor control system. Since motors skills do not require any conscious effort once mastered, the novel interaction concepts presented in this work could possibly lower the cognitive load for interacting with computing systems, and thus allow users to use their cognition for the task at hand.

DISSERTATION STATUS

At the time of writing, I have published two CHI full papers on the topic of my PhD research [9, 10]. Another full paper related to "End-User Fabrication of Tangible Systems" is in preparation for CHI 2016. This work was not included in this position paper for legal reasons, but will be presented at the UIST doctoral consortium. My Phd work builds on other tangible research that I conducted: Kickables [12]. One full paper [11] was published at UIST but is outside the scope of this dissertation.

ACKNOWLEDGEMENTS

I would like to thank my advisors Kris Luyten and Johannes Schöning for their support and guidance. I would also like to thank my internship supervisors Patrick Baudisch, Tovi Grossman, and George Fitzmaurice for all their advice and input.

REFERENCES

1. Baudisch, P., Pohl, H., Reinicke, S., et al. Imaginary reality gaming: ball games without a ball. In *Proc. UIST'13*, UIST '13 (2013), 405–410.

2. Fitzmaurice, G. W., Ishii, H., and Buxton, W. A. S. Bricks: laying the foundations for graspable user interfaces. In *Proc. CHI '95*, 442–449.

3. Ishii, H., and Ullmer, B. Tangible bits: towards seamless interfaces between people, bits and atoms. In *Proc. CHI '97*, 234–241.

4. Jones, L. A., and Lederman, S. J. *Human Hand Function*. New York: Oxford University Press, 2006.

5. Khalilbeigi, M., Lissermann, R., Kleine, W., and Steimle, J. Foldme: interacting with double-sided foldable displays. In *Proc. TEI '12*, 33–40.

6. Klemmer, S. R., Hartmann, B., and Takayama, L. How bodies matter: five themes for interaction design. In *Proc. DIS '06*, 140–149.

7. Lahey, B., Girouard, A., Burleson, W., and Vertegaal, R. Paperphone: understanding the use of bend gestures in mobile devices with flexible electronic paper displays. In *Proc. CHI '11*, 1303–1312.

8. Mueller, F., and Gibbs, M. A table tennis game for three players. In *Proc. OzCHI'06*, 321–324.

9. Ramakers, R., Schöning, J., and Luyten, K. Paddle: Highly deformable mobile devices with physical controls. In *Proc. CHI '14*, 2569–2578.

10. Ramakers, R., Todi, K., and Luyten, K. Paperpulse: An integrated approach for embedding electronics in paper designs. In *Proc. CHI'15*, 2457–2466.

11. Ramakers, R., Vanacken, D., Luyten, K., et al. Carpus: A non-intrusive user identification technique for interactive surfaces. In *Proc. UIST '12*, 35–44.

12. Schmidt, D., Ramakers, R., Pedersen, E. W., et al. Kickables: Tangibles for feet. In *Proc. CHI '14*, 3143–3152.

13. Underkoffler, J., and Ishii, H. Urp: a luminous-tangible workbench for urban planning and design. In *Proc. CHI '99*, 386–393.

Supporting Collaborative Innovation at Scale

Pao Siangliulue
Harvard School of Engineering and Applied Sciences
Cambridge, MA USA
paopow@seas.harvard.edu

ABSTRACT

Emerging online innovation platforms have enabled large groups of people to collaborate and generate ideas together in ways that were not possible before. However, these platforms also introduce new challenges in finding inspiration from a large number of ideas, and coordinating the collective effort. In my dissertation, I address the challenges of large scale idea generation platforms by developing methods and systems for helping people make effective use of each other's ideas, and for orchestrating collective effort to reduce redundancy and increase the quality and breadth of generated ideas.

Author Keywords

Creativity support system, Ideation, Collective intelligence.

ACM Classification Keywords

H.5.m. Information Interfaces and Presentation (e.g. HCI): Miscellaneous

INTRODUCTION

Innovation is a product of collaborative effort. When people create together, each person brings unique knowledge, experiences and points of view, which can be combined to achieve amazing things such as creating new technology, making new scientific discovery and solving social problems. Online innovation platforms allow their contributors to seek inspirations from a large collection of ideas by other members and to generate novel ideas that none of the contributors could have come up with alone. OpenIDEO.com and Quirky are examples of such platforms, whose members have shown the potential of collective idea generation in solving challenging problems.

However, large-scale collaborative idea generation also brings new challenges. The large number of ideas makes it difficult for a contributor to find non-redundant inspiring ideas. Contributors have to look through a lot of ideas with no effective way to discover the ideas they find inspiring. Moreover, there is no mechanism to coordinate effort among

contributors. Instead of working together, contributors generate ideas alone with no guidance on how to best contribute. They end up producing many instances of redundant common ideas while leaving many parts of the solution space unexplored [20]. To help a large community of contributors make full use of its size and diversity, we need new methods and tools that enable contributors to make effective use of each other's ideas, and work effectively together.

My dissertation focuses on developing intelligent systems that improve user experience and outcomes of large-scale collaborative idea generation by providing people with carefully selected inspiring ideas of others at appropriate time.

My work builds on studies of creativity from cognitive science. I have extended this body of work to further understand mechanisms that help people generate more creative and diverse ideas as they get inspired by ideas of others in an actual collaborative innovation platform. Building on these insights, I have developed automatic methods to provide ideators with inspirational ideas, leading to improved performance. Specifically, my work has thus far made the following contributions:

- I have demonstrated that presenting people with sets of *diverse* inspirational ideas results in people generating more diverse ideas than they would have if they were presented with a random selection of ideas [15]. To enable this intervention in real-world settings, I developed and evaluated an efficient, scalable and domain-independent method that can select a diverse set of ideas from a large set of ideas.

- I demonstrated the impact of timing of delivery of inspirational ideas on creative output. I showed that inspirational idea delivery mechanisms that attempt to deliver ideas when people are switching from generating ideas in one category to another can improve novelty and quantity of generated ideas [16].

- I am investigating mechanisms that select personalized set of inspirations to best inspire each contributor based on their solution path (ideas they have explored so far) and their cognitive state (focused exploration versus seeking new inspiration). Prior work suggests that providing a set of inspirations tailored to each individual might yield more creative ideas and improve the contributor's experience [12, 16].

I am now at the crucial point where I address technical challenges in building the system that embodies these findings.

UIST'15 Adjunct, November 08–11, 2015, Charlotte, NC, USA.
ACM 978-1-4503-3780-9/15/11.
http://dx.doi.org/10.1145/2815585.2815588

I plan to demonstrate the viability of my vision in an innovation platform that is open to public, and to proceed in the following directions:

- To select a set of ideas that are inspiring to ideators, the system needs some knowledge about the quality of ideas and semantic relationship between ideas. In my prior work [15], the system acquired this knowledge from paid crowd workers, which is not always viable. I am building a system that uses a self-sustainable "organic" approach where the system subtly extracts information about the quality and the semantics of ideas from users' natural interactions while they are generating ideas.

- In practice, idea generation spans a period of time. During this time, ideators might be incubating their ideas as they go about their other daily activities [3]. To support an ideation task that spans longer than one session, I plan to integrate the ideation task throughout the ideators' day by sending prompts or ideas of others through mobile devices to remind or inspire them to come up with new ideas.

- One main problem in existing innovation platforms is that they elicit many redundant ideas that represent a small fraction of possible solutions while leaving some promising solutions unexplored. I plan to develop novel algorithms that help the community coordinate individuals' efforts in parallel, reduce redundant contributions, and achieve a more thorough, diverse exploration of the solution space.

In the remainder of the paper, I first describe the theoretical findings of prior work and my own work. Then I propose how to integrate these findings into a real innovation platform.

UNDERSTANDING HOW TO HELP PEOPLE GENERATE CREATIVE AND DIVERSE IDEAS

Idea exchanges on large innovation platforms often occur when contributors get inspired by each other's ideas. But seeing ideas of others is not always helpful: depending on the choice of ideas and the timing of their delivery, the ideas that people see can either benefit or harm their creative output [12, 8, 6, 16]. An effective approach therefore should help a contributor find inspiring ideas from a large pool at an appropriate time.

Selecting a diverse set of inspirations

Prior laboratory studies have demonstrated that presenting people with diverse inspirational examples help people generate more diverse ideas themselves [12]. However, prior to my work, there was no robust, scalable and domain-independent method to dynamically identify a diverse set of ideas. Existing crowdsourced approaches designed to organize large collections of items are designed mainly for batch processing and not for the settings where new ideas keep trickling in [1].

I developed a method powered by human computation and machine learning for incrementally constructing an abstract spatial "idea map" (Figure 1) from simple human's judgement on similarity between ideas ("Is idea A more similar to B or C?") [15]. I developed this method based on prior work on multidimensional scaling and active similarity learning techniques [18, 17] to embed ideas in an idea space with

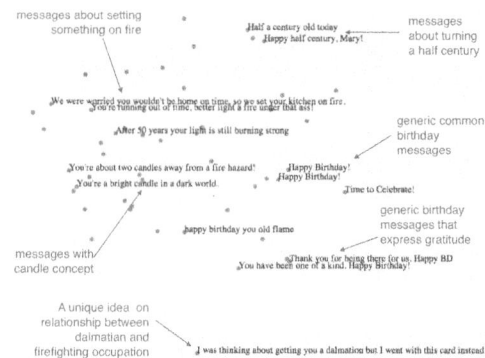

Figure 1. An idea map of birthday messages to a 50-year-old female firefighter. Similar ideas are placed close to each other and dissimilar ideas are kept far apart. See emergent clusters of ideas around different themes and sentiments.

as few human queries as possible. From the idea map, a system can algorithmically extract diverse sets of examples by selecting a set of ideas that are situated far apart from one another on the map. In contrast to some existing methods which use text mining algorithms to infer similarity between ideas in text form [4], my approach is domain independent. I also demonstrated that people generate more diverse ideas when they saw a set of diverse ideas selected by the algorithm compared to when they saw randomly selected ideas or no ideas at all [15].

Timing of inspiration delivery

The timing of example delivery, not just the choice of examples themselves, can impact creative outcomes [7]. Prior work on a theory of idea generation called SIAM (Search for Ideas in Associative Memory) [11] and the Prepared Mind theory of insight [14] suggested that new inspirations should be offered when people finish exploring ideas in one semantic category, as seeing ideas of others can direct them towards new parts of the solution space. Showing ideas of others while people are still exploring their current topics; however, can cut their train of thoughts short and reduce the quantity and quality of generated ideas [11].

In my recent work [16], I explored two timing mechanisms that attempt to offer ideas of others when people just finished exploring ideas in one category: (1) participants can request ideas on demand whenever they want, and (2) the system automatically infers when participants are stuck from their idle time and provides ideas at that moment. The results of evaluation of the two mechanisms show that people who requested examples themselves generated the most novel ideas and people who received ideas automatically when they were idle produced the largest quantity of ideas.

Providing personalized inspirations for individuals

While providing a diverse set of ideas at appropriate time is a sensible strategy in general, it does not take into account the differences between individuals. Prior work suggests the prior experience and the ideas they have already explored can impact how much individuals can benefit from ideas of others [20, 11]. In this case, inspiration delivery could be personalized to a user's current solution path. With an algorithm that adaptively shows ideas of others that are appropriately related to a user's current ideas, the system can either direct the person in new directions or suggest deep exploration within a category for highly creative ideas [11, 10, 13].

I am developing mechanisms for real-time semantic analysis of participants' solution paths, and I plan to conduct experiments to test whether personalized inspiration could further help people benefit from inspirational examples. The three main technical challenges for this approach are (1) the system needs to be able to identify the semantic relationships between ideas dynamically so that it knows the users' paths of exploration relative to other ideas, (2) the system should be able to infer the users' cognitive states—whether the users are receptive to ideas of others that are similar or different from their own ideas—to select appropriate suggestions, and (3) for each cognitive state, the system should have a mechanism to decide what kinds of examples should be shown.

SYSTEM SUPPORT FOR INNOVATION AT SCALE

Organic interactions
In my initial work [15], the system learned about relationships between ideas from outsourced microwork. This approach is domain-independent and scalable, but it has two disadvantages. First, paid crowd workers are not intrinsically motivated to produce high quality work. Second and more importantly, many types of creative tasks require special knowledge and thus cannot be outsourced.

Instead, I am designing interactions that encourage ideators to generate useful information about ideas for the system while engaging in meaningful activities for their own idea generation. For example, people usually spatially organize ideas and group ideas together to get a better sense of possible solutions [9]. These grouping activities reveal users' perceptions of similarity among ideas and can be used to generate an idea map without the need to resort to external crowds.

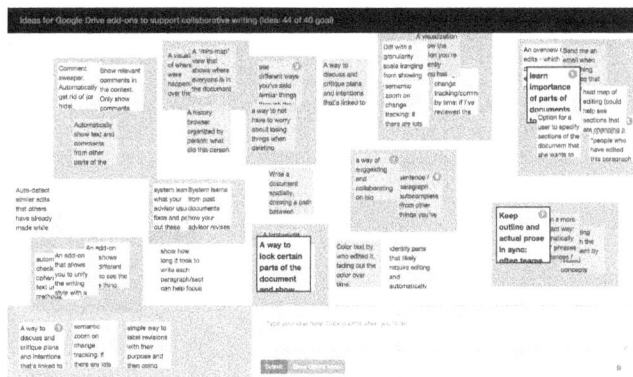

Figure 2. A prototype of an interface with organic interactions. The users can organize ideas on the whiteboards from which the system extracts information about relationships between ideas.

I am building an intelligent system that supports and leverages such "organic" interactions (Figure 2). The current prototype is a web application that allows users to create projects, invite people to contribute to their projects, submit ideas and request to see others' ideas. The users can organize ideas

on their personal "whiteboards", bookmark ideas that they want to easily access later and remove ideas that they no longer want to see from the board. These interactions give the system information about the quality of ideas (bookmarking, deleting from the work space) and how they are related to each other (spatial organization on the whiteboard) which the system uses to help select inspiring ideas when users request them.

Pilot user testing with small groups over several days showed that users naturally organize ideas into groups and bookmark ideas they consider interesting. I also learned that participants sometimes had other uses of grouping ideas other than organizing semantically similar ideas into clusters. Some created a separate group for their own ideas, while some had a pile for ideas that they do not want to organize yet. Such groups do not give meaningful information about semantic relation between ideas and introduce noise to the algorithm that selects ideas. I am working on a way to automatically identify which clusters are semantically meaningful.

Will such organic activities provide enough input for the system to reason reliably about the semantic relationships among ideas? To answer this question, I am designing a study to compare the idea maps generated organically, as ideators naturally go about their creative activities, to those generated using my previously validated method that relied on paid crowd workers performing explicit assessment tasks.

The pilot studies also revealed opportunities for other interaction designs. There are two in particular that I plan to explore. The first one is derived from my observation that participants sometimes submit rationales for their ideas on top of the idea itself. According to prior work, seeing the rationale is less likely to cause fixation than seeing the examples [21]. If the users can provide rationales or tag the interesting aspects of ideas, the system can intelligently provide these rationales as an alternative to showing the ideas themselves.

The second opportunity is based on participants' comments that it took some time for them to reorient themselves to their workspace in the following sessions. The system can allow users to put labels or notes on groups of ideas. These labels can help inform the system whether the grouping is meaningful and on which dimension it is based in case there are several ways to group the available ideas. Such information might help the system provide better explanation on how it selects to people. The explanation can increase trust in the recommendation by the system [19] and help ideators pinpoint which part of the inspirational ideas to focus on.

Making incubation more effective
Prior work in cognitive science suggests that idea generation is a long process that involves incubation periods where ideators take a break from actively thinking about the problems [3]. While people are not trying to come up with ideas, there is a solution searching process running in the background. To keep this process running, people need to be aware that they are returning to generate ideas later [5]. A system can help remind people of the task while they are not actively thinking about ideas by sending prompts or showing

inspiring ideas by others. However, the system also needs to be careful in choosing which reminders to send based on the context of ideators to avoid interfering with other tasks the users try to accomplish [2].

Mobile devices grant access to information about users' context such as location, activity and schedule. This information can help a system decide when and how to instigate interactions with the users. For example, knowing a user's schedule and location, a system can offer related inspirations or prompting her to record her ideas at a certain point in time. I plan to expand my prototype to include a mobile application that provides inspirational ideas of others and prompts users based on their contexts. This version of collective ideation platform can also better inform how people generate ideas in different situations for future creativity research as well.

Coordinating collaborative exploration of idea space

As the number of contributors increases, the more crucial and difficult it becomes to coordinate the community efforts. Without coordination, people are likely to generate redundant ideas that are very similar to one another instead of exploring a broader range of ideas [20]. However, the community also wants to avoid too much communication overhead that can take time away from generating ideas.

I plan to explore mechanisms that reduce idea redundancy in large creative communities and widen the breadth of ideas generated. One possible mechanism is to automatically identify the parts of the idea space that have not been explored as much as others and direct more people to generate ideas in those unexplored regions of the space. An algorithm can help the community decide whether the contributors should focus on generating ideas related to particular topics or exploring new ones. This mechanism can be integrated into a system as a form of an explicit todo list [22] or as a subtle nudge through judicious selection of inspirational examples. Another approach is to provide people with an overview of the community's idea generation along with a way for contributors to communicate so that they do not interfere with each other.

CONCLUSION

Large ideation platforms promise a huge opportunity for innovation, but are limited by lack of appropriate methods and tools to help people discover inspiring ideas and coordinate their efforts. By synthesizing knowledge and approaches from cognitive science, human computation and machine learning, we can create an intelligent system that addresses the existing challenges and improves the experience of ideators and quality of generated ideas at scale.

Acknowledgments This work was funded in part by gifts from Google and Adobe.

REFERENCES

1. Paul André, Aniket Kittur, and Steven P. Dow. 2014. Crowd Synthesis: Extracting Categories and Clusters from Complex Data. In *Proc. CSCW'14*. ACM, 989–998.
2. Brian P Bailey and Shamsi T Iqbal. 2008. Understanding changes in mental workload during execution of goal-directed tasks and its application for interruption management. *ACM TOCHI* 14, 4 (2008), 21.
3. Benjamin Baird, Jonathan Smallwood, Michael D Mrazek, Julia WY Kam, Michael S Franklin, and Jonathan W Schooler. 2012. Inspired by distraction mind wandering facilitates creative incubation. *Psychological Science* (2012).
4. Joel Chan, Steven Dow, and Christian Schunn. 2014. Conceptual distance matters when building on others' ideas in crowd-collaborative innovation platforms. In *Proc. CSCW'14*. ACM, 141–144.
5. Jason Gallate, Cara Wong, Sophie Ellwood, RW Roring, and Allan Snyder. 2012. Creative people use nonconscious processes to their advantage. *Creativity Research Journal* 24, 2-3 (2012), 146–151.
6. Nicholas W Kohn and Steven M Smith. 2011. Collaborative fixation: Effects of others' ideas on brainstorming. *Applied Cognitive Psychology* 25, 3 (2011), 359–371.
7. Chinmay Kulkarni, Steven P Dow, and Scott R Klemmer. 2014. Early and repeated exposure to examples improves creative work. In *Design Thinking Research*. Springer, 49–62.
8. Richard L Marsh, Joshua D Landau, and Jason L Hicks. 1996. How examples may (and may not) constrain creativity. *Memory & Cognition* 24, 5 (1996), 669–680.
9. Bill Moggridge and Bill Atkinson. 2007. *Designing interactions*. Vol. 14. MIT press Cambridge.
10. Bernard A Nijstad, Carsten KW De Dreu, Eric F Rietzschel, and Matthijs Baas. 2010. The dual pathway to creativity model: Creative ideation as a function of flexibility and persistence. *European Review of Social Psychology* 21, 1 (2010), 34–77.
11. Bernard A Nijstad and Wolfgang Stroebe. 2006. How the group affects the mind: A cognitive model of idea generation in groups. *Personality and social psychology review* 10, 3 (2006), 186–213.
12. Bernard A Nijstad, Wolfgang Stroebe, and Hein FM Lodewijkx. 2002. Cognitive stimulation and interference in groups: Exposure effects in an idea generation task. *Journal of experimental social psychology* 38, 6 (2002), 535–544.
13. Eric F Rietzschel, Bernard A Nijstad, and Wolfgang Stroebe. 2007. Relative accessibility of domain knowledge and creativity: The effects of knowledge activation on the quantity and originality of generated ideas. *Journal of Experimental Social Psychology* 43, 6 (2007), 933–946.
14. Colleen M Seifert, David E Meyer, Natalie Davidson, Andrea L Patalano, and Ilan Yaniv. 1994. Demystification of cognitive insight: Opportunistic assimilation and the prepared-mind hypothesis. (1994).
15. Pao Siangliulue, Kenneth C. Arnold, Krzysztof Z. Gajos, and Steven P. Dow. 2015a. Toward Collaborative Ideation at Scale—Leveraging Ideas from Others to Generate More Creative and Diverse Ideas. In *Proc. CSCW'15*.
16. Pao Siangliulue, Joel Chan, Krzysztof Z. Gajos, and Steven P. Dow. 2015b. Providing Timely Examples Improves the Quantity and Quality of Generated Ideas. In *Proc. Creativity and Cognition'15*.
17. Omer Tamuz, Ce Liu, Serge Belongie, Ohad Shamir, and Adam Tauman Kalai. 2011. Adaptively Learning the Crowd Kernel. *arXiv.org* (May 2011).
18. L van der Maaten and K Weinberger. 2012. Stochastic triplet embedding. *Machine Learning for Signal Processing (MLSP), 2012 IEEE International Workshop on* (2012), 1–6.
19. Weiquan Wang and Izak Benbasat. 2007. Recommendation agents for electronic commerce: Effects of explanation facilities on trusting beliefs. *Journal of Management Information Systems* 23, 4 (2007), 217–246.
20. Thomas B Ward, Merryl J Patterson, Cynthia M Sifonis, Rebecca A Dodds, and Katherine N Saunders. 2002. The role of graded category structure in imaginative thought. *Memory & Cognition* 30, 2 (2002), 199–216.
21. Lixiu Yu, Aniket Kittur, and Robert E Kraut. 2014. Distributed analogical idea generation: inventing with crowds. In *Proc. CHI'14*. ACM, 1245–1254.
22. Haoqi Zhang, Edith Law, Rob Miller, Krzysztof Gajos, David Parkes, and Eric Horvitz. 2012. Human computation tasks with global constraints. In *Proc. CHI'12*. ACM, 217–226.

Wait-Learning: Leveraging Wait Time for Education

Carrie J. Cai
MIT CSAIL
Cambridge, MA
cjcai@mit.edu

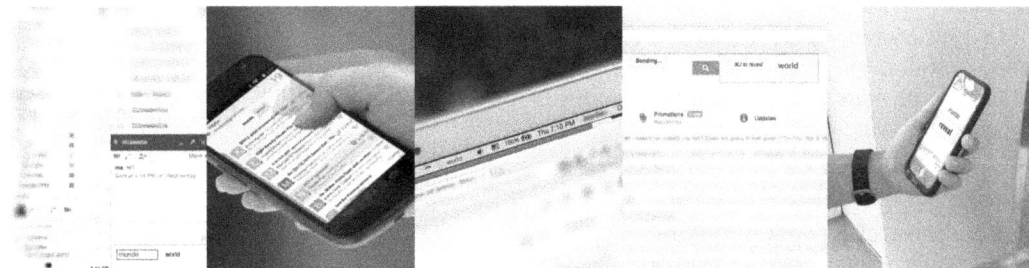

Figure 1. Wait-learning enables learning during micro-waiting moments. WaitChatter and FlashSuite enable learning across a variety of task contexts: (left to right) instant messaging, pull-to-refresh, wifi seeking, email sending, and elevator waiting.

ABSTRACT

Competing priorities in daily life make it difficult for those with a casual interest in learning to set aside time for regular practice. Yet, learning often requires significant time and effort, with repeated exposures to learning material on a recurring basis. Despite the struggle to find time for learning, there are numerous times in a day that are wasted due to micro-waiting. In my research, I develop systems for *wait-learning*, leveraging wait time for education. Combining wait time with productive work opens up a new class of software systems that overcomes the problem of limited time while addressing the frustration often associated with waiting. My research tackles several challenges in learning and task management, such as identifying which waiting moments to leverage; how to encourage learning unobtrusively; how to integrate learning across a diversity of waiting moments; and how to extend wait-learning to more complex domains. In the development process, I hope to understand how to manage these waiting moments, and describe essential design principles for wait-learning systems.

Author Keywords

wait-learning; micro-learning; attention management

UIST '15 Adjunct, November 08-11, 2015, Charlotte, NC, USA
ACM 978-1-4503-3780-9/15/11.
http://dx.doi.org/10.1145/2815585.2815589

ACM Classification Keywords

H.5.2. User interfaces: Interaction styles

INTRODUCTION

There are numerous times in a day when people wait, such as time spent waiting for an elevator, waiting for an instant message reply, or waiting for a lecture to start. Yet, these moments are rarely used for productive tasks due to the perception that long, uninterrupted periods of effort are required to make meaningful progress. At the same time, spaced, repeated exposure [3] to educational content is key for endeavors such as learning a foreign language or studying for a standardized exam. While people may have the desire or the *choice motivation* to form productive habits, many lack the *executive motivation* to actually perform these tasks on a repeated basis [4], due to barriers in finding time for practice. Given existing tendencies to fill wait time with less productive activities (e.g. compulsive email-checking), there is an opportunity for learning to occur during these daily gaps that may otherwise be spent unproductively.

This work presents *wait-learning*: leveraging wait time for education. I design and build interactive systems for learning during waiting moments, bringing in expertise from domains such as attention management, education, and task allocation. For example, **WaitChatter** delivers learning exercises while users wait for instant message (IM) replies, and **FlashSuite** (Figure 1) integrates learning across five different modalities and waiting contexts. Although user interaction should be seamless, the underlying systems may be complex in determining the optimal moment to intervene, and the kinds of learning exercises to deliver at that moment to maximize learning without sacrificing engagement.

13

Through my research, I aim to address the following research questions:

- Which waiting moments are more compatible with learning, given factors such as expected wait time and cognitive load?
- How do we design interfaces to encourage engagement in learning while minimizing intrusiveness?
- How can wait-learning serve as an entryway to continued learning or productive work, helping people ease in to more complex activities during longer periods of wait time?

THESIS STATEMENT

Wait-learning is a novel and effective way to learn, increases engagement in learning, reduces frustration in wasted time, and minimizes the perception that time spent learning is intrusive to daily life.

RELATED WORK

There is a growing body of work aiming to integrate micro-learning into existing daily activities, ranging from second language learning of location-relevant vocabulary [5] to displaying parts of a web article being read into a foreign language [12]. A common goal of this prior work is to lower the activation barrier of performing micro-tasks. However, prior work has tended to focus more on the *content* delivered rather than the *timing* of those deliveries. Moreover, these systems often leveraged *live* time, moments when the user is already engaged with an existing task, rather than *wait* time.

Micro-Learning and Micro-Work

Based on evidence that spaced and repeated exposure [3] to educational content results in greater learning gains, a rich thread of research on *micro-learning* [6] has explored methods to distribute learning into small units throughout a person's day-to-day life. Micro-learning has largely been implemented in the form of mobile applications that provide opportunities to learn contextually relevant second language vocabulary based on surrounding contexts [2,5]. Several desktop applications have also embedded learning programs into common daily activities, such as Lernschoner [6], in which learners complete a vocabulary flashcard before resuming activity on their computer screen, and Aloe, where some words within articles the user is browsing are displayed in a foreign language [12].

Despite the promising benefits of micro-learning, researchers found that some users discontinued usage due to the slower rate at which they could conduct their normal tasks on the Web [12]. Another also found that the quantity of vocabulary reviewed may depend as much on when users were available to learn as the contextual relevance of those vocabulary [5]. Challenges raised in prior work point to the necessity of identifying moments that are non-intrusive to a user's daily workflow, as even micro-diversions may be viewed as disruptive if the user feels that his or her tasks are being delayed. Motivated by these challenges, this work targets moments when users would ordinarily spend waiting, with the goal of minimizing perceived disruption of ongoing tasks. Because filled waiting periods are typically perceived to be shorter than unfilled waiting periods [8], wait-learning could also enhance a user's subjective experience beyond providing educational benefits.

Attention and Interruption

Although wait-learning aims to leverage idle time, previous work on interruptability suggests that the detailed manner and timing of delivery can still result in significant differences in task performance and levels of frustration. Because our minds dynamically allocate and release resources throughout task execution, the timing of information delivery relative to a user's ongoing task may affect interruption cost [7]. Since decreases in workload tend to be larger at boundaries corresponding to larger chunks of a task [7,9], a system that presents information during down time should favor boundaries that represent more salient breaks in workflow [7]. My research aims to understand how to design wait-learning experiences in a way that minimizes disruption.

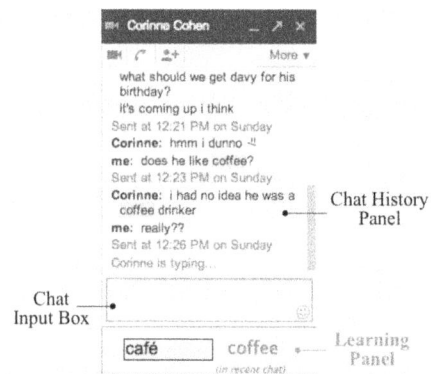

Figure 2. WaitChatter presents vocabulary exercises in the *learning panel* while the user awaits an IM response. Here, the user is being quizzed on a word and must enter the second language (French) translation given the native language (English) prompt. The word is highlighted in the chat history because it appeared in the context of the conversation.

WAITCHATTER

As a first instantiation of wait-learning, I developed an extension of instant messaging (IM) called WaitChatter [1] (Figure 2). WaitChatter presents second-language vocabulary exercises while the user awaits an IM response. Instant messaging offers a powerful opportunity for wait-learning due to its semi-asynchronous nature. Because messages being typed are unseen by the conversant, a user must often wait in anticipation of a response, with no guarantee that the other party will in fact reply [11].

In WaitChatter, users see vocabulary quizzes appear under their chatbox while waiting for an IM response, and can optionally complete these exercises while waiting. Because vocabulary retention hinges on repeated exposure to words across time, short spurts of waiting during instant messaging may be a low-barrier way to get repeated practice.

Implementation

WaitChatter automatically detects when a user might be waiting for a response in two ways. The first case occurs after a user has sent a chat message and is waiting to see whether his conversant will respond. The second case occurs when the conversant has started typing but not yet sent the message. WaitChatter triggers an exercise when the "[conversant] is typing…" indicator appears in the user's chat window and if the user if not still typing.

WaitChatter uses the Leitner flashcard algorithm to dynamically schedule the order of vocabulary exercises: repetitions occur at increasingly spaced intervals so that they are encountered just as they are about to be forgotten. WaitChatter extends the Leitner algorithm in two ways. First, aside from teaching learners commonly used words, WaitChatter also selects words from the IM conversation on-the-fly and automatically converts them into quizzes for just-in-time learning. In order to dynamically interleave between contextual and non-contextual vocabulary, WaitChatter modifies the Leitner algorithm to allow for timely injections of contextual vocabulary. Second, WaitChatter also modifies the algorithm to increase engagement by dynamically reordering words based on whether the user has previously ignored the exercise.

Engagement and Learning Value

My research on WaitChatter found that users were fastest to engage and most likely to engage with learning when exercises were delivered at the start of the waiting period, compared to other timing conditions. Results also showed that learning during wait time can serve as a viable channel for learning, at least for bite-sized information. After two weeks of casual WaitChatter usage during their regular IM activities, users on average retained 57 new Spanish and French words, the equivalent of learning approximately four new words per day.

WaitChatter's primary value to learners is the decreased effort involved in making time for learning. WaitChatter users cited time and ease of access as a major benefit, contrasting WaitChatter to mobile applications which required them to consciously set aside time and open the app to learn. Given the critical importance of time, I am continuing to examine how wait-learning systems can accommodate a wider range of waiting moments with varying amounts of wait time.

Live Deployment

After the initial research study, WaitChatter was deployed to the public as a Google Chat extension and has since been widely circulated, with over 900 installations. The substantial public interest in WaitChatter validates the need for learning despite limited time. At the same time, the abundance of people who voiced interest in wait-learning, but who could not use WaitChatter because they do not instant message, motivates a system for integrating learning into a diversity of waiting moments.

FLASHSUITE

In many educational disciplines, the key to retention is the ability to sustain repeated exposure to the same content over time. However, many learners only experience certain types of waiting on particular days, or may encounter unusual periods with limited access to particular platforms. To address this problem, I developed FlashSuite, a system that unifies a suite of wait-learning possibilities into a single, integrated learning experience. FlashSuite unifies learning across the following five apps: 1) **ElevatorLearner:** users learn while waiting for the elevator. 2) **PullLearner:** users learn after pulling to refresh mobile app content, while waiting for the content to load. 3) **WifiLearner**: users learn while waiting for their computer to connect to wifi. 4) **EmailLearner**: users learn after sending an email, a time when s/he has potentially just completed one task before transitioning to something new. 5) **ChatLearner**: users learn while awaiting IM responses ChatLearner is essentially the same as WaitChatter, but without contextual words.

Because different kinds of waiting can occur at different frequencies, the ability to maintain forward progress *across* apps is key. FlashSuite synchronizes data so that users can continue to make learning progress on the same set of vocabulary when switching from one app to another. For apps like WifiLearner which specifically target internet down time, handling offline usage is a necessity. FlashSuite caches data on the client side so that the user can continue to complete exercises while offline. Because apps targeting internet down time may fetch consistently stale exercises, FlashSuite also force-synchronizes to the server every time internet re-connects. In the case of a concurrency conflict, FlashSuite selects the state reflecting further progress.

DESIGN SPACE

Given the vast diversity of waiting moments, it is necessary to examine trade-offs between different kinds of waiting, and determine which ones are more suitable for wait-learning. I charted a design space that spans three critical dimensions: 1) wait time, 2) response time (time to begin responding to the learning exercise), and 3) cognitive and perceptual load (the likelihood of other processes competing for the user's attention).

Using the five instances of wait-learning described in FlashSuite, I gathered in-situ data on real usage patterns across apps to determine metrics such as wait time, response time, and engagement rate. I found that engagement rate is highest when typical response time is less than the wait time, and when cognitive load is low. I also found that wait-learning can reduce the frustration associated with certain kinds of waiting (i.e. waiting for wifi). In evaluating these systems, I am currently establishing design principles that can be used by other designers of wait-learning systems.

WORK IN PROGRESS: SELF-SOURCING

While waiting could conceivably accommodate simple tasks like vocabulary learning or photo labeling, it is more difficult to imagine how large, complex tasks such as learning calculus or writing a project proposal could be feasibly "self-sourced" [10] during down time. Even if large tasks can be broken down into micro-components, it is unclear how individuals can complete those smaller components without context of the bigger picture.

As a next step in my thesis, I plan to expand wait-learning beyond simple tasks, by examining how micro-tasks can serve as an entryway to more complex tasks. For example, a system could order tasks such that lightweight, context-free tasks are presented first. In completing these smaller tasks, the user may gain the contextual awareness necessary to complete the longer task. I am building a self-sourcing system component that automatically orders tasks based on a number of interdependent task parameters.

FUTURE WORK: GROUP WAIT-LEARNING

Waiting occurs not only in personal contexts, but also in group settings, such as in the minutes before a lecture starts, or at the start of a business meeting. In these situations, wait-learning could empower not only the completion of personal tasks, but also the education of groups with a common goal. However, group-waiting also bears a number of challenges, such as different arrival times between individuals and varying expertise. In the upcoming year, I plan to address these challenges. For example, a system could leverage the collective intelligence of the group, using differential arrival time as a way of progressively narrowing down answer options in a group learning exercise so that late arrivers benefit from early arrivers.

SUMMARY

My work thus far has sought to answer critical questions such as which design dimensions are more effective for wait-learning (FlashSuite), which moments maximize engagement within a particular domain (WaitChatter), and how to design the user interface to encourage learning while minimizing disruption (both). It has also demonstrated that wait-learning can be effective for bite-sized learning. In future work, I plan to understand how wait-learning can expand beyond simple, personal learning tasks, by developing systems that involve more complex goals and coordination among groups. At the conclusion of my graduate work, I hope to have built systems that enable users to more easily complete meaningful tasks, demonstrated the efficacy of these systems, and established essential design principles for wait-learning systems.

ACKNOWLEDGMENTS

I am grateful for the support and mentorship of my thesis advisor, Rob Miller, Professor of EECS at MIT CSAIL, as well as Shamsi Iqbal and Jaime Teevan at Microsoft Research. This research was funded by Quanta Computer and MIT Lincoln Laboratory.

REFERENCES

1. Carrie J Cai, Philip J Guo, James Glass, and Robert C Miller. 2015. Wait-learning: leveraging wait time for education. In CHI'15. ACM.

2. David Dearman and Khai Truong. 2012. Evaluating theimplicit acquisition of second language vocabulary using a live wallpaper. In CHI '12. ACM, 1391–1400.

3. Frank N Dempster. 1987. Effects of variable encoding and spaced presentations on vocabulary learning. Journal of Educational Psychology 79, 2 (1987), 162.

4. Zoltan Dornyei and Istv´an Ott´o. 1998. Motivation in action: A process model of L2 motivation. Working Papers in Applied Linguistics (1998), 43–69.

5. Darren Edge, Elly Searle, Kevin Chiu, Jing Zhao, and James A Landay. 2011. MicroMandarin: mobile language learning in context. In CHI '11. ACM, 3169–3178.

6. Gerhard Gassler, Theo Hug, and Christian Glahn. 2004. Integrated Micro Learning–An outline of the basic method and first results. Interactive Computer Aided Learning 4 (2004).

7. Shamsi T Iqbal and Brian P Bailey. 2005. Investigating the effectiveness of mental workload as a predictor of opportune moments for interruption. In CHI'05 Extended Abstracts. ACM, 1489–1492.

8. David H Maister. 1984. The psychology of waiting lines. Harvard Business School.

9. Yoshiro Miyata and Donald A Norman. 1986. Psychological issues in support of multiple activities. User centered system design: New perspectives on human-computer interaction (1986), 265–284.

10. Teevan, Jaime, Daniel J. Liebling, and Walter S. Lasecki. "Selfsourcing personal tasks." CHI'14 Extended Abstracts on Human Factors in Computing Systems. ACM, 2014.

11. Tree, J. E. F., Mayer, S. A., and Betts, T. E. Grounding in instant messaging. Journal of Educational Computing Research 45 , 4 (2011), 455–475.

12. Andrew Trusty and Khai N Truong. 2011. Augmenting the web for second language vocabulary learning. In CHI '11 . ACM, 3179–3188.

13. Stuart Webb. 2007. The effects of repetition on vocabulary knowledge. Applied Linguistics 28, 1 (2007), 46–65.

From Papercraft to Paper Mechatronics: Exploring a New Medium and Developing a Computational Design Tool

Hyunjoo Oh
ATLAS Institute
University of Colorado Boulder
430 UCB, Boulder, CO, 80309
hyunjoo.oh@colorado.edu

ABSTRACT
Paper Mechatronics is a novel interdisciplinary design medium, enabled by recent advances in craft technologies: the term refers to a reappraisal of traditional papercraft in combination with accessible mechanical, electronic, and computational elements. I am investigating the design space of paper mechatronics as a new hands-on medium by developing a series of examples and building a computational tool, *FoldMecha,* to support non-experts to design and construct their own paper mechatronics models. This paper describes how I used the tool to create two kinds of paper mechatronics models: walkers and flowers and discuss next steps.

Author Keywords
Paper mechatronics; computational design tool; papercraft; craft technology.

ACM Classification Keywords
H.5.2. Information interfaces and presentation: User Interfaces – *Prototyping*.

INTRODUCTION
Papercrafting invites a diverse range of people to investigate art, craft and mechanics through hands-on making. Paper, which is thin, lightweight, ubiquitous, and inexpensive, enables people who have only basic technical skills to work in this playful and creative medium. Making origami figures, paper automata, and myriad geometry artifacts motivates us to actively explore our ideas beyond the aesthetic and technical quality of our creation. For instance, one may build a tiny origami triangle and envision a giant pyramid.

Today, the design space of papercraft can be enlarged with recent high-low technology innovations. Small lightweight microprocessors can be embedded within paper constructions; sensors, actuators, electronic elements, and power sources may be connected to those processors by conductive inks, tapes, adhesives, and threads. We call this interdisciplinary domain "Paper Mechatronics"—the combination of mechanisms, electronics, and computation with the traditional cutting and folding activities of papercraft. An introductory level of electronic circuitry and programming enables novice users to build dynamically original and interactive paper machines. The widened medium represents a remarkable leap in the palette for creative exploration [7].

My research investigates two threads: exploring the design space of paper mechatronics as a new medium and developing a computational design tool to support this exploration. Although paper mechatronics affords the potential to move beyond traditional realm of papercraft, the inherently interdisciplinary nature imposes a barrier for novices. For instance, to design a paper mechatronics model, one must understand fundamental structures whereby mechanisms and physical forms combine to generate a movement, and then to plan the embedding of electronic parts to the structure. The enhanced expressiveness and required techniques present not only opportunities for learning and creativity but also more challenges than each individual discipline. I aim to provide solid design examples and establish guidelines that suggest a plausible creative strategy starting from traditional papercrafting, and to develop a computational tool to empower novices in designing and building their own paper mechatronics creations.

RELATED WORK
Paper mechatronics is rooted in several established domains. Perhaps most importantly, paper mechatronics is founded upon the field of electronic papercraft. Qi and Buechley [9] presented an interactive pop-up book using non-standard electronics components such as copper conductive tape, conductive ink, and shape memory alloy wires that resemble traditional craft materials. Also, Saul *et al.* [10] developed tools and techniques for building simple paper devices such as employing a nitinol wire with gold-leaf circuits. These examples illustrates a natural way in which ideas central to the study of electronics can arise in the context of constructing with paper.

UIST '15 Adjunct, November 08-11, 2015, Charlotte, NC, USA
ACM 978-1-4503-3780-9/15/11.
http://dx.doi.org/10.1145/2815585.2815590

Then, paper mechatronics combines electronically augmented paper with the field of playful and creative machines such as automata. Because building a moving craft artifact requires acquiring skills in mechanical construction, handcraft, and storytelling, it has been used as a popular educational medium for children. Rob Ives [4] has published books and hosts a website where educators and children can download printed kits to build, for example, the "Flying Pig". Also Robert Addams lays out an instructional approach to building automata with a craft sensibility [1]. Onn and Alexander [8] provide an illustrated textbook on the creation of mechanisms and automata aimed at young audience as well.

In addition, computational tools have been built to unfold virtual 3D models to assist building physical papercraft and designing and fabricating mechanical characters. An early entry into this space is Eisenberg & Eisenberg's HyperGami (later Javagami) [3]. This software supports creating and modifying three-dimensional polyhedra on the screen, and unfold it as a two-dimensional map. Mitani and Suzuki [6] developed a method for converting virtual meshes into a set of triangle strips, and producing the unfolded patterns. Beyond the realm of papercrafting, Zhu et al. [11] presented a system to design automata by selecting a mechanism from a parameterized set. Coros *et al.* [2] support designing and fabricating mechanical characters based on a motion library to identify appropriate mechanisms. ChaCra [5] supports rapid crafting of planar mechanical characters by simplifying the design of animated characters.

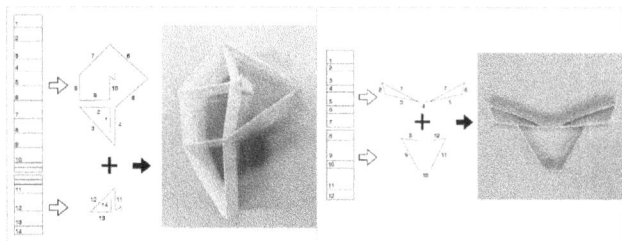

Figure 1. Design templates to construct walkers and flowers: the critical part of building a paper mechanical model is in the setting of rigid links, fixed pivots and moving pivots. By folding and unfolding, one can make these elements with paper strips. The models are strong enough to enable the construction to be pushed and pulled as a mechanical unit [7].

TWO DESIGN MODULES: BUILDING WALKERS AND FLOWERS

So far I have worked on two examples that illustrate the way in which paper mechatronics can develop into an engaging creative design medium, inspired by two kinetic art works, Theo Jansen's Strandbeest (www.strandbeest.com) and Matthew Gardiner's Oribotics (www.matthewgardiner.net). These mechanisms reflect a range of mechanical ideas. The walker constructions are based on Jansen's elegant mechanism: a rotating central disk with opposing quadrilateral-based legs. The rotating disk deforms the two quadrilaterals, producing the walking motion. The flower constructions are based on a rack and pinion mechanism: a pair of gears that convert rotation into linear motion. As the pinion (a circular gear) rotates, the rack (a linear gear) travels, generating the up and down motion of the sepal (base of the flower). This animates the opening and closing motion of the petals.

FoldMecha: a Computational Design Tool

Figure 3 shows sequential screen snapshots of FoldMecha simulating the opening and closing of a paper flower. Along with animating mechanisms integrated with forms, FoldMecha supports hands-on learning and designing.

A user begins with a default model to see how the mechanism works. Then the user modifies key design parameters (top left panel) and observes how this changes the movement. The simulation helps users understand how form and mechanical behavior are integrated and enables them to design their own working models by varying template parameters. After setting the design parameters, a user selects a mechanism (in building flowers: either "Rack and Pinion" or "Piston") to generate the movement, and then "View the Map" navigates to the next page, which displays folding nets of the parts in the selected color with default dimensions. The default size is 15-16 cm, but one can scale the width; the software changes the dimensions on the screen accordingly. The user can save and print the file in a PDF format, and build models by following the folding instruction on the left panel.

Customization using templates

Building a device with mechanical movement requires accurate structures, which in turn requires understanding both the physical forms and the mechanisms. Designing different models, not from scratch but by modifying parameters in a template, can lower the entry bar for novice users. Simple interactions (entering parameters, adding models, etc.) support users customizing the "look and feel" of a variety of forms within the working structure.

Simplified prototyping with paper strips

I simplified the design and construction process to support novices to reduce trial-and-error. Our system generates paper folding nets as paper strips with marked folding locations; after cutting, users fold the strips following the printed instructions to build the model they designed.

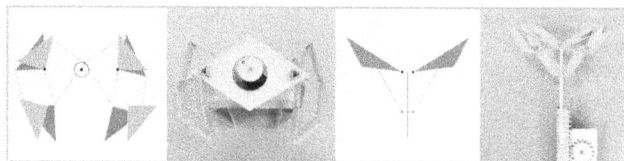

Figure 2. Simulation of mechanical structures in FoldMecha and paper prototypes generated by the system via the folding nets.

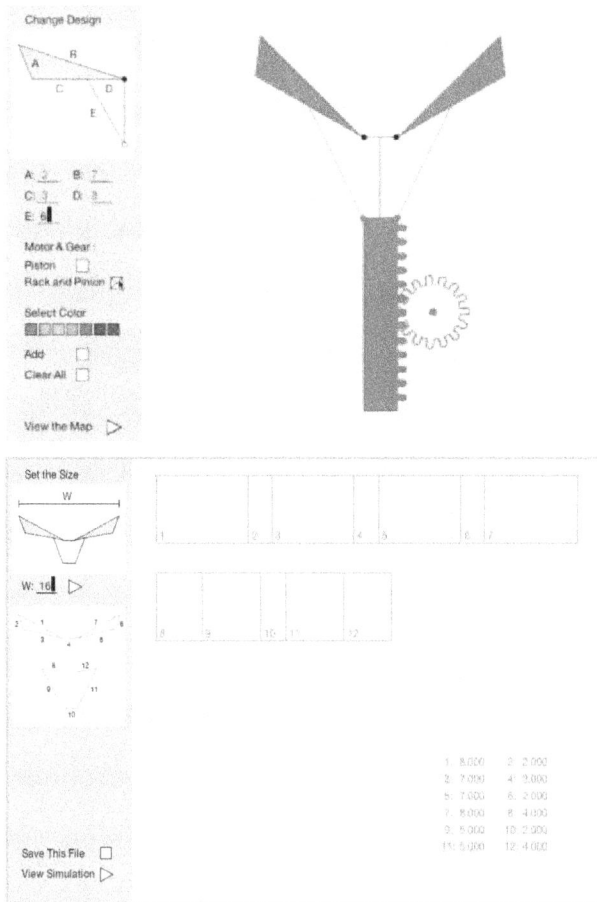

Figure 3. Sequential screen snapshots of FoldMecha.

Iterative Prototyping

Design guidelines for the physical prototyping are developed based on iterative three stages. The first (mechanical) stage starts from a simple papercraft automaton without electronic or computational elements. Then the second (electronics) stage introduces elements such as a motor (or motor with a switch), sensors and other actuators. The third (computational) phase, includes programming and interactivity are included. The iterative constructions illustrate a plausible method that can be adapted for novices' activities: a sequence of iterative steps through which students can create, test, and optimize these mechanical forms to include computational control through a mixture of planning and tinkering.

Stage 1: Simple hand-powered automata
I built the first prototypes using only craft materials – mainly paper with glue, tape, and a steel wire or wood sticks. As the walkers (the first study) employ a rather challenging mechanism, I found that doing the initial assembly with a steel wire (which is bendable but rigid) helped the trial-and-error process through repetitive revisions. In contrast, the second example (the mechanical flower) employs a relatively simple mechanism: a

straightforward vertical movement, so I used rigid wood sticks for the initial designs; as the work proceeds to subsequent iterations, these can be replaced with any long and fixed materials (such as straws). This first stage of prototyping enabled me to solidify my understanding of basic automata structures.

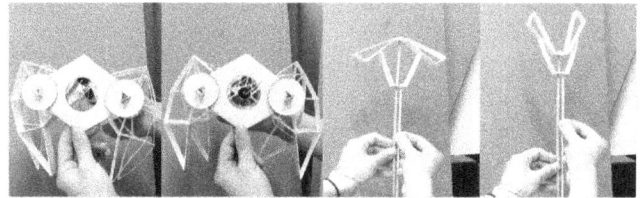

Figure 4. A steel wire connects each pair of paper legs and hand-rotating enables the walking motion (left); two wood sticks connected to the sepal and the center of petals enables the opening and closing motion (right).

Stage 2: Locomotion with a motor and exploration of forms with more modules

In order to automate the movements via a motor with gears, I needed to enhance the accuracy of the structure and adjust the forms so that they could accommodate the attached electronic elements. Specifically, motors and gears can influence the building at this stage. Motor sizes, weights, required power resources are diverse so I tested different motors, gear designs, and structure' configurations to decide suitable configurations. To operate the basic mechanism of each structure, the walkers required two pairs of legs and the flowers required one pair of petals to form each basic structure; but I extended these basic mechanisms, exploring the addition of extra petals or pairs of legs, and combining the flower and walker into larger composite forms. Figure 5 depicts important moments in this second (electronic component) phase of construction.

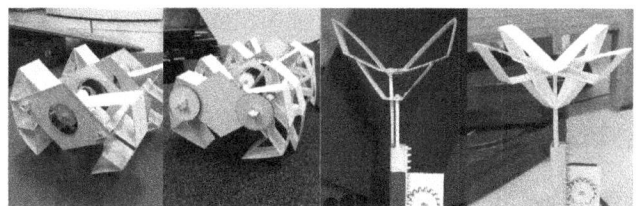

Figure 5. Motors are implemented to automate the movements and applied more modules (legs for the walkers and petals for the flowers) to enhance the three-dimensional effect of models.

Stage 3: Interactive mechatronics with a microcontroller
Finally, I moved to "computational paper mechatronics", with intermingled mechanical, electrical, and computational concepts that augment the realm of papercraft automata. This stage included an Arduino microcontroller in the constructions to control the walkers and flowers. I began with simple interactive scenarios for controlling the paper

machines that can lead a far greater range of "narratives", which can motivate one's creative exploration. For instance, in one of the walker constructions, two RGB LEDs are positioned as "eyes" with a light sensor; the overall model was a sort of mechanical "crab", which prefers darkness and thus stops walking in bright light (its blue eyes turned red as it responds with alarm to the presence of light). Also, in one of the flower constructions, an infrared proximity sensor was mounted at the center of the petals; this sent signals to respond to the motor (to close the petals) when the user's hands near approach the flower. The result is a mechanical paper "Venus fly trap". Figure 6 illustrates these ideas by showing illustrative moments from the third stage of constructions.

Figure 6. Integrating a microcontroller widens the design space of constructions from previous stages.

FUTURE WORK

I plan to add more design modules with different mechanisms so that FoldMecha can help users select multiple modules to explore a wide spectrum of their own creations. For instance, the preliminary two examples (walkers and flowers) can be each module and one can create another creature such as a walking flower (See Figure 7). At the same time, I plan to conduct workshops with novices using the FoldMecha to solidify design guidelines as well as to enhance accessibility of the tool. Thereby, my ultimate goal is to investigate paper mechatronics as a novel design medium that can support one's creative exploration via designing and to provide a computational design tool to make it more accessible.

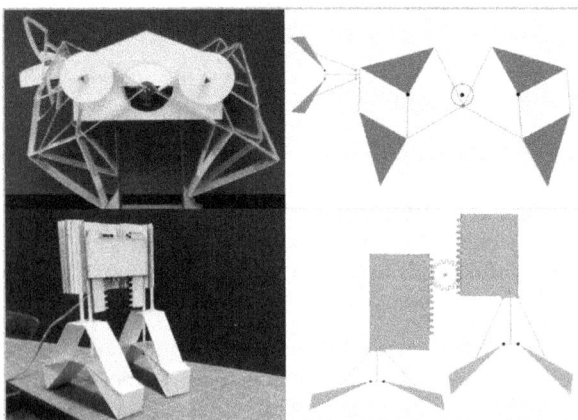

Figure 7. Prototypes (left) and FoldMecha simulation sketches (right) to represent the concept of assembling multiple modules to build more diverse models.

ACKNOWLEDGEMENTS

I am grateful for the guidance and support of my advisors, Mark D. Gross and Michael Eisenberg. This material is partly based upon work supported by the National Science Foundation under Grant No. IS1451463.

REFERENCES

1. Addams, R. How to Make and Design Automata. *Craft Education*, Dorset, UK. 2001.

2. Coros, S.; Thomaszewski, B.; Noris, G.; Sueda, S.; Forberg, M.; Sumner, R. W.; Matusik, W.; and Bickel, B. 2013. Computational design of mechanical characters. *ACM Trans. Graph.* 32: 4, Article 83 (July 2013), 12 pages. DOI=10.1145/2461912.2461953

3. Eisenberg, M. and Eisenberg, A, 1997. Creating polyhedral models by computer. *J. Comput. Math. Sci. Teach.* 16, 4 (November 1997), 477-511.

4. Rob Ives: http://www.robives.com

5. Megaro, V.; Thomaszewski, B.; Gauge, D.; Grinspun, E.; Coros, S.; and Gross, M. 2014. Chacra: An Interactive Design System for Rapid Character Crafting.

6. Mitani, M. and Suzuki, H. 2004. Making papercraft toys from meshes using strip-based approximate unfolding. *ACM Transactions on Graphics* 23:3 (August 2004), 259-263. DOI=10.1145/1186562.1015711

7. Oh, H.; Eisenberg, M.; Gross, M. and Hsi, S. 2015. Paper mechatronics: a design case study for a young medium. In *Proceedings of the 14th International Conference on Interaction Design and Children* (IDC '15). ACM, New York, NY, USA, 371-374. DOI=10.1145/2771839.2771919

8. Onn, A. and Alexander, G. 1998. *Cabaret Mechanical Movement*. London: Cabaret Mechanical Theatre.

9. Qi, J. and Buechley. L. 2010. Electronic Popables: exploring paper-based computing through an interactive pop-up book. In *Proceedings of Tangible, embedded, and embodied interaction (TEI '10)*. ACM, New York, NY, USA, 121-128. DOI=10.1145/1709886.1709909

10. Saul, G.; Xu, C.; and Gross, M. 2010. Interactive paper devices: end-user design & fabrication. In *Proceedings of Tangible, embedded, and embodied interaction* (TEI '10). ACM, New York, NY, USA, 205-212. DOI=10.1145/1709886.1709924

11. Zhu, L.; Xu, W.; Snyder, J.; Liu, Y.; Wang, G.; and Guo, B. 2012. Motion-guided mechanical toy modeling. *ACM Trans. Graph.* 31, 6, Article 127 (November 2012), 10 pages. DOI=10.1145/2366145.2366146

Enriching Online Classroom Communication with Collaborative Multi-Modal Annotations

Dongwook Yoon
Cornell University
Ithaca, NY 14850
dy252@cornell.edu

ABSTRACT

In massive open online courses, peer discussion is a scalable solution for offering interactive and engaging learning experiences to a large number of students. On the other hand, the quality of communication mediated through online discussion tools, such as discussion forums, is far less expressive than that of face-to-face communication. As a solution, I present *RichReview*, a multi-modal annotation system through which distant students can exchange ideas using versatile combinations of voice, text, and pointing gestures. A series of lab and deployment studies of RichReview promised that the expressive multimedia mixture and lightweight audio browsing feature help students better understand commentators' intention. For the large-scale deployment, I redesigned RichReview as a web applet in edX's courseware framework. By deploying the system at scale, I will investigate (1) the optimal group assignment scheme that maximizes overall diversities of group members, (2) educational data mining applications based on user-generated rich discussion data, and (3) the impact of the rich discussion to students' retention of knowledge. Throughout these studies, I will argue that a multi-modal anchored digital document annotation system enables rich online peer discussion at scale.

Author Keywords

Multi-modal annotation; online education; peer discussion; instructor feedback; massive open online courses.

ACM Classification Keywords

H.5.3 Group and Organization Interfaces: Collaborative computing; H.5.2 User Interfaces: Interaction styles; H.5.1 Multimedia Information Systems: Audio input/output.

INTRODUCTION

In massive open online courses (MOOCs) or large classes, it is impractical for instructors to give personalized and constructive feedback to individual students due to the high student-instructor ratio. As a scalable solution, prior

UIST '15 Adjunct, November 08-11, 2015, Charlotte, NC, USA
ACM 978-1-4503-3780-9/15/11.
http://dx.doi.org/10.1145/2815585.2815591

researches have suggested supporting inter-student interactions. However, communicational affordances of existing peer discussion systems, such as video chats [3] or anchored discussions [1,9], are far less expressive than what face-to-face (F2F) interaction can support with rich communication modalities, such as voice and gestures.

My dissertation aims to bring the richness of F2F-like communication into online education at scale. As a first step of this work, I designed RichReview, a tablet-based multi-modal annotation system that can record and replay a dynamic mixture of voice, digitizer inking, and gestural pen hovering. RichReview offers two major beneficial affordances for supporting online peer discussion. Firstly, RichReview benefits from expressivity of coherently combined multimedia mixture [6]. Secondly, RichReview facilitates contextualization of a comment by (1) placing it right below the referent text-line in a fluid document layout [7] and (2) supporting a deictic gesture over the text as an referential aid for speaking. A series of prior lab and deployment studies have confirmed the effectiveness of RichReview as a rich communication tool. For example, the users found it quick and easy to browse a voice recording in RichReview using its lightweight time indexing feature.

To draw out design implications of multi-modal annotation systems for peer discussion, we deployed RichReview into a class-wide discussion process. Since the original tablet app cannot be distributed to the students who do not have that specific platform, I redesigned and built RichReview as a web service that supports cross-platform access. From the study, we found out that an effective voice editing feature is key to a successful multi-modal peer discussion. For example, after making a mistake in a voice comment, students wanted to rerecord the section of the audio only, rather than start over and redo the entire recording. In the forthcoming study, I will focus on designing voice editing features, which are as versatile and lightweight as editing text, such as partial deletion and interim insertion of voice.

For a large-scale deployment of the system, I am working closely with edX, a MOOC provider with over 3 million learners worldwide, to integrate RichReview into their courseware platform. The rich discussion data aggregated from a number of students' online activities will constitute sources of big-data for various educational data mining (EDM) applications. For example, students' profile data, such as topical interest, extracted from their past discussion content can help develop a peer group assignment scheme that maximizes overall diversity of the group member composition for quality discussions [3].

Finally, our prior studies focused on the rich annotation system's communicational affordances rather than its impacts on learning. To measure the system's pedagogical efficacy, our large-scale evaluation will investigate how different feedback tools, including RichReview, affect students' understanding and retention of knowledge.

Thesis statement I will argue that multi-modal anchored digital document annotation system enables rich online peer discussion *at scale*.

DESIGNING RICHREVIEW
The design goal of the RichReview system was to empower writing feedback process with F2F-like communicational modalities by employing rich multi-modal inputs.

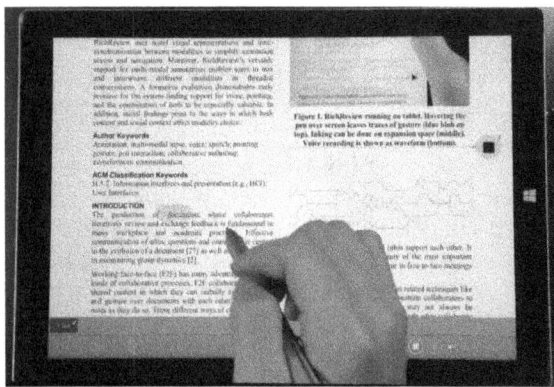

Figure 1. RichReview records and replays a combination of digitizer writing and hovering in sync with voice.

Choice of Modalities: Inking, Voice, and Gesture
In F2F conversation, people choose a versatile combination of communication modalities based on different affordances that they offer. Therefore, when designing RichReview, we chose the three input modalities to support each different use cases as follow. When fixing a simple typewriting error, digitizer inking is the easiest way to leave a written markup. Voice recording's high-throughput enables effective description of complicated ideas, with an additional advantage of nuanced expressions with voice pitch and tone. Additionally, we replicated 'finger-pointing action' as a referential aid to voice by recording and replaying the pen's hovering movement.

Design Principles and Features
In order to weave the multi-modal annotations together as a coherent whole without introducing additional complexities to the user interface, we set the following three principles:

Consistency and Simplicity We fought against the potential complexities of introducing several multi-modal inputs by keeping interactions consistent and mode-less. For example, users can tap any annotation entity to replay the recording from the time point when the queried entity was recorded.

Contextualization Putting comments close to the pertinent texts enriches the context of conversation, because then the discussant can see what they are talking about. RichReview employed the TextTearing representation [7] that places comments alongside the referent text.

Voice Consumption In [2], Grudin claimed that voice applications facilitate communication in favor of the speaker rather than the listener, because voice is easy to record but hard to browse or navigate through. To solve this voice consumption problem, we let users tap any of the recorded elements—voice waveforms, recorded inks, or pointing gesture traces—to navigate through the audio. In addition, overlaying auto-caption over the voice comments enabled visual skimming of audio contents.

Preliminary User Study and Findings
We conducted a formative user study in which participants performed writing feedback tasks [6]. The participants could mingle versatile combinations of modalities to generate expressive and nuanced comments. The recipients even felt telepresence of the speaker who spoke and pointed over the document at the same time. Additionally, deictic gestures could dramatically reduce communication costs when referring to a specific part of the texts.

DEPLOYMENT FOR RICH INSTRUCTOR FEEDBACK
Given the success of the preliminary study of the prototype system, we wanted to measure practical impacts of using RichReview in a real educational setting. We targeted an undergraduate course's term paper writing and feedback process. Most students in the class were using laptops, so we built a platform-independent web viewer for replaying RichReview comments generated from the tablet app by the instructor. We asked the students to compare the RichReview experience with the traditional pen + paper feedback and the office hour meeting experience.

Findings
The students preferred the RichReview feedback to longhand writing. From the tone and nuances of voice recording, they could better understand which part of manuscript the instructor really wanted them to revise. Surprisingly, some students even thought that exchanging the rich comments could potentially substitute office hour meetings. They especially liked RichReview's support for quick voice re-listening since they can replay the comments until they fully understand the instructor's intention, which is a luxury of the asynchronous communication that office hour meetings cannot offer. Nevertheless, some users still preferred in-person meeting for its conversational immediacy and prompt back and forth turn taking.

DEPLOYMENT FOR RICH ONLINE PEER DISCUSSION
As a step forward to the large-scale peer discussion, we conducted a dry run deployment study in a midsize real classroom [8]. The goal of this study was to obtain design

implications for supporting peer discussion through multi-modal annotations.

Discussion Support Features

In peer discussion, the students are the major bodies of people who create the multi-modal annotations. As such, we designed and built a desktop version of RichReview so that the students can record their voices through web browsers as an extension to the web viewer system built for the previous study. As the running environment moves to desktop, we also redesigned user interface to support desktop inputs. For example, textual comments in the new system were an integral part of the multi-modal mixture, which can be placed with voice or pointing gestures (see Figure 2).

As the system revolves around the iterative design process, we geared the system toward the peer discussion purpose by introducing several new features for supporting discussion. The Comment History feature offered a chronological summary of the existing comments of the document. Booklet UI was an overlay widget for prompt cross-document navigation, and the General Note feature offered a discussion space for higher-level topics.

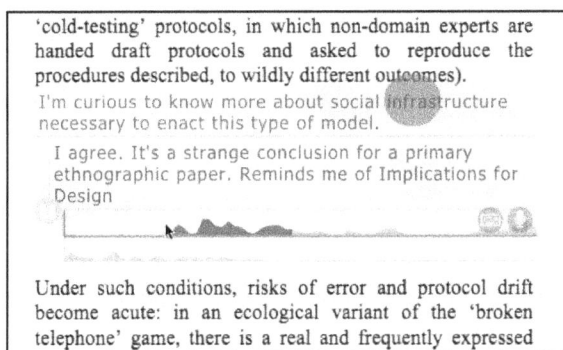

Figure 2. RichReview online discussion system. This example thread of comments presents a combination of textual annotation, speaking, and pointing gesture.

The RichReview discussion system was deployed for a weekly class-wide peer discussion activity for a graduate-level social science course.

Findings

The students encountered peers' comments as they read the body texts to where the RichReview comments were juxtaposed. This allowed socially driven learning in that students expanded their perspectives about the course topics by reading peer comments. The popularity of the Comment History and the Booklet features highlighted the importance of supporting comment skimming and cross-document browsing behaviors.

On the other hand, we found that the quality of voice comments might be inferior to text comments, because students feel compelled to keep speaking—not to have long pauses in the recording—which works against deep

thinking. Moreover, when a part of a recording was unsatisfactory, the entirety of it had to be rerecorded. We also observed other reservations from situational constraints, such as working in a library, missing headset, or self-consciousness. This leads to our next research plan for developing advanced semantic voice editing features.

FORTHCOMING STUDIES

In the coming 2015 fall, I will be entering the fourth year of my PhD. To finish my claim on the multi-modal peer discussion, I will delve into the following research topics for the rest of my study.

Semantic Voice Editing

Rubin et al. presented a caption-based audio editing UI by which audio can be edited in the same way as text [5]. Inspired by their approach, we will present a set of new live audio editing features so that the students can record and revise a voice comment at the same time.

The problem of auto-captioning is that it is not always readily available and it requires time for processing or networking. We can solve this by splitting the audio stream into chunks of pseudo-semantic tokens that are split by the pauses of the audio recording. The pause boundaries will provide snapping guidelines for voice editing on which the user can perform versatile editing operations, similarly to editing text, such as trimming, copying, and pasting.

Even after getting the voice recording done, some editing tasks can still be tedious jobs. For example, in our RichReview lab study, most of the users wanted to remove long pauses and 'Um's in their speech as a baseline cleanup. A semantic post-processing can ease such a burden of the repetitive but trivial removal tasks by automatically trimming non-content tokens.

Finally, words are sometimes wrongly transcribed as homophones—different words that sound similar to each other. To help users revising a mistranscription, we can interactively suggest alternative homophones of selected words. For example, when the user requests alternatives to the mistranscription 'too male,' the system can suggest 'to male' and 'two mail' by dynamically computing a space of homophone word combinations.

Toward Online Discussion at Scale

The final goal of my dissertation is a large-scale deployment of the multi-modal annotation system for peer discussion in MOOCs. I am targeting the peer discussion use-case in which a group of students grows threaded comments on shared course material as a means for exchanging their ideas on the subject matters.

We chose edX.org as a testbed for the study. The edX version of RichReview is a part of XBlock, a component architecture for building edX courseware. This means that the authors of edX courses will be able to employ

RichReview discussions as an integral part of their edX courseware contents.

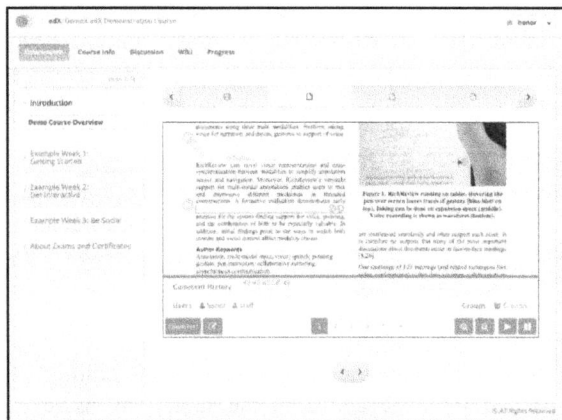

Figure 3. RichReview MOOC discussion system implemented as a course applet in edX.org

Since a number of students in MOOCs will conduct discussions *at scale*, the aggregated multimedia contents can be a source of big-data for various educational data mining applications. For example, when assigning a number of students into discussion groups, it is a challenge to minimize students' assignment waiting time while keeping the member compositions of overall groups heterogeneous enough to raise diverse perspectives [4]. For an optimal group assignment, we can leverage student profile data such as demographic information or a student's course enrollment history. In addition, computationally analyzing the contents of the past RichReview discussion can provide richer background information such as a student's discussion style and preferred topics.

Moreover, after a semester of students finish a round of discussion, analysis on the accumulated rich discussion data can offer collective insights about the underlying texts. For example, if many users made pointing gestures over the same sentence, this repeated referencing behavior may indicate the higher rate of interest pertaining to that part of the body text. In addition, applying natural language processing techniques can unearth the students' collective understanding on the underlying discussion materials. For example, running a topic modeling on aggregated discussion threads will provide information on the relevant topical keywords that subsequent students can find useful for understanding the texts.

Measuring of Pedagogical Effectiveness of Rich Feedback

We will evaluate efficacy of the rich feedback system as an educational tool by measuring how different feedback methods, including RichReview and pen + paper markup, affect students' retention of knowledge. Since peer assessment cannot offer a rigorous control on the quality of feedback and experimental conditions, we will instead

deploy RichReview for the instructor feedback process. A math course will be an optimal testbed, since we can track students' understanding on math concepts by repetitively measuring scores of quiz-assignment-prelim throughout a semester. The students will be split into two groups, which will alternatively get feedback using different tools. For example, two groups can go through three sections of studies with different feedback tools in the order of C-R-C vs. C-C-R (C for the control condition, and R for RichReview). This design will allow us to firstly measure from a baseline condition from both groups, and then to compare effects of different methods in a balanced way.

ACKNOWLEDGEMENT
I am grateful for the guidance of my advisor Prof. François Guimbretière. My study was made possible by the support from the Kwanjeong Educational Foundation and the generous gifts from FXPAL and Microsoft Research.

REFERENCES
1. Brush, A.J.B., Bargeron, D., Grudin, J., Borning, A., and Gupta, A. Supporting interaction outside of class: anchored discussions vs. discussion boards. CSCL, ACM Press (2002), 425–434.

2. Grudin, J. Why CSCW applications fail: problems in the design and evaluationof organizational interfaces. *CSCW*, ACM Press (1988), 85–93.

3. Kulkarni, C., Cambre, J., Kotturi, Y., Bernstein, M.S., and Klemmer, S.R. Talkabout: Making Distance Matter with Small Groups in Massive Classes. *CSCW*, ACM Press (2015), 1116–1128.

4. Kulkarni, C.E., Bernstein, M.S., and Klemmer, S.R. PeerStudio: Rapid Peer Feedback Emphasizes Revision and Improves Performance. *Learning @ Scale*, ACM (2015), 75–84.

5. Rubin, S., Berthouzoz, F., Mysore, G.J., Li, W., and Agrawala, M. Content-based tools for editing audio stories. *UIST*, ACM Press (2013), 113–122.

6. Yoon, D., Chen, N., Guimbretière, F., and Sellen, A. RichReview: Blending Ink, Speech, and Gesture to Support Collaborative Document Review. *UIST*, ACM (2014), 481–490.

7. Yoon, D., Chen, N., and Guimbretière, F. TextTearing: opening white space for digital ink annotation. *UIST*, ACM Press (2013), 107–112.

8. Yoon, D., Chen, N., Randles, B., Cheatle, A., Jackson, S., Loeckenhoff, C., Sellen, A., and Guimbretière, F. Deployment of a Collaborative Multi-Modal Annotation System for Instructor Feedback and Peer Discussion. *CSCW*, ACM Press (2016).

9. Zyto, S., Karger, D., Ackerman, M., and Mahajan, S. Successful classroom deployment of a social document annotation system. *SIGCHI*, ACM Press (2012), 1883.

Using Personal Devices to Facilitate Multi-user Interaction with Large Display Walls

Ulrich von Zadow
Interactive Media Lab
Technische Universität Dresden
Dresden, Germany
uzadow@acm.org

ABSTRACT

Large display walls and personal devices such as Smart-phones have complementary characteristics. While large displays are well-suited to multi-user interaction (potentially with complex data), they are inherently public and generally cannot present an interface adapted to the individual user. However, effective multi-user interaction in many cases depends on the ability to tailor the interface, to interact without interfering with others, and to access and possibly share private data. The combination with personal devices facilitates exactly this. Multi-device interaction concepts enable data transfer and include moving parts of UIs to the personal device. In addition, hand-held devices can be used to present personal views to the user. Our work will focus on using personal devices for true multi-user interaction with interactive display walls. It will cover appropriate interaction techniques as well as the technical foundation and will be validated with corresponding application cases.

Author Keywords

Cross-device interaction; data transfer; mobile phones; display wall; wearable display; multi-user; collaboration

ACM Classification Keywords

H.5.2. Information Interfaces and Presentation: User Interfaces: Input devices and strategies, Interaction styles

INTRODUCTION

Wall-sized interactive displays are becoming more common and have been shown to provide numerous benefits [2]. Their potentially very high resolution means that they are usable from a distance as well as in reach of the hands, making them suitable for the exploration of large amounts of data. Collaboration is well-supported and physical navigation – moving around to access data – becomes possible, exploiting human spatial awareness [4]. At the same time, they have inherent

limitations. Data shown is generally visible by all collaborators and thus public. It is hard to identify the user and provide a user-specific interface. In addition, it is unclear where user interface elements such as tool palettes should be placed on a very large display [2].

Contrast this with devices such as smartphones and tablets: They are inherently personal devices that connect users with their digital ID, providing easy access to private data in everyday situations. Due to their small size, personal devices have limited ability to show large amounts of data; also, sharing views with other people is hard at best. The combination of both device classes makes it possible to use the modalities – display output, touch input, sound and haptic feedback – available on the personal device to extend interaction with the large display. It also allows personalized interaction and access to private data when using the large display: User interface components such as palettes can be offloaded to the personal device, and data can be transferred in both directions, essentially moving it from private to public space and back (e.g., [13]).

PREVIOUS WORK

Interaction with large displays and personal mobile devices is an active research field. We first discuss work that examines relevant aspects of interactions with large vertical displays. The second section focuses on interaction with large displays using personal devices.

Interaction with Wall Displays

For a general introduction to interaction with high-resolution wall-sized displays, we refer to two overviews. Ni et al. [10] provide a comprehensive survey that covers rendering technology, interaction techniques and application domains. Among others, they mention transitioning between working within touching distance and further away as interaction challenge. Andrews et al. [2] give an overview of data visualization on large displays. Like other work of this group (e.g., [3, 4]), this work asserts that physical navigation (moving around in front of the wall to access content) has advantages in speed and maintaining context. They emphasize that the "design of other interactions must afford or even exploit physical navigation" and argue that interaction should be localized: The user's position and focus should determine the location of interaction effects. For a different perspective on the effects of physical navigation, see [9]. Related to this is Greenberg et

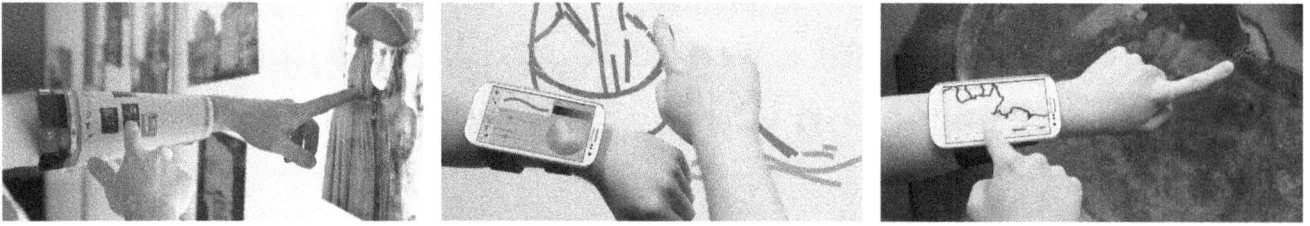

Figure 1. SleeD: e-Ink mockup (left), smartphone-based prototype with tool palette (center) and interactive personal view using the non-dominant SleeD hand to provide a frame of reference (right).

al.'s notion of Proxemic Interaction (e.g., [7]), in which interactions are based on spatial relationships between people and devices.

Multi-Device Interaction with Large Displays

There is a large body of work that covers interaction at close distance between personal devices and large displays. For space reasons, we restrict ourselves to a selection that covers a wide range of interaction techniques. Alt et al. [1] analyse content exchange techniques with public displays, comparing direct interaction with remote website and mobile phone interaction. Schmidt et al. [13] examined cross-device interaction between phones and interactive surfaces, building on the ability to detect touches by phones on a tabletop. They proposed a collection of interaction techniques in areas such as data transfer, personalization, or localized feedback. Using a mobile device to personalize interfaces was also investigated by Spindler et al. [15], who offload user interface palettes onto secondary hand-held displays and thereby free the associated display space. The idea of using mobile personal palettes is also found in Haller et al.'s work on the NiCE Discussion Room (e.g., [8]), who use pen interaction with static, palm-sized printed menus to interface with a large interactive whiteboard.

Interaction from a distance has also been examined, among others by Dachselt and Buchholz [6], who use expressive phone gestures for data transfer and interaction with large screen content. With CodeSpace, Bragdon et al. [5] integrate multi-device interaction and distal pointing into a realistic application scenario. In PointerPhone [14], Seifert et al. investigate the interactions possible when remote pointing is combined with interactions on the phone. Significantly, Peck et al.'s work [11] is to our knowledge the only one that combines pointing and physical navigation. In general, only few works propose interaction techniques that exploit the advantages of physical navigation. Finally, several authors (among them Rashid et al. [12]) investigate the effects of attention switches between small devices and large displays and find them time-consuming and disrupting. Interaction techniques that explicitly address this issue have not been investigated.

RESEARCH OBJECTIVES

The main goal of our work will be to assess the implications of using personal devices in the context of multi-user interaction with large display walls. A necessary prerequisite for this (and a research goal in itself) is enabling the association of touches on the wall to individual users. A further central objective is the development of appropriate interaction techniques. In this context, the following issues need to be taken into account:

- We agree with Andrews et al. [2] that techniques should adjust to a user's changing physical location and work hand-in-hand with physical navigation. As a user moves from overview distance to a close detail view, the enabled interactions need to follow perception in scale and precision as well as adjust to the user's level of engagement [7].

- Gaze switches are an inevitable part of multi-device interaction but have been shown to disrupt users and slow them down (e.g., [12]). They therefore need to be considered explicitly when designing interactions.

- Interactions need to enable smooth transitions between working directly with the wall (using, e.g., touch) and interaction at a distance (using the personal device or gestures) [10].

The work above will enable us to analyze the tradeoffs involved in different device configurations: What benefits and drawbacks do different types of personal devices have when compared to direct interaction with the display wall? A number of tradeoffs are involved here: While personal devices make working with private data easy, provide an implicit user identification, and afford interaction at a distance without changing modalities, directly interacting with the wall avoids gaze switches entirely and enables larger personal views. Our work should enable us to provide a well-founded analysis of these tradeoffs as well as associated recommendations for application designers.

WORK TO DATE

Work until now has focused on the one hand on development of a solid technical foundation. On the other hand, we have explored interaction between arm-worn devices and large display walls in the SleeD project [16].

As a technical foundation, we wanted a framework that allows rapid prototyping of novel user interfaces and offers support for seamless multi-device development. Furthermore, we required access to all needed input modalities: touch and position information for all connected devices. To fulfill these requirements, we extended the libavg framework[1]. Significant work went into supporting development of distributed user interfaces. The UI streaming component we wrote renders all user interfaces on a central server and streams the display contents via h264 over RTP to attached mobile devices.

---

[1]https://www.libavg.de

Figure 2. Exploring cross-device data transfer: Integrating layout support (left), transfer based on geolocation (center), and transfer of continuous streams of items (right).

Conversely, input events are streamed to the server. To the application developer, the different devices appear as local windows; all networking is abstracted away entirely. These components have been deployed successfully. As a result, libavg is being used as basis for nearly all wall and multi-device research at our lab.

With SleeD [16], we presented a concept for combining interactions on touch-sensitive sleeve displays (the SleeD) with large display walls. In wall interaction, a SleeD inherits the advantages (such as complex personalized interaction and access to private data) that other personal devices have. Additionally, it is quicker in activation and makes seamless switching to bimanual work on the wall possible. In our publication, we discuss different levels of coupling between wearable and wall. A focus is on close physical coupling, where the SleeD hand provides a frame of reference for the dominant hand (Figure 1, right). In addition, we propose novel user interface techniques that support data transfer, user-specific interfaces, and arbitrary personal views (Figure 1) that we verified using a qualitative study.

SleeD is a first major step in tackling the overall research objectives and lays the foundation for comparing use of personal devices with direct wall interaction. However, while it supports multi-user interaction conceptually, a multi-user capable implementation is still missing since the wall does not distinguish between users.

CURRENT AND FUTURE WORK
Current and future work will focus on three areas: the technical foundation that enables the remainder of the research, development and assessment of interaction techniques, and applications that validate the techniques.

Technical Foundation
Work on the technical foundation is for the most part done. However, one unsolved issue remains: How do we correlate users with touches at a display wall? Without this capability, personalized multi-user touch interaction is not possible. Numerous solutions for touch user identification have been proposed for tabletop displays, but most of these do not generalize to wall displays because they are either specific to the orientation, rely on viewing the touch from above or are limited to small displays.

We are developing a practically usable technical solution that serves as a basis for our development of application use cases, besides being a novel contribution in itself. This precludes

development of custom hardware. We aim to have robust user detection and thus temporary user IDs for the duration of a typical usage session. This is complemented with state-of-the-art login procedures when a user enters the session to correlate persistent user IDs with the temporary IDs.

Interaction Techniques
We are currently investigating bidirectional data transfer techniques between smartphone and display wall (Figure 2) that make use of the phone's position and orientation. The techniques we are developing support multi-item transfer and layout, allow casual as well as precise interaction, work well with physical navigation, and are designed to minimize gaze switches between the devices. Our work includes a comprehensive qualitative study as well as an analysis of the underlying design space.

A second – related – project is a pointing technique that adapts to varying distances and thus works well with physical navigation. By seamlessly varying the pointing parameters, we can support casual and imprecise pointing at a distance and very precise pointing when close to the wall, while maintaining an imperceptible transition between the two.

Furthermore, we intend to use the work on SleeD as a basis for a comparison of using different modalities (smartphones, direct wall interaction and different arm-worn devices) for interaction with a display wall. We will build state-of-the-art interfaces for these modalities that support handling of personal data and data transfer, tool palettes, and individualized views on data and use these interfaces to conduct a comprehensive qualitative study. Our goal is to analyze the tradeoffs: How do the differences in the modalities with respect to private data handling, disruption through gaze switches, bimanual interaction on the wall, and user identification affect users?

Applications
In this part of the work, we will build application cases that validate the concepts and interaction techniques presented above. Currently, two application cases are planned: A game and a biological visualization application. The first is a time-critical cooperative multiplayer game (Figure 3, left) that we will use to evaluate behavior when using a variety of input modalities. Interesting questions include communication channels, awareness of other player's actions, and modes of cooperation.

The second application case involves visualization of biological data (Figure 3, right). In cooperation with biologists from

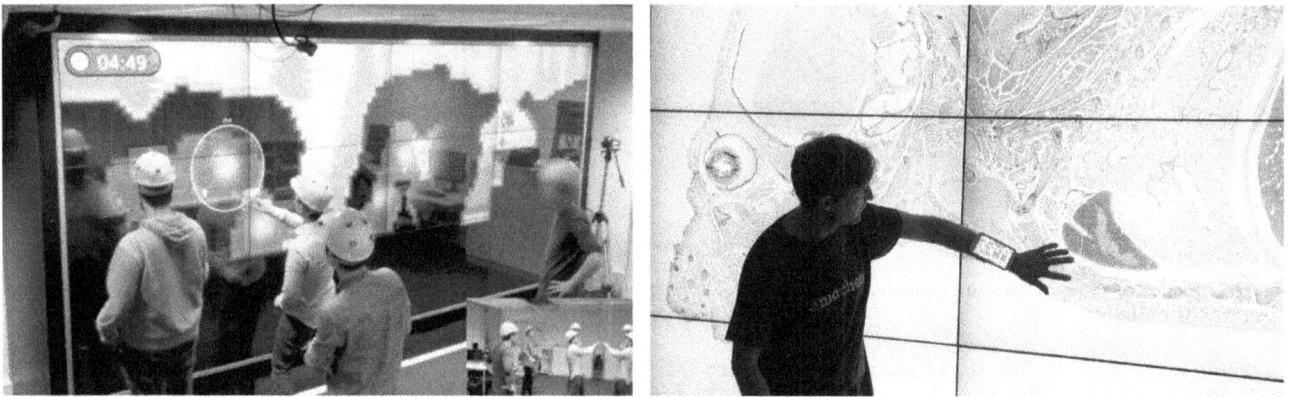

Figure 3. Application cases: Cooperative game (left) and focus-context interaction using biological data.

the Max Plank Institute for Molecular Cell Biology and Genetics, we plan to build a visualization application for light sheet microscopy images. Development will proceed in close cooperation with prospective users. The work on interaction techniques described above should on the one hand be a solid foundation for this work. On the other hand, we can use the application case to verify their practical usefulness.

CONCLUSION

Personal devices have the potential to enable true multi-user interaction with large display walls, and we have identified a number of research questions in this area that remain unsolved. We are confident that we can make a significant contribution in this area with the combination of technical foundation, interaction techniques, and verification using application cases.

ACKNOWLEDGEMENTS

I thank my advisor, Raimund Dachselt, for his indispensable help and guidance. Furthermore, I thank Ulrike Kister and Ricardo Langner for their significant assistance with the camera ready version.

REFERENCES

1. Alt, F., Shirazi, A. S., Kubitza, T., and Schmidt, A. Interaction techniques for creating and exchanging content with public displays. In *Proc. CHI*, ACM (2013), 1709–1718.

2. Andrews, C., Endert, A., Yost, B., and North, C. Information visualization on large, high-resolution displays: Issues, challenges, and opportunities. *Information Visualization 10*, 4 (2011), 341–355.

3. Andrews, C., and North, C. The impact of physical navigation on spatial organization for sensemaking. *IEEE Transactions on Visualization and Computer Graphics 19*, 12 (2013), 2207–2216.

4. Ball, R., North, C., and Bowman, D. A. Move to improve: promoting physical navigation to increase user performance with large displays. In *Proc. CHI*, ACM (2007), 191–200.

5. Bragdon, A., DeLine, R., Hinckley, K., and Morris, M. R. Code space: Combining touch, devices, and skeletal tracking to support developer meetings. In *Proc. ITS*, ACM (2011), 212–221.

6. Dachselt, R., and Buchholz, R. Natural throw and tilt interaction between mobile phones and distant displays. In *Proc. CHI EA*, ACM (2009), 3253–3258.

7. Greenberg, S., Marquardt, N., Ballendat, T., Diaz-Marino, R., and Wang, M. Proxemic interactions: the new ubicomp? *Interactions 18*, 1 (Jan. 2011), 42–50.

8. Haller, M., Leitner, J., Seifried, T., Wallace, J. R., Scott, S. D., Richter, C., Brandl, P., Gokcezade, A., and Hunter, S. The NiCE discussion room: Integrating paper and digital media to support co-located group meetings. In *Proc. CHI*, ACM (2010), 609–618.

9. Jakobsen, M. R., and Hornbæk, K. Is moving improving?: Some effects of locomotion in wall-display interaction. In *Proc. CHI*, ACM (2015), 4169–4178.

10. Ni, T., Schmidt, G., Staadt, O., Livingston, M., Ball, R., and May, R. A survey of large high-resolution display technologies, techniques, and applications. In *Virtual Reality Conference, 2006* (march 2006), 223 – 236.

11. Peck, S. M., North, C., and Bowman, D. A multiscale interaction technique for large, high-resolution displays. In *Proc. 3DUI*, ACM (2009), 31–38.

12. Rashid, U., Nacenta, M. A., and Quigley, A. The cost of display switching: a comparison of mobile, large display and hybrid ui configurations. In *Proc. AVI*, ACM (2012), 99–106.

13. Schmidt, D., Seifert, J., Rukzio, E., and Gellersen, H. A cross-device interaction style for mobiles and surfaces. In *Proc. DIS*, ACM (2012), 318–327.

14. Seifert, J., Bayer, A., and Rukzio, E. PointerPhone: Using mobile phones for direct pointing interactions with remote displays. In *Proc. INTERACT*. Springer, 2013, 18–35.

15. Spindler, M., Cheung, V., and Dachselt, R. Dynamic tangible user interface palettes. In *Proc. INTERACT*. Springer, 2013, 159–176.

16. von Zadow, U., Büschel, W., Langner, R., and Dachselt, R. Sleed: Using a sleeve display to interact with touch-sensitive display walls. In *Proc. ITS*, ACM (2014), 129–138.

Graphical Passwords for Older Computer Users

Nancy Carter
College of William & Mary
Williamsburg, VA 23187 USA
njcarter@cs.wm.edu

ABSTRACT

Computers and the internet have been challenging for many computer users over the age of 60. We conducted a survey of older users which revealed that the creation, management and recall of strong text passwords were some of the challenging aspects of modern technology. In practice, this user group based passwords on familiar facts such as family member names, pets, phone numbers and important personal dates. Graphical passwords formed from abstract graphical symbols or anonymous facial images are feasible, but harder for older computers users to grasp and recall. In this paper we describe initial results for our graphical password system based on recognition of culturally-familiar facial images that are age-relevant to the life experiences of older users. Our goals are to design an easy-to-memorize, graphical password system intended specifically for older users, and achieve a level of password entropy comparable to traditional PINs and text passwords. We are also conducting a user study to demonstrate our technique and capture performance and recall metrics for comparison with traditional password systems.

Author Keywords

Graphical Passwords; Authentication; Older Adults; Human Factors; Human Cognition; Face Recognition

ACM Classification Keywords

H.5.2. [User Interfaces]: User-centered Design.

INTRODUCTION

User authentication, through the creation and memorization of strong passwords, poses a challenge for older computer users [3][6]. The sequences of letters, numbers and symbols forming traditional strong passwords can be abstract, with less meaning to the user than a personalized text or image sequence. This project resulted from a survey of older users who revealed that text passwords were challenging to create and use. We

have created and are currently evaluating an image-based graphical password technique designed specifically for the over-60 population. In contrast to previous work, which required the user to memorize anonymous facial images, abstract icons, points on a map or works of art, this project allows the user to choose a personally meaningful set of images to form their password.

The images chosen by the user are termed the "target images" and will be selected by the user from the display presentation. Target images are displayed embedded within a set of "decoy images" all on a single screen. All images showing in the display presentation are randomly placed. Figure 1 shows the case of a single four-image sequence that is contained within the representative screen displays. Decoy images are carefully chosen to match the external appearance characteristics of the password image set. Decoy images are drawn from the set of images within our database that are not meaningful to the user. The user typically has decades of familiarity with the subjects in the chosen password images, making those images easier to pick out from the decoy images.

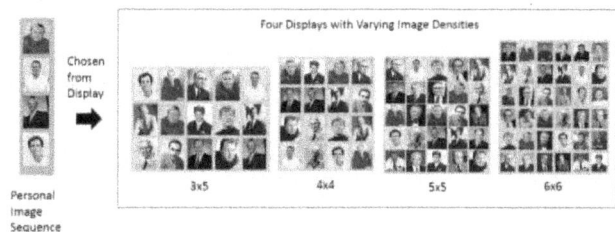

Figure 1: Graphical password login screens. Left to Right: 4 image personal sequence, 3x5, 4x4, 5x5 and 6x6 displays.

The selection of decoy images is restricted to images sharing physical characteristics with the target image set. The resulting display presentation is resistant to an in-person guessing attack. An observer looking at the display sees multiple images sharing common physical attributes and cannot identify the password target sequence by looking for unique aspects of the subjects in the images. As an example, a user choosing four males in business attire for their personal sequence will see a display randomly populated with images of males with ties wearing dark suits photographed against a light background.

If the user selects their sequence of personal images in the correct order, that constitutes a successful login. If the user is unsuccessful at selecting their sequence, then the login request is considered a failure and the display is refreshed with a re-randomized display of images. Because the arrangement of the images changes with each presentation, a casual observer will not see a geographic pattern to the location of the target images. Re-randomizing the arrangement of images also prevents a pattern from forming on touchscreen surfaces, a defense against a smudge attack [1]. Three successive failures should lock-out the user, providing a further defense against a guessing attack.

During our experiment, volunteers shared that they often developed a mental story to aid recall of their image sequences in the correct order. The mental story is formed from the user's personal association with the subjects in the images. These personal associations are not discoverable from written records or the results of web searching. It is the meaning behind the images that make the images an easily remembered password. Only the user knows which images are meaningful to them personally and therefore constitute the correct image sequence.

BACKGROUND
Much work has been done with graphical passwords [2] but none with solutions that are personalized to each individual older user. Previous work with graphical password systems was based on images of artwork, computer icons such as emoji, and facial images of anonymous persons [3][7]. All are somewhat abstract and require effort to memorize. Writing down the images or icons required detailed descriptions, enabling anyone with access to the note to execute the described password sequence [4]. Older users are open to creative computing opportunities [8] and have shown they perform better at memorizing age-appropriate materials [4]. Our personalized password technique is also usable with a touchscreen [5] to facilitate those with hand and finger disabilities.

Survey of Older Computer Users
We conducted an open-ended interview-style technology survey of more than twenty computer users over the age of 60 with the goal of identifying technology areas that could be meaningfully enhanced for this user population. The study revealed a common concern with creating and managing text-based passwords. Some representative comments from study participants are shown in the upper half of Figure 2. Fifteen of the study participants answered more detailed questions focusing on password creation, management and recall. Eleven of the fifteen stated they used a password creation strategy based on such familiar and comfortable components as a child's name, previous phone number, pet name, or spouse's birthdate. None of the surveyed users employed strong passwords meeting the definition of a series of characters including upper/lower case, numbers and symbols that did

not contain a meaningful text sequence. Thirteen of the fifteen participants normally wrote down their passwords. Of the remaining two participants, one refused to use more than one password "in order to keep life simple." The other participant refused to use more than two specific passwords in their computing life. Both of these persons accepted the resulting lifestyle limitations on internet and computer use resulting from their password limitation decisions.

Overwhelmingly, older users in our study wrote down their passwords, and were careful to safeguard their written records. They recognized that access to the written passwords potentially resulted in compromise of their important personal online records. In the current situation, loss of the written records constitutes an immediate password compromise.

The study results motivated us to design an easy-to-use password scheme based on personally familiar images that will foster user confidence and increasing acceptance of computing and internet use. By relying on personally meaningful images, we hope that the tendency to write down explicit password image sequence descriptions will be lessened. If a user does write down a list describing image subjects, an attacker will have to understand the description to make a match possible to a specific image subject name. If a subject is identified, the attacker will still have to conduct sufficient research to identify each subject in the display presentation images. For example a music fan may choose images of Kate Smith, Glenn Miller, Dizzy Gillespie and Louis Armstrong for his password sequence images. The attacker finding this list of names will have to look up the names and learn what each person looks like before attempting to select this image sequence as a password.

> *"It is annoying to create passwords, it is an extra effort and hard to memorize."*
>
> *"It is hard to make a password that is halfway safe."*
>
> *"It was easy to quickly recognize my chosen images because I have followed the careers of those individuals all my life."*
>
> *"It has been a week and I cannot forget my password image sequence."*
>
> *"This [password image technique] is interesting!"*

Figure 2: Volunteer Comments.

Graphical Password Entropy
One goal of our graphical password technique is to achieve a level of entropy comparable or superior to the traditional text password or PIN code systems. Entropy is the unpredictability of possible values in a password sequence. A system with higher entropy is more resistant to guessing attacks but harder to memorize. A text-based

password, N characters long, using the alphabet a to z, A to Z, 0 to 9 and symbols !@#$&*+%, has 70N possible values. Each character having one of seventy possible values. A graphical password based on images has as many possible values as the choices available on the screen to the user. The more images on the display, the greater the entropy of the password system. Given N images and password length M, our technique's entropy is N^M. As shown in Figure 3, an 8 character text password system with entropy of 5.7 x 10^14 is comparable to an 8 image password sequence chosen from a display with 70 images. Both have greater entropy than a traditional PIN code system.

Our challenges are that increasing the number of images on the display forces each image to be smaller, and therefore harder to see and discern image details. Our display consists of a single screen to eliminate the need for scrolling, a challenge for those with finger and hand disabilities. Longer password sequences result in greater entropy but add to the memorization and recall challenge. The time needed to hunt and select the chosen target password images within the surrounding decoy images increases. The probability of choosing the correct images in incorrect order also increases. One goal of our experiment is to understand how users search the displayed images. Are there techniques available to speed up the visual search pattern for the target images and thereby make the graphical password system faster? Does peripheral vision aid in speeding up the search for the target images? Do users remember the current locations of subsequent target images while searching for the initial members of the target image set? Do target image sequences become too long for effective recall and search? Can display screens have too many or too small images for effective search?

Graphical Password System Design

We use a laptop computer equipped with a touchscreen and mouse for this project. A large collection of images is organized into categories based upon the occupation of the subject. Participants selected categories based on personal interests and then chose personal image sequences by browsing. One question our experiment hopes to answer is to find out if users who spend more time selecting meaningful target images, perform faster and have better recall than users who spend less time selecting their target images? Each participant identified images which were unknown to them in a separate session. The set of decoy images was chosen from the set of personal unknown images.

Our study participants selected target sequences in lengths of 4, 7 and 10 images. Password sequences were presented in screens of 3x5, 4x4, 5x5, 6x6 and 7x10 images. Each display shows a random image placement to aid in defense against touchscreen smudge attacks [1] and in-person guessing attacks.

Image Database

The images in the database are carefully chosen of subjects who were famous during the early working years of the over-60 user. All of the images are black and white, focusing on the subject's upper torso or face. Identifying features such as team or corporate logos have been removed. Each image has been coded as to sex, race, posture, attire, foreground color, background color, gaze direction and brightness level. The coding facilitates composing a set of decoy images that match the feature set and color spectrum of the password target images. An attacker cannot guess the password sequence based on visible attributes of the images. Each user's personal history motivated the choice of images for their password target sequence. That motivation is in effect an internal "secret key" to the password image sequence and is unique to each individual.

Pin Length	10 Symbol Alphabet
4	10E+04
5	10E+05
6	10E+06
7	10E+07
8	10E+08
9	10E+09
10	10E+10

Text Length	10 Symbol Alphabet
4	2.40E+07
5	1.68E+09
6	1.18E+011
7	8.24E+012
8	5.77E+014
9	4.04E+016
10	2.82E+018

(a)   (b)

Sequence Size	Display Screen Density			
	16	25	36	70
4	6.55E+04	3.91E+05	1.68E+06	2.40E+07
5	1.05E+06	9.77E+06	6.05E+07	1.68E+09
6	1.68E+07	2.44E+08	2.18E+09	1.18E+011
7	2.68E+08	6.10E+09	7.84E+010	8.24E+012
8	4.30E+09	1.53E+011	2.82E+012	5.77E+014
9	6.87E+010	3.81E+012	1.02E+014	4.04E+016
10	1.10E+012	9.54E+013	3.66E+015	2.82E+018

(c)

Figure 3: Entropy Comparison of Multiple Graphical Password Systems. Clockwise from upper left: PIN Code (a), Text Password (b) and Graphical Password Systems (c).

Interim Results

Participants completed a series of exercises that utilized self-chosen 4, 7 and 10 image target sequences. Each experiment recorded timing and success/failure rates for varying sequence lengths of 4, 7 and 10 images, and varying display image densities of 15, 16, 25, 36 and 70 images. Each participant also prepared and typed text-based passwords of varying lengths for comparison purposes. Participants repeated the exercises at intervals of at least a week after choosing their target images to determine recall.

Volunteers are typically able to select their four-image password image sequences easily and quickly in the lower density screen displays. Often they did this more quickly than some volunteers would take to look up, recall and type a text password. Figure 4 provides a comparison of the individual timing differences between the first and last exercises performed by nine volunteers using five display image densities. Volunteers performed no more than two intermediate experiments at each density level. Selection times and group variance improved with this minor amount of experience.

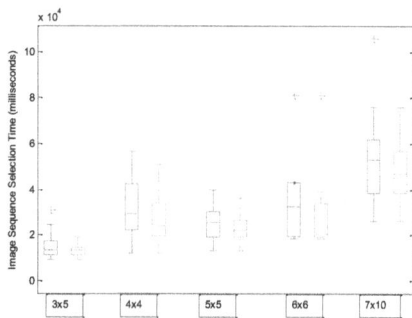

Figure 4: Login timing data for nine volunteers using a mouse to select a personal four image sequence from display grids of increasing density. From left to right: 3x5, 4x4, 5x5, 6x6 and 7x10 display grids. Blue identifies the first experiment result. Red identifies the last result.

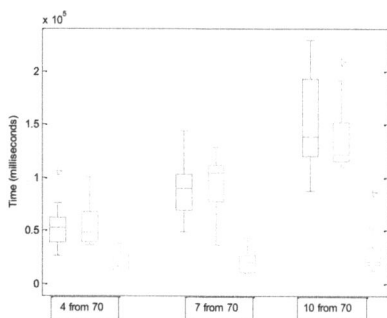

Figure 5: Average login timing for nine volunteers using a mouse to select an increasing size image sequence from a 7x10 display grids. From left to right: 4, 7 and 10 image sequences. Blue is the first attempt. Red is the last. Green is the comparable size text password result.

Figure 5 provides a comparison of the median timing differences at a single density of 70 images. In order to compare mouse with touchscreen performance, we used results from 11 volunteers running 138 exercises with their four-image sequences and a 4x4 display. The median time login with the mouse was less than twenty seconds, and less than fifteen seconds using the touchscreen.

Participants often provided positive comments such as those shown in the lower half of Figure 2. Their comments are a marked contrast to the concern many older users associate with the formation, management and use of traditional strong text passwords.

CONCLUSION
Our initial results show that a culturally-relevant, personally meaningful, image-based graphical password solution is promising as a technically effective, socially accepted and easier-to-use alternative to text-based passwords for older computer users. Our study will continue to evaluate this technique with more volunteers to assess timing and recall effects of peripheral vision, effects of color contrast patterns and image hunting techniques.

ACKNOWLEDGMENTS
We gratefully acknowledge the contributions of colleagues Ed Novak, Cheng Li, Zhengrui Qin, and Qun Li, along with our volunteer participants who willingly shared their opinions about computing and internet technologies.

REFERENCES
1. Aviv, A., Gibson, K., Mossop, E., Blaze, M., and Smith, J. Smudge Attacks on Smartphone Touch Screens. In Proc. WOOT 2010, USENIX Assn, Article No. 1-7.

2. Biddle, R., Chiasson, S. and Van Oorschot, P.C. Graphical Passwords: Learning from the First Twelve Years. ACM Computing Surveys (CSUR), Volume 44 Issue 4, August 2012, Article No. 19.

3. Brostoff, S. and Sasse, M. Are Passfaces More Usable Than Passwords? A Field Trial Investigation. In People and Computers XIV-Usability or Else!, SprinkerLink (2000), 405-424.

4. Chowdhury, S., Poet, R. and Mackenzie, L. Passhint: Memorable and Secure Authentication. In Proc. CHI 2014, ACM (2014), 2917-2926.

5. Findlater, L., Froehlich, J., Fattal, K., Wobbrock, J., and Dastyar, T. Age-Related Differences in Performance with Touchscreens Compared to Traditional Mouse Input. In Proc. CHI 2013, ACM (2013), 343-346.

6. Nicholson, J., Coventry, L. and Briggs, P. Age-Related Performance Issues for PIN and Face-Based Authentication Systems. In Proc. CHI 2013, ACM (2013), 323-33.

7. Passfaces Corporation. The science behind Passfaces. http://www.passfaces.com/enterprise/resources/white_papers.htm accessed April 2015.

8. Waycott, J., Vetere, F., Pedall, S., Kulik, L., Ozanne, E., Gruner, A. and Downs, J. Older Adults as Digital Content Producers. In Proc. CHI 2013, ACM (2013), 39-48

Scope+ : A Stereoscopic Video See-Through Augmented Reality Microscope

Yu-Hsuan Huang[1]
yush.huang@gmail.com

Tzu-Chieh Yu[2]
tzuchieh928@gmail.com

Pei-Hsuan Tsai[1]
ha31535@gmail.com

Yu-Xiang Wang[2]
vovo5558@gmail.com

Wan-Ling Yang[1]
b00611032@ntu.edu.tw

Ming Ouhyoung[1,2]
ming@csie.ntu.edu.tw

[1]Graduate Institute of Networking and Multimedia, National Taiwan University
[2]Department of Computer Science and Information Engineering, National Taiwan University

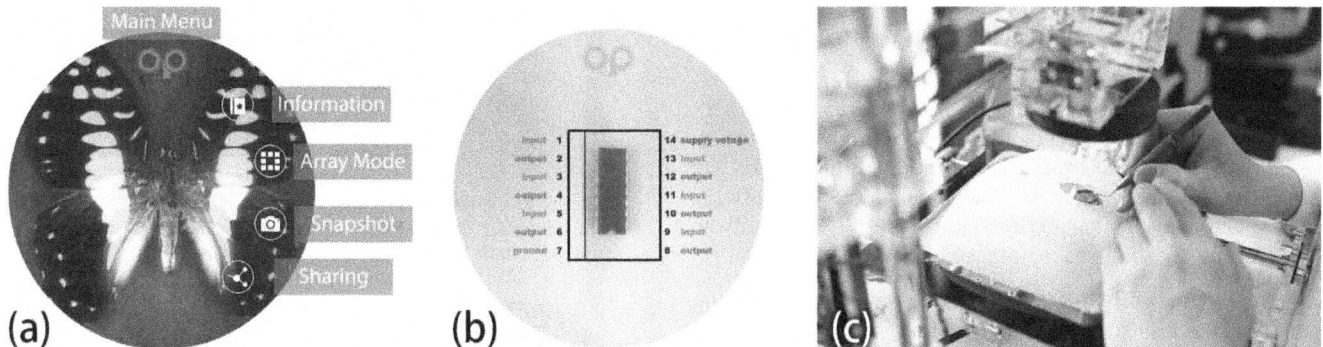

Figure 1. (a) An Interactive User Interface: Users can active applications by using instrument with special color tip. (b) Diagram of IC layout is added on the real image while assembling. (c) Surgical Training: A doctor is practicing Cataract surgery with this system.

ABSTRACT

During the process of using conventional stereo microscope, users need to move their head away from the eyepieces repeatedly to access more information, such as anatomy structures from an atlas. It happens during microsurgery if surgeons want to check patients data again. You might lose your target and your concentration after this kind of disruption. To solve this critical problem and to improve the user experience of stereo microscope, we present Scope+, a stereoscopic video see-through augmented reality system.

Scope+ is designed for biological procedures, education and surgical training. While performing biological procedures, for example, dissection of a frog, anatomical atlas will show up inside the head mounted display (HMD) overlaid onto the magnified images. For education purpose, the specimens will no longer be silent under Scope+. When their body parts are pointed by a marked stick, related animation or transparent background video will merge with the real object and interact with observers. If surgeons want to improve their techniques of microsurgery, they can practice with Scope+ which provides complete foot pedal control functions identical to stan-

dard surgical microscope. Moreover, cooperating with special designed phantom models, this augmented reality system will guide you to perform some key steps of operation, such as Continuous Curvilinear Capsulorhexis in cataract surgery.

Video see-through rather than optical see-through technology is adopt by Scope+ system, therefore remote observation via another Scope+ or web applications can be achieved. This feature can not only assist teachers during experiment classes, but also help researchers keep their eyes on the observables after work. Array mode is powered by the motor-driven stage plate which allows users to load multiple samples at the same time. Quick comparison between samples is possible when switching them by the foot pedal.

Figure 2. Array mode: Multiple samples can be observed on the same plate.

UIST'15 Adjunct, November 08-11, 2015, Charlotte, NC, USA
ACM 978-1-4503-3780-9/15/11.
http://dx.doi.org/10.1145/2815585.2817775

Author Keywords

3D Interaction and Graphics; Augmented Reality; VirtualReality; Tutorial and Help Systems.

INTRODUCTION

We use an Oculus Rift HMD and a modified Prusa i3 3D printer (SciBot) as the main components of this system, and then replace the extruder of 3D printer by a special designed stereo microscope module. When a user observing through the HMD, this module can provide stereo vision (Figure 3). A joystick was remodeled to an integrated foot pedal controller of Scope+. Users can translate the observation field, magnify the target, change the position of focal plane, adjust the intensity of light source and traversal through sample array without occupying their hands.

Two high resolution (1600 1200 pixels) industrial cameras and two mutually perpendicular reflection mirrors were assembled to build the microscope module compatible with Prusa i3. Working distance of camera and interpupillary distance can also be changed individually using our hardware design and algorithm to maintain a comfort stereo vision.

Surgeons can barely tolerate the visual latency during the operation and surgical simulation. To meet this demand, Scope+ adopted GPU acceleration pipeline and multi-thread rendering to reduce the latency and keep high frame rate (30 frames per second) even with dual full HD resolution cameras.

We designed several methods to interact with Scope+ applications. Besides recognizing special colors or patterns, surgeons need a markerless way while holding real surgical instruments. A motion sensitive method was developed by counting the change of image flow obtained by the cameras. Social networking is another feature in our design. Users can not only share the special finding to others immediately but can also get helps from remote devices while doing difficult operations.

APPLICATIONS

1. Biological research

With this application, students can get multimedia information such as texts, photos or videos (Figure 4a) while observing the samples without disruptions. If you are dissecting small animals, you can reach the atlas from the HMD by simply waving the knife or forceps in the corner.

2. Electronics assembly

Can you memorize the color code of resistors? Have you ever confused by the polarity of LED or capacitor? You can not only read the color code of resistors but also the layout diagram of an IC chip (Figure 1b) under Scope+. With augmented PCB layout on the true PCB board, you wont mess up the positive and negative end of the electronics again (Figure 4b).

3. Surgical training

Continuous Curvilinear Capsulorhexis (CCC) is a very difficult step in cataract surgery, therefore surgeons can use image guided system to achieved an optimal sized, well centered CCC during operation. However, there is no such kind of system for surgical training till now. Scope+ can not only provide a similar control experience as a real surgical microscope by using the foot pedal controller, but also provide the image guided function by AR technology for young surgeons to practice (Figure 1c, 4c).

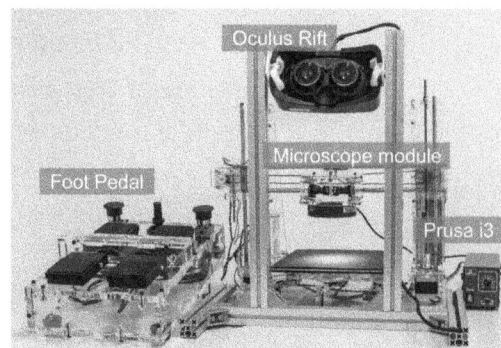

Figure 3. Hardware overview of Scope+. Left to right: integrated foot pedal controller, Oculus Rift fixed on a special designed rack, stereo microscope module and modified Prusa i3 3D printer.

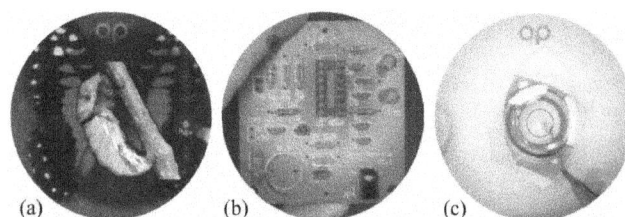

Figure 4. (a) Biological research: Augmented video overlaid on the butterfly sample. (b) Electronics assembly: Augmented PCB layout for electronics assembly. (c) Surgical training: Image guided training system of CCC in cataract surgery. Surgeon can practice CCC by following the augmented green circle on the artificial eye model.

CONCLUSION

We provide a comprehensive solution to build an AR stereo microscope and develop several new ways to use it. By using Scope+, user can get information from HMD without move their head away from the eyepieces repeatedly.

These applications are not only for professional use, but also provide a creative platform for further developments. With Scope+, a new and more intuitive user experience of stereo microscope is bringing to you.

REFERENCES

1. Birkfellner, W., Huber, K., Watzinger, F., Figl, M., Wanschitz, F., Hanel, R., Rafolt, D., Ewers, R., and Bergmann, H. Development of the varioscope ar. a see-through hmd for computer-aided surgery. In *Augmented Reality, 2000. (ISAR 2000). Proceedings. IEEE and ACM International Symposium on* (2000), 54–59.

2. Rolland, J. P., and Fuchs, H. Optical versus video see-through head-mounted displays in medical visualization. *Presence: Teleoper. Virtual Environ. 9*, 3 (June 2000), 287–309.

Creating a Mobile Head-mounted Display with Proprietary Controllers for Interactive Virtual Reality Content

Kunihiro Kato
Meiji University
Nakano, Tokyo, Japan
kkunihir@meiji.ac.jp

Homei Miyashita
Meiji University
Nakano, Tokyo, Japan
homei@homei.com

ABSTRACT

A method to create a mobile head-mounted display (HMD) a proprietary controller for interactive virtual reality (VR) content is proposed. The proposed method uses an interface cartridge printed with a conductive pattern. This allows the user to operate a smartphone by touching on the face of the mobile HMD. In addition, the user can easily create a mobile HMD and interface cartridge using a laser cutter and inkjet printer. Changing the form of the conductive pattern allows the user to create a variety of controllers. The proposed method can realize an environment that can deliver a variety of interactions with VR content.

Author Keywords

Interface Cartridge; Mobile HMD; Conductive Ink.

ACM Classification Keywords

H.5.2. Information Interfaces and Presentation (e.g. HCI): User Interfaces Input Devices and Strategies.

INTRODUCTION

In recent years, head-mounted displays (HMD), such as Oculus Rift and Samsung Gear VR, have become increasingly popular. Such devices allow users not only to experience virtual reality (VR) easily but also to create and deliver VR content. Acceleration sensors in HMD devices enable movement of the observation point in a VR world and allow users to experience highly immersive VR content. In addition, the sensors enable head tracking and realize an interface that provides rich user interactions. For example, Oculus Rift with LeapMotion can use hand gestures to control VR content. Gear VR has a touch pad that can be used to control VR content.

We propose another method to create a mobile HMD with a proprietary controller for interactive VR content (Figure 1). Google Cardboard [1] is a mobile HMD with a particularly simple structure. Essentially, it is a cardboard box with optical

---

[1] https://www.google.com/get/cardboard/

UIST'15 Adjunct, November 08-11, 2015, Charlotte, NC, USA.
ACM 978-1-4503-3780-9/15/11.
http://dx.doi.org/10.1145/2815585.2817776

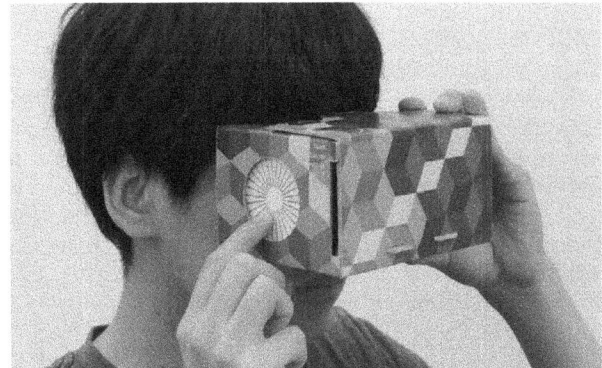

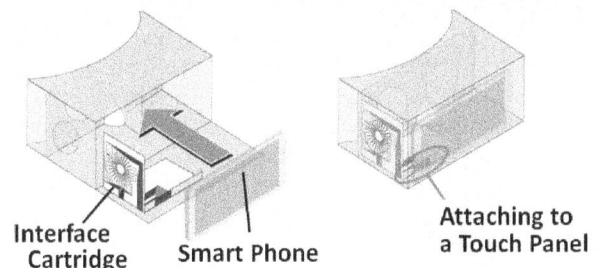

Figure 1. Mobile HMD with Proprietary Controller.

lenses. Google Cardboard uses a smartphone display. Simply by installing VR applications on a smartphone, users can have the same quality VR experience as that offered by Oculus and Gear VR. Therefore, we can realize VR interactivity for this type of HMD by using smartphone sensors or the touch panel. For example, Google Cardboard has a magnetic interface for VR content control. It has a magnet ring on the side of the HMD and senses the movement of the magnet using a smartphone sensor. It also has a near field communication (NFC) tag for launching an application. Recently, another type of Google Cardboard has been released; it has a physical button interface on the top of the HMD box. When the user pushes this button, touch-input can be activated on the touch panel through conductive material on the button. Note that users have to consider the limitations of the HMD devices when creating VR applications.

Other devices, such as Acoustruments, can extend the functionality of a smartphone interface to enable use with a mobile HMD [1]. This device allows the user to operate a smartphone without directly touching the touch panel. The Acoustruments product video shows that the device can be used with a mobile HMD device made of cardboard [2].

Our proposed method can be realized by putting an interface cartridge printed with a conductive pattern into the mobile HMD. The user can easily create an interface cartridge by using an inkjet printer with conductive ink. This allows the user to design not only VR content but also a proprietary controller that can be used with particular VR content. In addition, delivering the applications and the HMD developed figure and controller pattern data realizes an environment in which users can easily have a VR experience.

PROPOSED METHOD

The proposed method uses an inkjet-printed conductive pattern. This allows the user to operate a smartphone that is external to the mobile HMD. We used the Extension Sticker method to create the conductive pattern [2]. A conductive pattern has multiple thin lines. By activating the conductive pattern, continuous touch input can be generated on the smartphone. This allows the user to control the VR contents by tapping or scrolling on the face of the mobile HMD. In addition, changing the form of the conductive pattern allows a variety of interactions in response to user gesture input.

Interface Cartridge

The proposed method uses a conductive pattern printed on a piece of cardboard as a controller for the mobile HMD. We refer to this as an interface cartridge. The interface cartridge is folded and inserted into the mobile HMD. One side of the conductive pattern can be connected to a with touch panel (Figure 1, Bottom). Changing the interface cartridge allows other types of controllers to be used. In addition, including a QR code or NFC tag enables easy access to application URLs. The user can use the device in the same way as they would use a video game cartridge.

APPLICATION

Here we describe application examples that can be realized using the proposed method. Changing the form or a portion of the conductive pattern can realize various interactions related to specific VR content.

A dial controller can be used for interactions that require rotation actions. For example, a dial controller can be used to assign forward and backward rotation actions to an accelerator and brake, respectively, or for hand-wheel control in car racing game content. In addition, the proposed method can realize fishing games. The method allows the user to control a fishing rod using an acceleration sensor, and reel in a fish using a rotation operation. A dial controller can also be used to search for a video interface or select an interface for music. In addition, scrolling operations on the interface cartridge allows the user to perform swipe interactions on the side or back of the HMD box. For example, throwing interactions can be realized by a swiping action on the side of the HMD box.

---

[2]Acoustruments:
http://www.disneyresearch.com/publication/acoustruments/

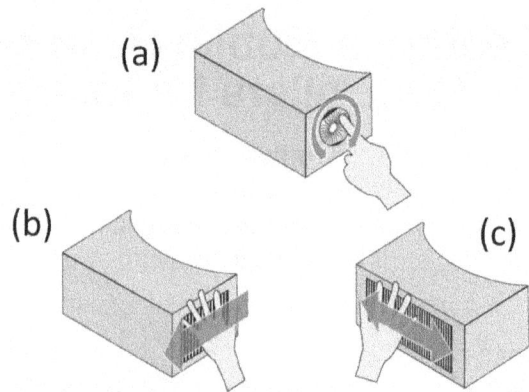

Figure 2. (a) Rotating action, (b) Swiping action on the side of the HMD, (c) Swiping action on the back of the HMD.

DISCUSSION

In this paper, we propose a method for creating a mobile HMD with proprietary controllers for interactive VR content.

To create high immersive interactive VR content, it is necessary to provide a controller that works with particularly content. For example, to realize a fishing game, we can use rotation actions as the input gesture (Figure 2 a), to realize a throwing interaction, we can use a swiping hand movement as the input gesture (Figure 2 b), and to flip a page or open a window, we can use a side-to-side hand movement (Figure 2 c).

The proposed method allows users to easily create an interface cartridge using an inkjet printer with conductive ink. However, we found that the conductive lines could break when the interface cartridge was folded. Therefore, we checked robustness against folding for several conductive materials (silver, carbon, and aluminum). The results of this test confirmed that carbon or silver were most suitable. In addition, users can create an HMD box using a laser cutter. The user can also design the exterior of the HMD. Therefore, the proposed method allows application developers to deliver their applications with a mobile HMD with proprietary controllers. In addition, because the HMD is made of cardboard, applications developers also can design the exterior of HMD.

The proposed method allows the user to be creative. They can design all aspects of VR content, including the application, hardware, and user interactions. We believe that the proposed method can contribute to the realization of an environment that allows many people to participate in interactive VR experiences.

REFERENCES

1. Gierad Laput, Eric Brockmeyer, Scott E. Hudson, and Chris Harrison. Acoustruments: Passive, Acoustically-Driven, Interactive Controls for Handheld Devices, In *Proc. CHI'15*, pp.2161-2170, 2015.

2. Kunihiro Kato, Homei Miyashita. ExtensionSticker: A Proposal for A Striped Pattern Sticker to Extend Touch Interfaces and its Assessment, In *Proc. CHI'15*, pp.1851-1854, 2015.

Spotlights: Facilitating Skim Reading with Attention-Optimized Highlights

Byungjoo Lee
Aalto university
Helsinki, Finland
byungjoo.lee@aalto.fi

Antti Oulasvirta
Aalto university
Helsinki, Finland
antti.oulasvirta@aalto.fi

ABSTRACT

This demo presents Spotlights, a technique to facilitate *skim reading*, or the activity of rapidly comprehending long documents such as webpages or PDFs. Users mainly use continuous rate-based scrolling to skim. However, visual attention fails when scrolling rapidly due to excessive number of objects and brief exposure per object. *Spotlights* supports continuous scrolling at high speeds. It selects a small number of objects and raises them to transparent overlays (spotlights) in the viewer. Spotlights stay static for a prolonged time and then fade away. The technical contribution is novel method for "brokering" user's attentional resources in a way that guarantees sufficient attentional resources for some objects, even at very high scrolling rates. It facilitates visual attention by (1) decreasing the number of objects competing for divided attention and (2) by ensuring sufficient processing time per object.

ACM Classification Keywords

H.5.2 Information Interfaces and Presentation (e.g. HCI): User Interfaces–Interaction styles

Author Keywords

Skim Reading; Comprehension; Scrolling Techniques; Attention Brokering; Visual Attention; Attentional Blink.

INTRODUCTION

This demo presents *Spotlights*, a novel technique to facilitate *skim reading*. The explosion of digital contents in Internet has made it important for users rapidly comprehend complex documents [1]. Our goal is to improve the most commonly used interaction technique, *continuous scrollling*, which has become the de facto standard in browsers and viewers. The rate is typically controlled by a scrolling wheel, scrollbar, touchpad, or touchscreen.

The design of Spotlights addresses two issues that degrade information gain in continuous scrolling at high scrolling speeds. (1) Motion blur [5]; (2) Too brief exposure times per object. Visual processing degrades when attention is forced to

UIST'15 Adjunct, November 8–11, 2015, Charlotte, NC, USA.
ACM 978-1-4503-3780-9/15/11.
http://dx.doi.org/10.1145/2815585.2817777

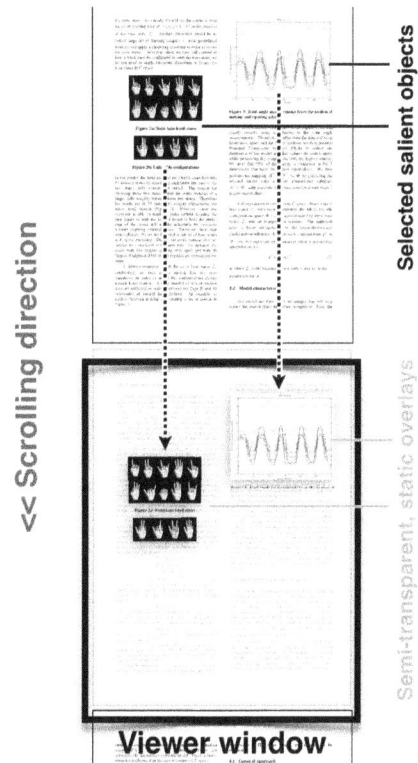

Figure 1. Spotlights supports rapidly scrolling long documents for comprehension. When scrolling down, Spotlights selects important objects into semi-transparent overlays (spotlights) that stay static for a prolonged time before fading away. Visual attention can be maintained on objects from previous pages.

re-shift before 500 ms of processing time (*attentional blink*) [4]. When scrolling faster than 2 pages/sec, it is impossible to avoid the blink.

Spotlights is designed to complement continuous scrolling. Below the rate of 2 pages per second (pps), continuous scrolling takes place as normal. Above this rate, Spotlights is triggered. It selects a few objects for static, semi-transparent layers (spotlights) rendered on the viewer window (Figure 1). That the overlays are static eliminates motion blur, yet transparency allows the user to maintain a global view of the scrolling document and spot potentially interesting objects there. The spotlights stay on for some time before fading away and attention is guided to another one. The benefit of our implementation is that it can be integrated to any viewer using continuous scrolling. No additional hardware is

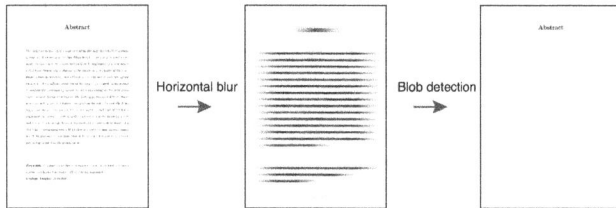

Figure 2. Spotlights extracts objects for overlays using horizontal gaussian blur and blob detection. This identifies objects that are larger than their context.

required, the only requirement is (lightweight) preprocessing of documents.

CONTENT OVERLAYS: DESIGN AND IMPLEMENTATION

The overlays in Spotlights are transparent, rendered in or near the place of the corresponding object on the original page, and fade out as a function of time. We implemented the technique for documents consisting of textual and graphical elements. However, the principles can be adapted to other types.

Extracting and Prioritizing Objects on a Page

To decide which objects are important enough for overlays, we assume that at scrolling speeds over 2 pps, a maximum of 1-2 objects per page can be attended due to effects like attentional blink. Our approach is informed by results [1] showing that users spend more time gazing title, headings, pictures, and figures than plain text. We automatically parse objects that are likely to be interesting and descriptive.

Our parser extracts headings and figures from a PDF page using a two-step process. First the PDF is converted to a set of images. Then, *horizontal* gaussian blur is applied to each image. The result is a set of "smudged" horizontal lines shown in Figure 2. In the second step, we group these lines by a blob detection process. We assume that there is a standard line spacing defined for a document, and those blobs having larger height than this line spacing is selected as possible important objects. In this process, titles, headings and figures have larger height than plain text and are likely to be selected. Lastly, we sort objects on a page in the order of descending height. Finally, this allows us to select only the largest 1-2 objects are selected for overlays. This parser is implemented in Java. It reaches a processing speed of 100 pages per 40 seconds on a regular laptop.

Dynamic Overlay Control

After choosing objects, we render them in the same place they were originally in a static overlay. Importantly, we adapt exposure time of an ovelay dynamically, in real-time, depending on scrolling speed. When speed exceeds 2 pps, the overlay function is triggered. After triggering the overlay, its transparency is linearly decreased until the time expires. When transparency is high, it works as a trigger for visual attention to move on to the next object. Also, when it is not, the attention can easily select the "freshest" objects to attend to.

Our overlay control is content-specific. Appreciating the fact that textual information takes longer to comprehend [3], we

obtain optimal parameters separately for graphical vs. textual objects with a calibration study. Objects with width-to-height ratio over 20 were regarded as a textual objects and given 1500 ms of exposure time. Others were treated as figures and provided 1250ms. The overlay functions were implemented on framebuffer object of openGL. A framerate of 60 Hz was achieved for 1050 pixel height, A4 or letter sized documents.

Minimizing Masking with Transparency

During scrolling, the movement of the document in the background layer is not meaningless but indicates scrolling speed and global position to the user. Hence, an overlay should not mask too much of the scrolling background. To minimize masking, and yet achieve high legibility in the overlay, we adapted an empirical result from a past study [2]. According to this result, the foreground opacity of 20 per cent is required for obtaining good performance on both focused and divided attention. In our case, the overlay should be gain more focus than the background layer.

Stacking Objects

We also deal with competition of highlighted objects for the same space. This can occur when two overlays from two or more previous pages have overlapping positions. Titles and figures, for example, tend to be in the top half of a page. In this case, Spotlights tries to retain original positions. However, it treats the vertical and the horizontal dimensions differently. Vertical positions of overlays are filled sequentially in first-come-first-served fashion, starting from the top of the display. In contrast, the horizontal position is kept as it was to retain some memory for object locations. When the document is crowded, the overlays may thus appear stacked. The fact that the overlays are static and close to each other may actually help selective attention to find next targets.

REFERENCES

1. Duggan, G. B., and Payne, S. J. Skim reading by satisficing: evidence from eye tracking. In *Proc. CHI11*, ACM (2011), 1141–1150.

2. Harrison, B. L., Ishii, H., Vicente, K. J., and Buxton, W. A. Transparent layered user interfaces: An evaluation of a display design to enhance focused and divided attention. In *Proceedings of the SIGCHI conference on Human factors in computing systems*, ACM Press/Addison-Wesley Publishing Co. (1995), 317–324.

3. Kline, T. J. B., Ghali, L. M., Kline, D. W., and Brown, S. Visibility distance of highway signs among young, middle-aged, and older observers: Icons are better than text. *Human Factors: The Journal of the Human Factors and Ergonomics Society 32*, 5 (1990), 609–619.

4. Shapiro, K. L., Raymond, J., and Arnell, K. The attentional blink. *Trends in cognitive sciences 1*, 8 (1997), 291–296.

5. Valsecchi, M., Gegenfurtner, K. R., and Schütz, A. C. Saccadic and smooth-pursuit eye movements during reading of drifting texts. *Journal of vision 13*, 10 (2013), 8.

WearWrite: Orchestrating the Crowd to Complete Complex Tasks from Wearables

Michael Nebeling[1], Anhong Guo[1], Alexandra To[1], Steven Dow[1], Jaime Teevan[2], Jeffrey Bigham[1]
[1] Human-Computer Interaction Institute, Carnegie Mellon University, Pittsburgh, PA, USA
[2] Microsoft Research, Redmond, WA, USA
{ mnebelin, anhongg, aato, spdow, jbigham }@cs.cmu.edu, teevan@microsoft.com

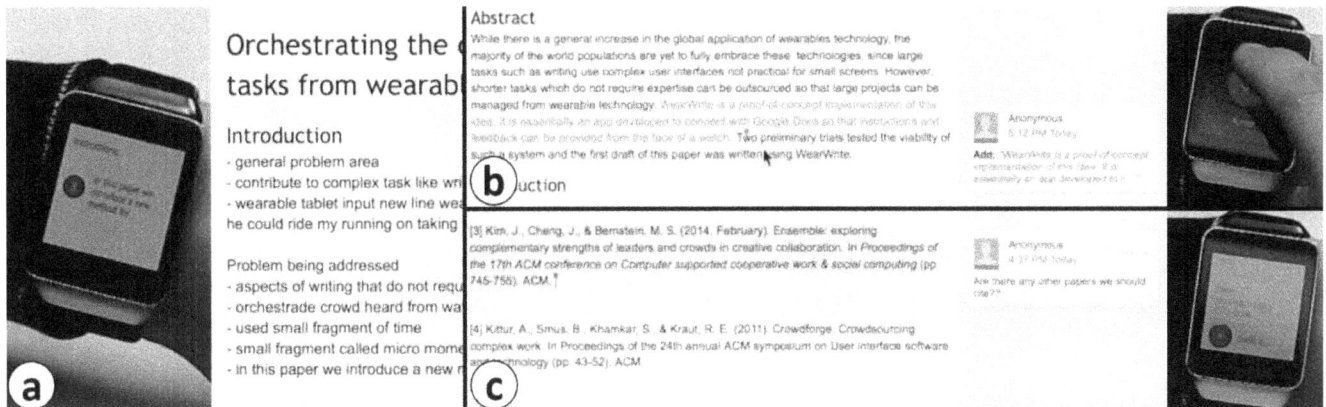

Figure 1. WearWrite allows a watch user to contribute to three paper writing tasks from a smartwatch: *(a)* outlining a document via simple speech commands, *(b)* accepting or rejecting crowd worker edits, and *(c)* replying to comments and questions left by crowd workers in the document.

ABSTRACT

Smartwatches are becoming increasingly powerful, but limited input makes completing complex tasks impractical. Our WearWrite system introduces a new paradigm for enabling a watch user to contribute to complex tasks, not through new hardware or input methods, but by directing a crowd to work on their behalf from their wearable device. WearWrite lets authors give writing instructions and provide bits of expertise and big picture directions from their smartwatch, while crowd workers actually write the document on more powerful devices. We used this approach to write three academic papers, and found it was effective at producing reasonable drafts.

Author Keywords

Crowdsourcing; wearables; smartwatch interaction; writing

ACM Classification Keywords

H.5.m. Information interfaces and presentation

UIST '15 Adjunct, November 08-11, 2015, Charlotte, NC, USA
ACM 978-1-4503-3780-9/15/11.
http://dx.doi.org/10.1145/2815585.2817782

MOTIVATION

Smartwatches are quickly becoming powerful computing devices, but performing complex tasks with them remains difficult because of physical constraints. Text input is particularly difficult from a watch, and very little content can be displayed on their tiny screens at one time. While it is not possible to retain the full range of functionality available with large screens and keyboards, we hypothesize that complex tasks can still be supported on wearable devices by orchestrating crowd workers to complete complex tasks on one's behalf. Domain experts can contribute bits of expertise and maintain global context, while crowd workers actually perform the task.

The specific task we explored is academic writing. This is a challenging domain for crowdsourcing because the technical content of an academic paper requires expertise to explain, and writing a complex document such as a paper requires maintaining global context. We present the WearWrite system (Figure 1) that allows authors who do not have access to large devices, but want to take advantage of free micromoments, to contribute their domain expertise and big picture directions from their watch, while directing crowd workers using more powerful devices to implement the changes suggested by the author. By using crowd workers to write content and only requiring the author to review it, WearWrite exploits the fact that it is easier to read compared to writing new text on a wearable device.

The contribution of WearWrite is not in crowdsourcing complex tasks, but in how it allows end-users to complete complex tasks from wearables by sending instructions to crowd workers. Systems such as CrowdForge enable non-expert crowds to complete complex tasks by breaking them down into smaller context-free subtasks [3]. Crowd shepherding was introduced to help give workers feedback so they could improve over time [1]. Flash Teams bring together on-demand teams of experts from the crowd to complete complex tasks [6]. Finally, Ensemble uses a team leader to direct crowd writing projects [2]. The complementary writing skills of individuals produce better results in less time with higher creativity. WearWrite enables an expert user to guide the crowd through a lightweight wearable interface.

Wearable devices have recently received increased attention in the literature. Prior work has attempted to both increase the input capabilities of smartwatches and to increase the amount of information that can be entered by a smartwatch user [5, 7]. Despite this, text input remains much slower than from other types of devices; an author would not want to write an entire academic paper this way. Speech recognition is the current standard for input for smartwatches, but it can be error prone, especially for long sequences of text. WearWrite overcomes these limitations by integrating wearable input with crowd workers' input from more powerful devices.

WEARWRITE

WearWrite enables watch-based interactions to give writing instructions and direct crowd workers (Figure 1). Firstly, it supports direct authoring of new content such as inserting sections, paragraphs, and bullets via simple speech commands. Secondly, as crowd workers edit the document, their changes become suggestions and are displayed on the watch where the expert can review them. Edits are sent along with a screenshot of the page on which they were made to provide context. Finally, comments written by crowd workers are sent to the watch and the author can reply using speech. To keep the process manageable for the watch user, the watch interface can be configured to notify of changes at varying levels of granularity and frequency. Only substantial changes of a certain text length and Levenshtein edit distance may be reported, and notifications can be snoozed for custom time intervals. The whole document can be browsed in a thumbnail representation showing the document as is or highlighting edits and comments to see where actions are required.

WearWrite uses a three-step iterative workflow: **1. Recruit**—The watch user recruits crowd workers from oDesk.com. While ideally done directly from the watch, our implementation requires pre-recruitment so that the watch user only needs to communicate with crowd workers who are on standby. **2. Outline**—The watch user efficiently uses free micro-moments as well as time spent waiting for crowd responses to outline the document. The seed document is created with Google Docs and authored exclusively from the watch. It contains the basic structure of the document, the key points it should include, and references for crowd workers to use. **3. Co-Author**—The watch user and crowd workers engage in an iterative authoring process and transform the seed document into the desired final document. A task queue is dynamically generated that contains generic paper-writing tasks (e.g., "turn the bullets in the 'Introduction' into paragraphs", "find the paper that each bullet in the 'Related Work' section refers to and create a reference to it") as well as new specific tasks set by the watch user to be prioritized.

INITIAL WEARWRITE EXPERIMENTS

WearWrite was successfully used by three authors to write papers. The first was a 2-page paper on a simple crowdsourcing experiment, the second attempted to duplicate an existing published paper [1], and the third was a report on the WearWrite system itself (see [4] for details). The authors were surprised by the quality of the content produced, and it was sufficient to occasionally provide the crowd workers with suggestions and feedback on edits. The experiments guided us in designing the system to provide necessary context to the watch user as well as the crowd workers while reducing the need for communication to a minimum. They revealed a number of interesting issues that we are currently addressing. Speech recognition often struggled with terminology so that we decided to send recorded audio and let crowd workers do the transcription instead. Other issues were related to task generation and queuing given the highly dynamic writing process. The question of who is actually writing the document—the watch user or the crowd—is a challenging one. We are developing new mechanisms to ensure the watch user remains in control when workers engage in intellectually intensive tasks.

DEMONSTRATION

Our demo allows attendees to experience the WearWrite system both from the watch user's and the crowd workers' perspective at different stages of the document authoring process. Crowd worker input can be replayed to the system from data recorded from previous document writing experiences, or fed live to the system from a laptop running Google Docs in the worker role. Additionally, we will demonstrate the results of our WearWrite experiments conducted so far.

REFERENCES

1. Dow, S., Kulkarni, A., Klemmer, S., and Hartmann, B. Shepherding the crowd yields better work. CSCW 2012.
2. Kim, J., Cheng, J., and Bernstein, M. S. Ensemble: exploring complementary strengths of leaders and crowds in creative collaboration. CSCW 2014.
3. Kittur, A., Smus, B., Khamkar, S., and Kraut, R. E. Crowdforge: Crowdsourcing complex work. UIST 2011.
4. Nebeling, M., Guo, A., Murray, K., Tostengard, A., Giannopoulos, A., Mihajlov, M., Dow, S. P., Teevan, J., and Bigham, J. P. WearWrite: Orchestrating the Crowd to Complete Complex Tasks from Wearables (We Wrote This Paper on a Watch). arXiv:1508.02982, 2015.
5. Oney, S., Harrison, C., Ogan, A., and Wiese, J. Zoomboard: a diminutive qwerty soft keyboard using iterative zooming for ultra-small devices. CHI 2013.
6. Retelny, D., Robaszkiewicz, S., To, A., Lasecki, W. S., Patel, J., Rahmati, N., Doshi, T., Valentine, M. A., and Bernstein, M. S. Expert Crowdsourcing with Flash Teams. UIST 2014.
7. Xiao, R., Laput, G., and Harrison, C. Expanding the input expressivity of smartwatches with mechanical pan, twist, tilt and click. CHI 2014.

Zensei: Augmenting Objects with Effortless User Recognition Capabilities through Bioimpedance Sensing

Munehiko Sato[1], **Rohan S. Puri**[1], **Alex Olwal**[1]*, **Deepak Chandra**[2], **Ivan Poupyrev**[2], **Ramesh Raskar**[1]

[1]MIT Media Lab
Cambridge, MA, USA
{munehiko, rohan, olwal, raskar}@media.mit.edu

[2]Google ATAP
Mountain View, CA, USA
{dchandra, ipoupyrev}@google.com

Figure 1. *Zensei* enables effortless and uninterrupted user identification and personalization with almost any object, such as a smartphone.

ABSTRACT

As interactions with smart devices and objects become increasingly common, a more seamless and effortless identification and personalization technique will be essential to an uninterrupted user experience. In this paper, we present *Zensei*, a user identification and customization system using human body bioimpedance sensing through multiple electrodes embedded into everyday objects. *Zensei* provides for an uninterrupted user-device personalization experience that is difficult to forge because it uses both the unique physiological and behavioral characteristics of the user. We demonstrate our measurement system in three exemplary device configurations that showcase different levels of constraint via environment-based, whole-body-based, and handheld-based identification scenarios.

ACM Classification Keywords

H.5.2. Information interfaces and presentation: User Interfaces - Graphical user interfaces; Input devices & strategies.

Author Keywords

User identification; bioimpedance sensing; customization

INTRODUCTION

People interact with more and more smart devices every day. This includes personal electronics, such as mobile phones, tablets, laptops, desktop computers, and public displays. In scenarios in which user interactions are frequent, such as with personal devices, it is critical that user recognition procedures do not repeatedly interrupt the interaction. The ideal interaction should not be interrupted by toggling a switch, inputting

*Secondary affiliations: KTH – Royal Institute of Technology (Stockholm, Sweden); Google Inc.(Mountain View, CA, USA)

UIST'15 Adjunct, November 8–11, 2015, Charlotte, NC, USA.
ACM 978-1-4503-3780-9/15/11.
http://dx.doi.org/10.1145/2815585.2817786

a password, or any other explicit procedure. There are interesting opportunities now that everyday objects are being augmented with computational power and network connectivity, and we envision that implicit identification and automated customization will be of significant importance for human-computer interaction.

Zensei is a fundamental sensing technology that enables physical objects to identify their user instantly by sensing the user's touch behavior and bioimpedance. It makes almost any object capable of effortless identification – for example, a smartphone that recognizes you as soon as you pick up your phone, a car that knows who is sitting in the drivers seat so it can change to custom user settings, or a shared tablet that toggles into the child-safe mode when a child is holding it. With *Zensei*, one does not need to type in a username or password, scan an ID, or even align the correct fingertip with the fingerprint scanner.

SYSTEM AND IMPLEMENTATION

Bioimpedance and capacitive sensing technologies have been used for various applications including tomography [1], multi-user touch surfaces [3], and wearable devices [2]. Unlike conventional capacitive sensing, *Zensei* peers into the body tissue by measuring the bioimpedance between a pair of electrodes. Therefore, *Zensei* can know who is touching the object using the differences in body tissue composition. We advocate an approach to capture a user's electrical characteristics by implementing a sensor into the physical objects around us. Our approach shares some similarity with SFCS [5, 4], however, we measure both the amplitude and phase components of electrical frequency response and do so among all combinations of six embedded electrodes (Figure 3) with shielded cables. Our implementation uses an AD5932 wave generator, custom analog circuitry, and AD8302 RF gain and phase detector to capture the frequency response over a wide range of frequencies (1 KHz to 1.5 MHz in 150 linear steps) (Figure 4).

In our approach, we created three prototypes to demonstrate three different form factors that evaluate and exhibit *Zensei*'s versatility. These include static sensing with relatively stable and controlled user touch behavior (hand pad), semi-static

Figure 2. Three prototypes of Hand Pad, Chair, and Smartphone, and their electrode arrangements.

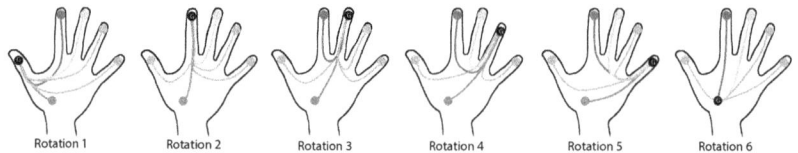

Figure 3. Electrode demultiplexing and ground electrode rotation.

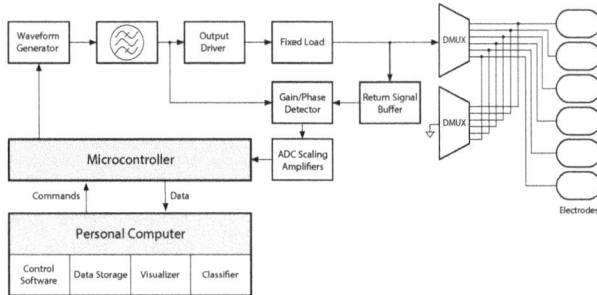

Figure 4. *Zensei* system block diagram.

sensing with somewhat variable touch behavior due to user posture and changes in clothing (chair), and variable sensing with highly variable user touch behavior (smartphone) as shown in Figures 1 and 2 as well as the Video Figure.

To prepare the data for classification, the thirty vectors of 150 frequency response values were first smoothed using a moving average filter (n=5). It was empirically determined that good performance was achieved by feeding just this smoothed data into an SVM classifier with Polynomial Kernel (E = 1.0, C = 1.0). We trained our classifier using SMO implementation in WEKA Toolkit.

APPLICATION SCENARIOS

Various applications can be realized with *Zensei*'s versatile user recognition technology. Specifically, it is particularly useful for "casual" biometrics. When an individual wants to gain access to a system such as an informational kiosk, they just need to place a hand on a hand-shaped pad. As *Zensei* uses multiple embedded electrodes for sensing, users could grab a doorknob in a certain way to unlock the door (Video Figure). By doing this, we can create a powerful user-specific key that is a combination of *physiological* and *behavioral* features. Furthermore, users can *generate* multiple temporary tokens by changing the way in which the doorknob is grabbed.

DATA COLLECTION

Data on all three arrangements was collected on 12 subjects over a time period of 30 days excluding weekends (22 days of data collection, two sessions each day, five samples per session on each arrangement) to evaluate their classification accuracies (CA), false acceptance rates (FAR), and false rejection rates (FRR). Subjects were instructed to touch each arrangement five times in series per session, removing themselves from the arrangement between each sample. The first four days of results of the hand pad were not used in the analysis because its circuit board had malfunctioned and had to be switched. Although a few sessions were missed, each subject participated in at least one session per day.

DATA ANALYSIS

To evaluate the overall performance of the system, we performed a hold-one-day-out validation by training our classifier on 21 days of data and testing on the remaining day for every combination of days and averaging the results of all combinations. As shown in Table 1, the more constrained arrangements (hand pad) tend to outperform those with more user variability. Additionally, the chair showed lower performance likely because of the strong influence of the subject's clothing in the collected signal. Overall, the high accuracies and low FAR prove promising considering the realistic long-term and variable scenarios in which the data was collected.

Table 1. Classification Accuracy

	Hand Pad	Phone	Chair
Classification Accuracy (SD)	96.0% (2.41%)	88.5% (5.51%)	78.6% (7.71%)
FAR (SD)	0.37% (0.20%)	1.04% (0.51%)	2.05% (0.83%)
FRR (SD)	3.97% (2.41%)	11.47% (5.50%)	21.30% (7.88%)

DEMONSTRATION

In this highly interactive demonstration, we will set up all three of our arrangements next to each other (hand pad, phone, and chair) for training and real-time classification on an attached laptop computer as shown in the Video Figure, with a minimum of three participants trained on any given arrangement.

CONCLUSION

We have presented a technique to augment objects to enable automatic personalization through wide-spectrum bioimpedance sensing of the human body. We developed a multi-electrode sensing system and evaluated it with three form-factors with six electrodes each. We then proposed diverse interaction scenarios to highlight the capability of sensing technology along with a long-term evaluation with promising results. We hope *Zensei* will be a useful tool for designing more seamless customized user interactions with a variety of objects.

REFERENCES

1. Bayford, R. H. Bioimpedance tomography (electrical impedance tomography). *Annu. Rev. Biomed. Eng. 8* (2006), 63–91.

2. Cornelius, C., Peterson, R., Skinner, J., Halter, R., and Kotz, D. A wearable system that knows who wears it. In *Proc. MobiSys '14*, 55–67.

3. Dietz, P., and Leigh, D. DiamondTouch: a multi-user touch technology. In *Proc. UIST '01*, 219–226.

4. Harrison, C., Sato, M., and Poupyrev, I. Capacitive fingerprinting. In *Proc. UIST '12*, 537–543.

5. Sato, M., Poupyrev, I., and Harrison, C. Touché: enhancing touch interaction on humans, screens, liquids, and everyday objects. In *Proc. CHI '12*, 483–492.

Form Follows Function(): An IDE to Create Laser-cut Interfaces and Microcontroller Programs from Single Code Base

Jun Kato   **Masataka Goto**

National Institute of Advanced Industrial Science and Technology (AIST), Tsukuba, Japan

{jun.kato, m.goto}@aist.go.jp

ABSTRACT

During the development of physical computing devices, physical object models and programs for microcontrollers are usually created with separate tools with distinct files. As a result, it is difficult to track the changes in hardware and software without discrepancy. Moreover, the software cannot directly access hardware metrics. Designing hardware interface cannot benefit from the source code information either. This demonstration proposes a browser-based IDE named *f3.js* that enables development of both as a single JavaScript code base. The demonstration allows audiences to play with the *f3.js* IDE and showcases example applications such as laser-cut interfaces generated from the same code but with different parameters. Programmers can experience the full feature and designers can interact with preset projects with a mouse or touch to customize laser-cut interfaces. More information is available at http://f3js.org.

Author Keywords

Integrated development environment; personal fabrication; laser-cut interface; microcontroller.

ACM Classification Keywords

H.5.2. Information interfaces and presentation (e.g., HCI): User Interfaces – GUI; D.2.6. Software Engineering: Programming Environments – Integrated environments.

INTRODUCTION

Physical computing, or the development process of the so-called Internet of Things (IoT), involves iterative cycles of modeling hardware and programming software. The recent proliferation of personal fabrication techniques reduces the cost and time of printing physical objects. Microcontrollers are becoming more powerful, and some are capable of running programs written in dynamically-typed languages such as JavaScript, allowing more software enthusiasts to create their prototypes easily.

Development of hardware and software is usually done with different tools, making it cumbersome to keep track of both changes synchronously. Moreover, tool separation prevents the software from accessing the hardware metrics and vice versa. For instance, modeling an object that has holes to support sensors and actuators requires manual input of their metrics. The source code contains 'import'-like statements for their drivers and thus might know which sensors and actuators are used, but it is not aware of the metrics, such as the size of the printed objects.

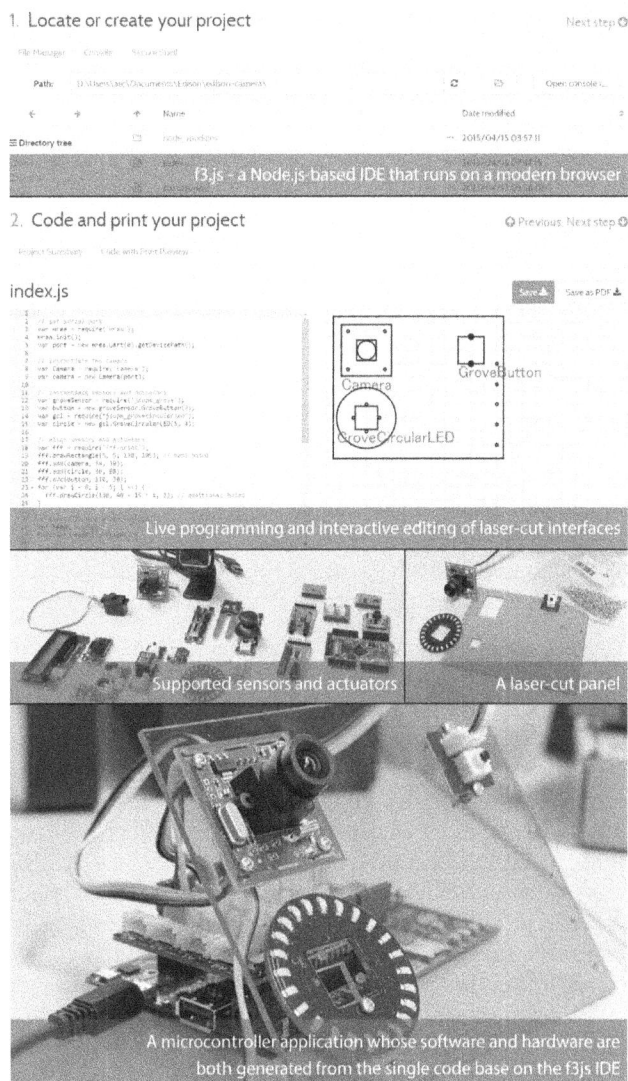

Figure 1. Overview of the development workflow with *f3.js*, completed in a single web page, language and code base.

UIST '15 Adjunct, November 08-11, 2015, Charlotte, NC, USA

ACM 978-1-4503-3780-9/15/11.

http://dx.doi.org/10.1145/2815585.2817797

We aim to address these issues and leverage the potential of microcontroller applications aware of the hardware metrics. This demonstration proposes an integrated development environment *f3.js* that stands for *"form follows function(), written in JavaScript."* It allows development of both a physical user interface (*form*) and its behavior by writing JavaScript code (*function*) on a browser (Figure 1). The programmer can write the same code that runs in a browser as well as on a microcontroller to allow customization of the layout of laser-cut interfaces and to define its behavior, respectively. Such *double-meaning* source code is achieved by utilizing two different JavaScript interpreters – one running on the *f3.js* and the other on the microcontroller.

FORM FOLLOWS FUNCTION() – F3.JS

The main interface of *f3.js* is rendered as a single web page as shown in Figure 1. The top of the page presents general information (such as the project directory) and becomes more detailed as the page progresses. While common commands are provided as links under the Operations menu in the file manager, the user can always switch to Console or Secure Shell tabs and input any command.

The current system supports Tessel.io[1] and Intel Edison[2] microcontrollers, which can run Node.js-based JavaScript applications. Once the user chooses a directory on the system, existing code in the project is analyzed, and its overview is shown in the 'Project Summary' tab. While most of the information is specified in `package.json` and can be edited in-place, the platform type is automatically detected by analyzing the JavaScript source code.

The current *f3.js* library contains Node.js packages that drive Grove and Tessel.io modules. These are sensors and actuators encapsulated with standardized connectors, easily attached to the supported microcontrollers. The next tab 'Code with Print Preview' shows the source code editor and the print preview. The programmer can write JavaScript application code that imports the *f3.js* library and creates the hardware module instances on the code editor.

The *f3.js* library does not only enable controlling the hardware modules but also provides the metrics information and supports live programming of laser-cut interfaces. The print preview is dynamically rendered by executing the source code with the sandboxed *f3.js* JavaScript interpreter on the browser. The interpreter ignores any calls to undefined functions meant to run on the microcontrollers. When a change is made to the source code, the system instantly evaluates the code and updates the preview. With this live programming support, the programmer can easily design the laser-cut interface as well as the interactive GUI on the print preview. With this interactivity, end-users including designers can use a mouse or touch to customize the laser-cut interfaces to fit their needs.

When the user is satisfied with the source code and the laser-cut interface, the system generates a PDF file and allows the user to laser-cut the acrylic panels. Finally, the assembled hardware can be connected to the host computer, and the user can upload the source code to start running the program on the microcontroller. The *f3.js* library on the microcontrollers does the same calculation as on the browser but does not render anything nor provide any interactivity (since there is no canvas to draw graphics) – therefore only allows to retrieve the metrics information. During execution of the program, *f3.js* shows a console with which the user can monitor the console output and input commands if needed.

RELATED WORK AND DISCUSSION

There exists prior work on programming tools for either physical objects or microcontroller applications. The former work includes DressCode [1] that allows designers to write code in a domain-specific language that generates two-dimensional artifacts. ShapeJS [2] provides JavaScript API that enables generating three-dimensional printer-ready objects. Our interaction design does not only allow the design of the hardware but also its behavior and can be integrated into these techniques. Recent work from the latter category includes .NET Gadgeteer [3] and Autodesk 123D Circuits [4], both of which support programming microcontrollers along with the graphical representations of the circuits. While these environments only care logical connections between microcontrollers and other modules, our system provides print preview that can be interactively edited by the designers and outputs laser-cut interfaces.

As discussed above, the novelty of our work resides in the integration of hardware and software design using a single programming language and single code base. The potential benefits include fast iterative development of applications aware of hardware metrics, simple version control, loose learning curve, and easy collaboration, whose validations remain as our future work. Whether JavaScript is suitable for designing layout of physical objects or not is an open question. Upon the choice of the language, we attached importance to the fact that it is popular, used for various purposes, and has a defacto standard package manager. Further details on the f3.js IDE and library are available on http://f3js.org.

REFERENCES

1. Jacobs, J., and Buechley, L. Codeable Objects: Computational Design and Digital Fabrication for Novice Programmers. In *Proc. of CHI'13*, 1589-1598.

2. Shapeways. ShapeJS. http://shapejs.shapeways.com

3. Villar, N., Scott. J., Hodges, S., Hammil, K., and Miller, C. .NET Gadgeteer: A Platform for Custom Devices. In *Proc. of Pervasive'12*, 216-233.

4. Autodesk. Autodesk 123D Circuits. http://www.123dapp.com/circuits

---

[1] Tessel. https://tessel.io

[2] Intel Edison. https://www.intel.com/content/www/do-it-yourself/edison.html

RFLOW: User Interaction Beyond Walls

Hisham Bedri
MIT Media Lab
Cambridge MA,
USA
hbedri@mit.edu

Otkrist Gupta
MIT Media Lab
Cambridge MA,
USA

Micha Feigin
MIT Media Lab
Cambridge MA,
USA

Andrew Temme
MSU
East Lansing MI,
USA

Gregory Charvat
MIT Media Lab
Cambridge MA,
USA

Ramesh Raskar
MIT Media Lab
Cambridge MA,
USA

ABSTRACT

Current user-interaction with optical gesture tracking technologies suffer from occlusions, limiting the functionality to direct line-of-sight. We introduce RFlow, a compact, medium-range interface based on Radio Frequency (RF) that enables camera-free tracking of the position of a moving hand through drywall and other occluders. Our system uses Time of Flight (TOF) RF sensors and speed-based segmentation to localize the hand of a single user with 5cm accuracy (as measured to the closest ground-truth point), enabling an interface which is not restricted to a training set.

Author Keywords
Radio-frequency; Hand-tracking; 3D; Through-wall

ACM Classification Keywords
H.5.m. Information interfaces and presentation.

INTRODUCTION

There is a growing demand for context aware, wireless, human-machine interfaces. Optical techniques are high in resolution, but are limited by occluders such as walls. Magnetic tracking works through occluders, however is sensitive to static-clutter and requires instrumentation of the user. Radio Frequency techniques enable contact-less tracking of features.

Recently the field of RF based interactive systems has exploded with innovation. Researchers have used various RF signals to perform non-contact un-instrumented interaction. Often this work centers around classifying a set of predefined gestures, however this limits the vocabulary of interaction and requires large training sets [4,5,7,8]. Other work has focused on localization and has produced results in tracking bodies and course arm-motions [1-4]. We demonstrate a system which extends these results in order

UIST '15 Adjunct, November 08-11, 2015, Charlotte, NC, USA
ACM 978-1-4503-3780-9/15/11.
http://dx.doi.org/10.1145/2815585.2817801

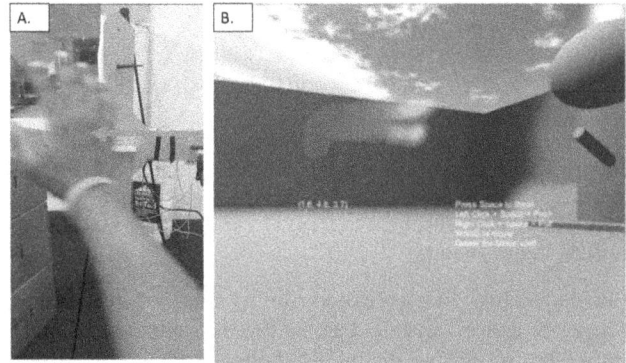

Figure 1: A live demo of a user moving their hand in front of the system. A) A user moves their hand in front of the system to control the position of an orb in B). Note that the wristband plays no role in the tracking.

to track smaller objects, such as a hand, with 5cm accuracy.

We rely on measuring the TOF between our transmitter, reflectors in the scene, and 4 antennas to localize objects. The accuracy of our localization system is linked to time resolution (bandwidth), signal to noise ratio, and aperture size (distance between antennas). While other systems broadcast high power into smaller bandwidth FCC gaps (2GHz), our system utilizes low-power transmitters across a wide gap (6GHz). This increases the time accuracy of our system while limiting the range of operation to <2 meters in front of the device. This enables our system to localize with greater accuracy and track reflective objects, such as a user's hand, water-based objects, and metallic objects.

IMPLEMENTATION

Our setup consists of an ultra-wideband transceiver which transmits a pulse of 10GHz bandwidth (100ps in duration). This pulse is repeated while the transceiver uses Continuous Time Binary Value (CTBV) architecture [6] to sample in the time-domain at 36GHz and thus measure the time of flight of the radar pulse. The transceiver is multiplexed between four antennas and the user's hand is localized.

SEGMENTATION

The system is designed to only track a single moving hand raised towards the interface. We implement a segmentation algorithm to separate the user's hand response from that of

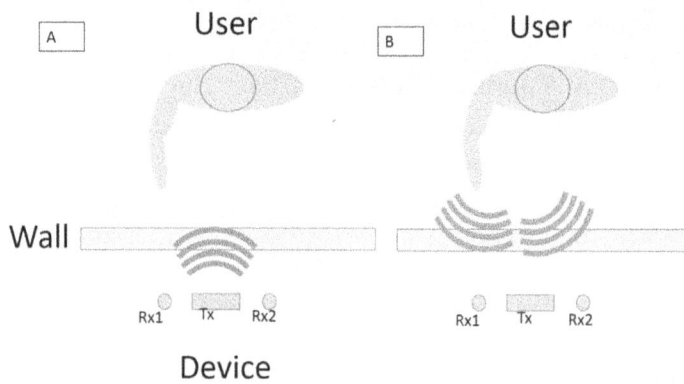

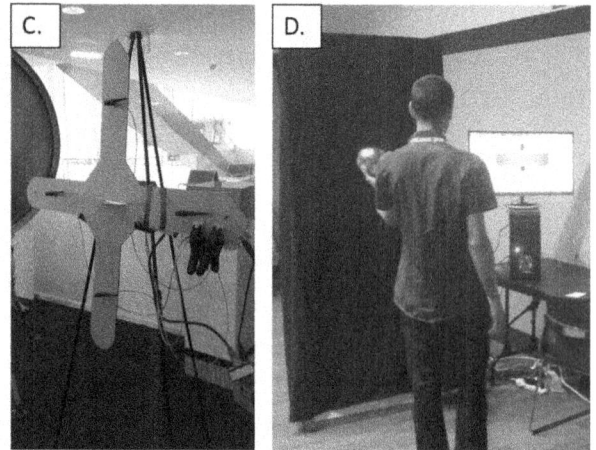

Figure 2: The system can operate behind walls and obstructions. A) The system transmits through the wall. In B), the signal reflects off of a user hand and returns to the system. In C), one can see a photo of the system which is light and compact. In D) a user moves a metal sphere in front of a wall with the system positioned behind the wall, demonstrating the capability to track other objects besides hands.

the body and other reflectors. First, static objects in the scene are cancelled, thus leaving the user's hand and body response. In order to distinguish between these, the system tracks the faster of the two moving objects, with the prior that the hand is usually closer to the system than the body. The result of the measurements is placed through a Kalman filter, leading to smoother results at the cost of signal delay.

EVALUATION

In order to evaluate the accuracy of the system, a user moved their hand along a predifined track while the system made continuous measurements of the user's hand location. We exploited the transparent nature of styrofoam to create a predefined pattern (circle) the user moved their hand along. Accuracy was measured as the closest distance between a measured point and a ground truth point and is shown in figure 3. The mean error is <5cm between the ground-truth measurements and the system's measurements. The system is accurate while tracking a single target in front of the system, however there are interesting cases for future work, such as multi-user, multi-hand, and objects with

Figure 3: In A) a histogram shows the mean error in localizing the moving hand in front of the system. In B), the result of recovering the motion of a user hand in a circle. The user moved their hand along a predefined path printed onto RF-transparent styrofoam.

complicated shapes which can appear stealth at particular orientations.

ACKNOWLEDGEMENTS
This work was supported in part by the National Science Foundation Graduate Research Fellowship under Grant No. 0802267. Thanks to Munehiko Sato and Jaimie Schiel for insightful comments, discussions, and guidance.

REFERENCES
1. Adib, Fadel, and Dina Katabi. See through walls with WiFi!. Vol. 43. No. 4. ACM, 2013.
2. Adib, Fadel, Zachary Kabelac, and Dina Katabi. "Multi-Person Motion Tracking via RF Body Reflections." (2014).
3. Adib, Fadel, et al. "3d tracking via body radio reflections." Usenix NSDI. Vol. 14. 2014.
4. Chetty, Kevin, et al. "Target detection in high clutter using passive bistatic WiFi radar." Radar Conference, 2009 IEEE. IEEE, 2009.
5. Cohn, Gabe, et al. "Your noise is my command: sensing gestures using the body as an antenna." Proceedings of the SIGCHI Conference on Human Factors in Computing Systems. ACM, 2011.
6. Hjortland, Håkon A., and Tor Sverre Lande. "CTBV integrated impulse radio design for biomedical applications." Biomedical Circuits and Systems, IEEE Transactions on 3.2 (2009): 79-88.
7. Pu, Qifan, et al. "Whole-home gesture recognition using wireless signals."Proceedings of the 19th annual international conference on Mobile computing & networking. ACM, 2013.
8. Zhao, Chen, et al. "SideSwipe: detecting in-air gestures around mobile devices using actual GSM signal." Proceedings of the 27th annual ACM symposium on User interface software and technology. ACM, 2014.

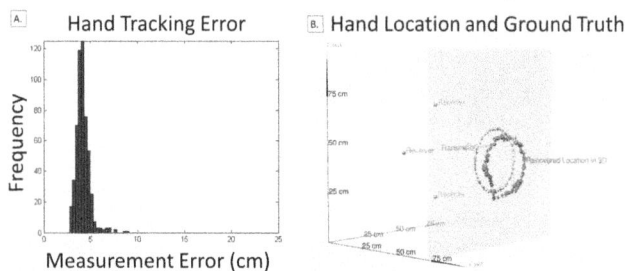

MetaSpace: Full-body tracking for immersive multiperson virtual reality

Misha Sra
MIT Media Lab
Cambridge, MA, 02142 USA
sra@media.mit.edu

Chris Schmandt
MIT Media Lab
Cambridge, MA, 02142 USA
geek@media.mit.edu

ABSTRACT

Most current virtual reality (VR) interactions are mediated by hand-held input devices or hand gestures and they usually display only a partial representation of the user in the synthetic environment. We believe, representing the user as a full avatar that is controlled by natural movements of the person in the real world will lead to a greater sense of presence in VR. Possible applications exist in various domains such as entertainment, therapy, travel, real estate, education, social interaction and professional assistance. In this demo, we present MetaSpace, a virtual reality system that allows co-located users to explore a VR world together by walking around in physical space. Each user's body is represented by an avatar that is dynamically controlled by their body movements. We achieve this by tracking each user's body with a Kinect device such that their physical movements are mirrored in the virtual world. Users can see their own avatar and the other person's avatar allowing them to perceive and act intuitively in the virtual environment.

Author Keywords

Multi-person Virtual Reality; Full-body immersion; First person view; Locomotion; Physical to virtual mapping.

ACM Classification Keywords

H.5.1. Information Interfaces and Presentation (e.g. HCI): Multimedia Information Systems

INTRODUCTION

New VR head-mounted devices (HMDs) are light, have dual high resolution screens, provide spatial audio, allow a wide field of view, offer head tracking with low latency, and use custom hand-held haptic input/output devices for navigation and interaction in the virtual world. Despite these characteristics, the lack of proprioceptive cues related to locomotion could limit a user's sense of presence in the virtual environment. Our focus in this demonstration is related to active situations where two users are moving in physical and virtual

UIST'15 Adjunct, November 8–11, 2015, Charlotte, NC, USA.
ACM 978-1-4503-3780-9/15/11.
http://dx.doi.org/10.1145/2815585.2817802

Figure 1. Two people wearing Oculus Rifts with their full body being tracked by two Kinect devices in a MetaSpace multiuser VR experience.

space while interacting with each other in the real world (see Figure 1). Their real world interactions are mirrored by their avatars in the virtual world.

First person experiences of the real world represent a standard to which all mediated experiences are compared, either mindfully or otherwise [3]. Our awareness of our body in space i.e. our body image is a *gestalt* through which all external space appears meaningful [1, 2]. Third person video games allow us to control a marionette through the physical extension of the game controller, making the avatar part of that through which the game world comes into existence. Bodily immersion in VR is rooted in the way the body is able to redirect a perception of itself as an object into virtual space (e.g. proprioception) and through this mirror image, the familiar body is also made the embodied subject during interaction [2].

Presence in VR is based on the perception of input through visual, auditory, or kinesthetic senses. For an enhanced sense of presence, VR needs to incorporate the participant as a part of the environment such that, head movements result in motion parallax, locomotion results in translation in space, proprioceptive cues are incorporated, vestibular responses are stimulated, and the user has agency. In most existing VR experiences, a seated user is presented with two contradictory motion cues; the visual stimulus signals movement to the brain, while the vestibular system indicates a lack of movement. These conflicting inputs can produce motion sickness and postural instability resulting in a sub-optimal immersive experience. For exploring VR environments, walking in place is not sufficient as it lacks the proprioceptive cues of actual walking [4]. In MetaSpace users can move in physical space

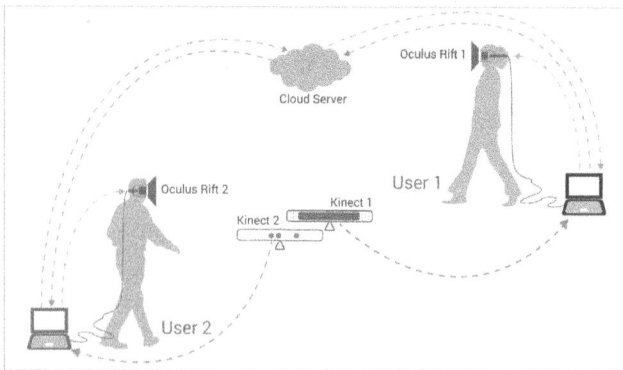

Figure 2. MetaSpace system configuration. Each user wears an Oculus Rift virtual reality head mounted display and can see themselves (first person view) and the other user's avatar on their screen. Each user is fully tracked with a Kinect and body movements like walking, waving etc of each user are transmitted through the cloud server such that everyone can see everyone and feel their presence in the virtual world similar to that in the real world.

(Figure 4), thereby maintaining coherence between the visual and vestibular inputs and experiencing VR in a more natural way. We use two Microsoft Kinect devices to track the full-body of each user and map their movements to an avatar in the virtual world. This allows users to see (first person perspective) their hands and legs move as they walk as well as see other users move around in a shared multi-person virtual world. In this demo we focus on the full body tracking and movement in real and virtual space while leaving the physical to virtual mapping for a separate full writeup.

METASPACE SYSTEM

The MetaSpace system consists of two parts (Figure 2). The first is two Oculus Rift head mounted display devices, one for each person, to view the virtual world. The second is skeleton tracking of each user using Kinect devices (Figure 4). In skeletal tracking, a human body is represented by a number of joints that represent body parts such as head, neck, shoulders, and arms. Each joint is represented by its 3D coordinates and mapped to the joints in a rigged 3D model. For a synchronous multiuser virtual experience, it is essential that all persons receive the same exact system state at all times. Therefore, MetaSpace features a client-server architecture that is made of four main entities: multiuser middleware and service (Photon Server), local clients (laptops), Microsoft Kinect devices, and HMDs (Oculus Rift). Data between the server and laptops is transmitted over wireless technology. The HMDs are wired to the laptops (for now) and present virtual world state such that each user can see the other move in real-time. Communication between the users and the virtual world happens through physical movement tracked using Microsoft Kinect devices. These mechanisms help create a natural hands-free immersive multiuser experience.

The demo VR was created by doing a 3D reconstruction of the hallway outside our offices using depth data, cleaning up and texturing the resulting 3D model of the space and objects, and adding other 3D elements like mountains and a valley to build a scene that is visually different from the hallway (Figure 3). Physical world barriers like walls and storage cabinets

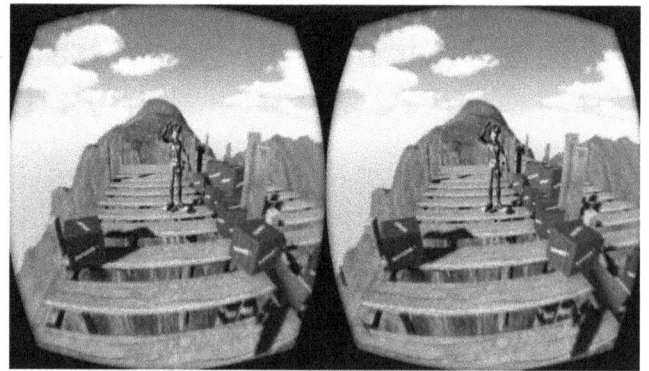

Figure 3. Virtual scene showing a bridge with one drop off corresponding to a physical wall and the crates corresponding to storage cabinets in the real world. The view through the first users' HMD shows the second user waving to them.

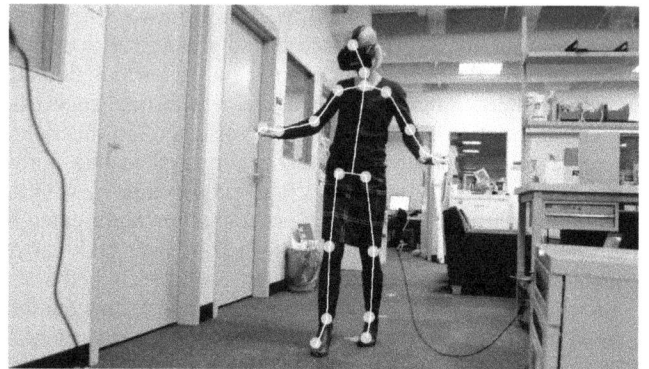

Figure 4. User 1 walking down the hallway (real) and bridge (virtual) toward User 2 (Figure 3) waving at them. User 1's skeleton is tracked by the Kinect and their physical movements are mapped to their avatar's movements.

appear in the virtual world as bridge edges and crates at the right locations and users avoid running into them intuitively as they do in real life. In the demo, the audience will have the opportunity to embody an avatar and walk in physical space to navigate a virtual bridge while wearing the Oculus Rift. They will also be able see another person's avatar and interact with them in the real world as well as the virtual world.

REFERENCES

1. Merleau-Ponty, M., and Smith, C. *Phenomenology of perception*. Motilal Banarsidass Publishers, 1996.

2. Sageng, J. R., Fossheim, H. J., and Larsen, T. M. *The Philosophy of Computer Games*, vol. 7. Springer Science & Business Media, 2012.

3. Steuer, J., Biocca, F., and Levy, M. R. Defining virtual reality: Dimensions determining telepresence. *Comm. in the age of virtual reality* (1995), 33–56.

4. Williams, B., Narasimham, G., Rump, B., McNamara, T. P., Carr, T. H., Rieser, J., and Bodenheimer, B. Exploring large virtual environments with an hmd when physical space is limited. In *Proc. of the 4th symp on Applied perception in graphics and visualization*, ACM (2007), 41–48.

GaussStarter:
Prototyping Analog Hall-Sensor Grids with Breadboards

Rong-Hao Liang*   **Han-Chih Kuo**†   **Bing-Yu Chen***
*† National Taiwan University
*{rhliang,robin}@ntu.edu.tw   †andikan@cmlab.csie.ntu.edu.tw

ABSTRACT

This work presents *GaussStarter*, a pluggable and tileable analog Hall-sensor grid module for easy and scalable breadboard prototyping. In terms of ease-of-use, the graspable units allow users to easily plug them on or remove them from a breadboard. In terms of scalability, tiling the units on the breadboard can easily expand the sensing area. A software development kit is also provided for designing applications based on this hardware module.

Author Keywords

Analog Hall-Sensor Grid, Breadboard, GaussSense

ACM Classification Keywords

H.5.2. Information Interfaces and Presentation (e.g. HCI): User Interfaces

INTRODUCTION

Camera-based object tracking techniques have been applied for years, but the thin-film magnetic field camera, GaussSense [4], is indeed an unusual one. With a dense grid of Hall-sensor deployed, GaussSense functions as a short-depth camera that tracks the 3D position and orientation [3], shape [2], and ID [5] of multiple magnetic objects nearby it by seeing the magnetic field distribution; GaussSense also functions as an X-ray camera that sees the magnetic object, which can be coated in non-ferrous materials and/or expressive forms, through users hands. Therefore, GaussSense can be attached to the back of prevalent portable displays for TUI design, or attached to human body for on-body input [1]. Although the design and application spaces are well-explored, theres still one fundamental challenge remains: *How to build an analog Hall-sensor grid from scratch?*

The challenge motivates us to consider breadboard, a common construction base for prototyping of electronics. Because prototyping electronics with breadboard does not require soldering, it is easy to use for creating temporary prototypes and experimenting with circuit design with electronic components that are in Dual In-line Packages (DIP); the structure of breadboard also support making tidy circuits –

UIST'15 Adjunct, November 8–11, 2015, Charlotte, NC, USA.
ACM 978-1-4503-3780-9/15/11.
http://dx.doi.org/10.1145/2815585.2815742

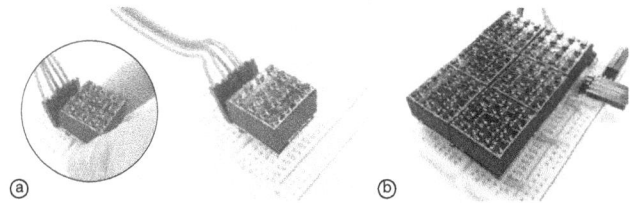

Figure 1. (a) *GaussStarter* is an analog Hall-sensor grid module that is compatible with breadboard. (b) Tiling the modules can easily extend the sensing area.

Figure 2. Hardware design of *GaussStarter*. (a) Top view and (b) bottom view of the Hall-sensor grid. (c) Overview of the assembled module.

which is essential for an effective sensor grid. However, the major limitation of breadboard is its capacity – makers can only build a relatively sparse sensor grid because they can only plug one sensor to each 5-hole row. A sparse sensor grid only supports tracking relatively large magnets with relatively low resolution, and thus limits the applications.

GAUSSSTARTER: GAUSSSENSE FOR BREADBOARD

This work introduces *GaussStarter* (Figure 1), a breadboard-compatible, tileable Analog Hall-Sensor Grid module for breadboard prototyping. In terms of *breadboard-compatible*, each 2cm-width×2cm-height×1cm-thick module consists of a grid of 4×4=16 Winson WSH136 analog Hall-sensors[1] and an 1-to-16 multiplexer (Figure 2), which reduces each module's I/O pin to 7: *VCC*, *ground*, 4 *selection inputs* and *1 analog output*. With the cuboid form and the 7 standard 1" pitch Dupont male connector at the bottom, users can easily grasp and plug the module to a breadboard. In terms of *tileable*, the 4×4 sensor grid that is located in the center of each module allows users to easily expand the sensing area by tiling them on the breadboard, which also aligns them physically. Although a 0.8mm gap may occurs between each unit, the effect on signal processing is negligible. This novel hardware module, therefore, allows novice users to prototype interactive devices with an analog Hall-sensor grid easily.

WORKFLOW: USING THE GAUSSSTARTER

1. Wire the circuit with breadboard: Users power up the sensor grid by connecting the *VCC* and *ground* pins between a micro-controller and the GaussStarter module, connect the

---

[1] http://www.winson.com.tw/

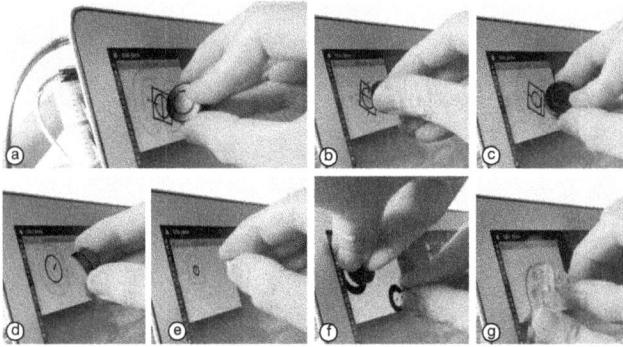

Figure 3. (a) The gridded GaussStarters attached to the back of a displays track the (b) roll, (c) pitch, (d) pitch and yaw, (e) hover height of a magnetic token, (f) the ID of different magnetic tokens, and (g) the shape of a magnetic construction.

digital output pins of the micro-controller to the four *selection* pins of each module, and connect the analog input pin of the micro-controller to the *analog out* pin of each modules. Additional multiplexers are useful if the amount of modules is more than the number of analog pins provided by the micro-controller. Figure 1(b) shows utilizing the structures of the breadboard effectively reduces the clutter of wiring.

2. Upload the firmware to the micro-controller: The signal processing firmware uploaded to the micro-controller designates the digital out pins and the analog input pins while initialization. After initialized, the firmware switches the selection pins to get all sensor data from the sensor grid, and then records the collected data as an integer array. Once requested, the firmware sends the data to the client software via serial connection.

3. Build software applications with GaussSense SDK: The *GaussSense SDK*[2] is available online for software application developers. In the software applications, users initialize the gridded GaussStarters with the height, width of the grid as well as the name of the serial port information provided. For example, a 3×2 GaussStarter grid to *COM*3 can be initialized by the following method:

```
GaussSense gs = new GaussSense(3,2,COM3);
```

To refresh the sensor data, users obtain the target magnetic field image in an array of sensor data with the height, width, and the up-sampling rate provided. For example, a $600 \times 400px$ magnetic field image that is up-sampled using the bicubic interpolation in a sample rate of 5 can be obtained by the following method:

```
float[][] Image = getUpsampledImage(600,400,5);
```

Figure 3 shows the gridded GaussStarters attached to the back of a display device can sense magnetic objects on and above the display surface. The obtained magnetic-field image is used for extracting the 3D position and orientation of multiple magnetic tokens by applying the feature extraction algorithms introduced in *GaussBits* [3], identifying multiple magnetic objects by extracting the area-intensity profiles as *GaussStones* [5], and extracting the geometry and skeleton of

----

[2]http://developers.gausstoys.com

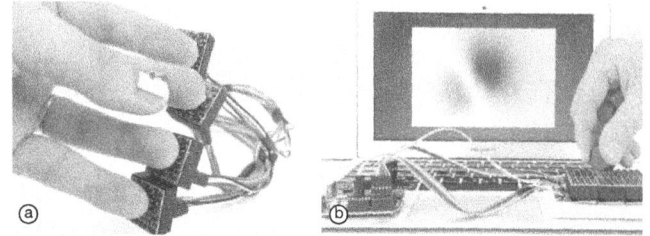

Figure 4. Use *GaussStarter* to prototype (a) wearable input devices, and (b) standalone devices for 3D interactions.

a magnetic construction as *GaussBricks* [2]. The APIs and examples are available online as well.

DISCUSSION AND FUTURE WORK

GaussStarter is an analog Hall-sensor grid module that is compatible with breadboards, thus is easy-to-use and reusable for iterative prototyping. Applying the concept presented in this work is also useful for fabricating the analog Hall-sensor grids in different sizes and resolutions, and the thickness can be further reduced to 2mm or less for more portability [4]. Figure 4 also shows developers can consider using this toolkit for prototyping wearable interactions or standalone devices for high-degree-of-freedom interactions with ease. The proposed hardware module and the software toolkit have been tried in several design workshops and used by a few artists and programmers. Future work will gather the results and user feedback to inform researchers and practitioners the novel uses of this technology.

ACKNOWLEDGMENTS

This work was supported in part by the Ministry of Science and Technology, National Taiwan University, and Intel Corporation under Grants MOST 103-2911-I-002-001, NTU-ICRP-104R7501, and NTU-ICRP-104R7501-1.

REFERENCES

1. Chan, L., Liang, R.-H., Tsai, M.-C., Cheng, K.-Y., Su, C.-H., Chen, M. Y., Cheng, W.-H., and Chen, B.-Y. Fingerpad: Private and subtle interaction using fingertips. In *Proc. ACM UIST '13* (2013), 255–360.

2. Liang, R.-H., Chan, L., Tseng, H.-Y., Kuo, H.-C., Huang, D.-Y., Yang, D.-N., and Chen, B.-Y. GaussBricks: Magnetic building blocks for constructive tangible interactions on portable displays. In *Proc. ACM CHI '14* (2014), 1391–1400.

3. Liang, R.-H., Cheng, K.-Y., Chan, L., Peng, C.-X., Chen, M. Y., Liang, R.-H., Yang, D.-N., and Chen, B.-Y. GaussBits: Magnetic tangible bits for portable and occlusion-free near-surface tangible interactions. In *Proc. ACM CHI '13* (2013), 1391–1400.

4. Liang, R.-H., Cheng, K.-Y., Su, C.-H., Weng, C.-T., Chen, B.-Y., and Yang, D.-N. GaussSense: Attachable stylus sensing using magnetic sensor grid. In *Proc. ACM UIST '12* (2012), 319–326.

5. Liang, R.-H., Kuo, H.-C., Chan, L., Yang, D.-N., and Chen, B.-Y. Gaussstones: Shielded magnetic tangibles for multi-token interactions on portable displays. In *Proc. ACM UIST '14* (2014), 365–372.

Enhanced Motion Robustness from ToF-based Depth Sensing Cameras

Wataru Yamada, Hiroyuki Manabe, Hiroshi Inamura
Research Labs, NTT DOCOMO
3-6, Hikarinooka, Yokosuka, Kanagawa, Japan
{wataruyamada, manabehiroyuki}@acm.org, inamura@nttdocomo.com

ABSTRACT

Depth sensing cameras that can acquire RGB and depth information are being widely used. They can expand and enhance various camera-based applications and are cheap but strong tools for computer human interaction. RGB and depth sensing cameras have quite different key parameters, such as exposure time. We focus on the differences in their motion robustness; the RGB camera has relatively long exposure times while those of ToF (Time-of-flight) based depth sensing camera are relatively short. An experiment on visual tag reading, one typical application, shows that depth sensing cameras can robustly decode moving tags. The proposed technique will yield robust tag reading, indoor localization, and color image stabilization while walking and jogging or even glancing momentarily without requiring any special additional devices.

Author Keywords
Depth sensing camera; exposure time; visual tag;

ACM Classification Keywords
H.5.2. Information interfaces and presentation (e.g., HCI): User Interface

INTRODUCTION
The performance of cameras embedded in smartphones is being continuously and rapidly improved. For example, 4K or 240 frames per seconds (fps) movie capture is already supported. Adding new functionality such as depth sensing is another direction in camera evolution. Since the adoption of depth sensing cameras for video games, the cost of depth sensing continues to fall precipitously and new applications that use RGB and depth information have been developed.

UIST '15 Adjunct, November 08-11, 2015, Charlotte, NC, USA
ACM 978-1-4503-3780-9/15/11.
http://dx.doi.org/10.1145/2815585.2817807

Among the several depth sensing techniques, ToF-based cameras ease the form factor and lower the computation cost. Smartphones with depth sensing cameras in addition to RGB have been already developed and the integration of RGB and depth sensing cameras into one image sensor is being addressed. These efforts will continue and we assume that ToF-based depth sensing will be adopted by most camera-equipped devices in the future.

The principles of ToF-based depth sensing cameras and regular RGB cameras are quite different. While regular RGB cameras integrate values over the exposure time, depth sensing cameras emit single IR pulses and measure the time difference between the radiated and received IR pulse. In practice, the depth value is measured more than once to improve the signal-to-noise ratio (SNR) [1]. The time taken is called the integration time; it corresponds to the exposure time of regular RGB cameras.

The integration time introduces motion blur, the same as regular RGB cameras. RGB cameras can suppress motion blur by setting short exposure times. This is effective when capturing a still image of a moving object. Unfortunately, short exposure times are not suitable for capturing movies. There are several reasons; first, they require high sensitivity and decrease SNR. Second, they emphasize the rolling shutter effect. Finally, proper motion blur makes color sequences more natural to humans [2]. Thus, shorter exposure times will not be used due to technical difficulties as well as the issue of human perception.

On the other hand, there is no human-related limitation on using short integration times for depth sensing cameras. The integration time will shorten as sensing techniques improve so the depth sensing camera will provide blur-free images. This will provide high motion robustness to several applications in the future.

For example, one indoor localization proposal uses IR cameras and invisible tags in the environment [3]. Accurate indoor localization will be possible while walking, jogging or momentary glances by applying the proposed method. Tracking fast moving objects with tags will be also possible.

IMPLEMENTATION AND EVALUATION

The motion robustness of three cameras was investigated by reading a rotating tag.

The tag has a rectangular frame (160 x 160 mm) holding several small retroreflector dots (5 x 5 mm), and dot placement on the 3 x 3 grid indicates ID and orientation. This configuration is almost the same as that described in [3].

We captured the tag while it was rotated at 2, 5, 10, and 15 rps using various cameras that were placed 50 cm from the tag. The tested cameras were Intel RealSense 3D Camera F200 and SoftKinetic DS325. Apple iPhone 6 was also used to record 240 fps movies with automatic parameters.

Figure 1 shows the images. While both color and depth images basically recorded the object accurately when the rotating speed was low, the difference between them became visible as the speed increased. For example, the iPhone 6 images show that it was difficult to well capture objects rotating at over 10 rps even at the high capture speed of 240 fps. Strong blur was found in the color images of F200, while the shapes are clear in the IR images. DS325 outputs saturated values for each pixel in the depth image when the reflected IR is too strong to permit depth measurements. The depth images of DS325 were simply binarized to indicate whether each pixel was saturated or not. DS325 exhibited only motion blur in binarized depth images while the rolling shutter effect and motion blur were found in the color images with rotation speeds over 5 rps. These results confirm that depth images have higher motion robustness than color images.

We also implemented a simple tag reading application using the DS325 and evaluated its accuracy. The rotating speeds and tag positions were the same as in the previous experiment. The reading algorithm is quite simple. Rectangular outer frame is extracted from the binarized depth images after finding contours, approximation by polylines, and thresholding by dimensions. In addition, the dots were read to decode the tag's ID. Tag reading was performed frame by frame.

We conducted 2400 trials (300 frames x 4 speeds x 2 tags) in total. The results for both tags were almost the same and the average reading accuracy is shown in Figure 1. Tag reading was almost completely successful; the speed of 15 rps lowered the accuracy to 80%. Errors were due to the failure to extract the outer frame and failure to accurately read the dot arrangement. Although failures increased with rotation speed, the results show that the proposed method supports robust tag reading.

CONCLUSION

A technique that uses ToF-based depth sensing cameras to enhance motion robustness was proposed. Such cameras offer robustness because of their short integration times. We captured images of a rotating tag with various cameras

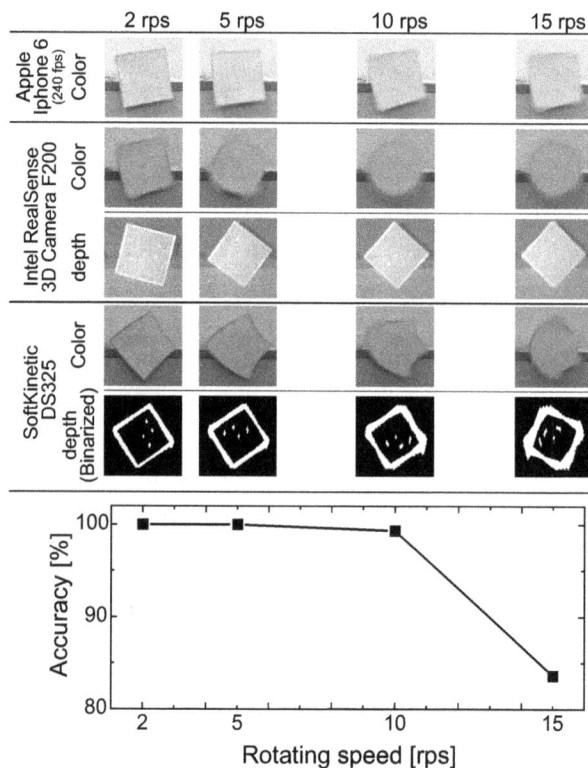

Figure 1. Captured images and the results of tag reading. iPhone 6 images exhibited motion blur at over 10 rps. Shapes of the tag were clear in depth images of F200. Depth images of DS325 were binarized (each pixel was saturated or not). The depth image of a tag captured by DS325 was almost perfectly decoded except at rotation speeds of 15 rps. On the other hand, the color images exhibited strong rolling shutter effect.

and confirmed that RGB cameras suffer rolling shutter effect and motion blur while depth sensing cameras could clearly capture the object. Moreover, an experiment was conducted in which a depth sensing camera decoded a rotating tag. Tag reading was successful (80%) even when the tag was rotated rapidly (15 rps). Therefore, it is concluded that depth sensing cameras offer strong motion robustness to tag reading applications. We intend to explore other applications of the proposed technique, for example, indoor localization and stabilization of color images.

REFERENCE

1 S. Foix, G. Aleny`a, and C. Torras. Lock-in Time-of-Flight (ToF) Cameras: A Survey. IEEE J. Sensors Vol.11. (2011), 1917–1926.

2 F.Navarro, F.J.Ser´on, and D.Gutierrez. Motion Blur Rendering: State of the Art. Computer Graphics Forum Vol.30. (2011), 3–26.

3 Y.Nakazato, M.Kanbara, and N.Yokoya. Localization of wearable users using invisible retro-reflective markers and an IR camera. In Proc. SPIE, Vol.5664. (2005), 563-570.

Workload Assessment with eye Movement Monitoring Aided by Non-invasive and Unobtrusive Micro-fabricated Optical Sensors

Carlos C. Cortes Torres[1], Kota Sampei[1], Munehiko Sato[2], Ramesh Raskar[2], Norihisa Miki[1,3]

[1]Keio University
Yokohama, Japan

[2]MIT Media Lab
Cambridge, MA, USA

[3]JST PRESTO
Tokyo, Japan

cortestc@a6.keio.jp, sampei521@a8.keio.jp, munehiko@acm.org, raskar@media.mit.edu, miki@mech.keio.ac.jp

ABSTRACT

Mental state or workload of a person are very relevant when the person is executing delicate tasks such as piloting an aircraft, operating a crane because the high level of workload could prevent accomplishing the task and lead to disastrous results. Some frameworks have been developed to assess the workload and determine whether the person is capable of executing a new task. However, such methodologies are applied when the operator finished the task. Another feature that these methodologies share is that are based on paper and pencil tests. Therefore, human-friendly devices that could assess the workload in real time are in high demand. In this paper, we report a wearable device that can correlate physical eye behavior with the mental state for the workload assessment.

Author Keywords

Dye-sensitized photovoltaic devices; Transparent sensors; Line-of-sight; NASA TLX; Workload assessment; Optical interface; Wearable.

ACM Classification Keywords

H.1.2. User/Machine Systems: Human Factors, Human Information Processing. H.5.2. User Interfaces: Evaluation/methodology. J.3. LIFE AND MEDICAL SCIENCES: Health.

INTRODUCTION

The workload is defined as the cost of accomplishing mission requirements for the human operator to achieve a particular level of performance. Yet this is a hypothetical construction, the workload is influenced by several factors such as operator skills, experience, and time to accomplish the task. The failure of accomplishing a task due to high workload could have disastrous results, i.e.

UIST '15 Adjunct, November 08-11, 2015, Charlotte, NC, USA
ACM 978-1-4503-3780-9/15/11.
http://dx.doi.org/10.1145/2815585.2817808

when piloting a commercial aircraft or operating a crane.

To properly assess this hypothetical construction, NASA has developed a framework that includes the factors mentioned above and organized them into six subscales and weight these subscales according to each subject [1]. Nevertheless, the application of this methodology is based on paper and pencil or a computerized test and applied once the task is done. While the operator is executing the determined task, we cannot know until what point, the operator is still capable of doing it. There is a considerable amount of time between the termination of the task and the application of the NASA-TLX test [1]; therefore human-friendly devices that could assess the workload in real time are extremely useful.

The position and movement of the eyes reflect the physical and mental state, and various techniques have been developed based on this characteristic. One of such techniques is the electrooculography (EOG) in which the eye is modeled as a dipole; a sensor is fixed on the cornea (positive pole) and the retina (negative pole). This technique has been being used for health monitoring.). Although it is proposed as non-invasive, it is not lightweight [2].

DESIGN

Dye-Sensitized Solar Cells (DSSC)

In this paper, we proposed a non-invasive, unobtrusive, and transparent micro-fabricated optical sensor for eye tracking/line-of-sight (LOS) affixed on eyeglasses (Figure 1) and combined with NASA-TLX methodology [1] in order to correlate and determined eye behavior with the mental state of a subject. We use dye-sensitized photovoltaic cells (DSSC) as optical sensors arrayed. The sensor array detects the difference in the light intensity reflected from the pupil and the white of the eye (sclera) and then determines the pupil position. Each sensor consists of two electrodes encapsulated and fills the capsule with electrolyte. The proposed design is confirmed by four semi-circular shaped sensors arrayed on eyeglasses. Because we micro-fabricated the sensors on indium tin oxide (ITO) sheet glasses, we do not block the user's LOS. It is also very thin and light-weight as the sensor is about 1mm thick piece of glass plates. The sensor requires very low power to operate as the sensor modules actually generate electrical power, and we only need to operate Analog-to-Digital converters to measure

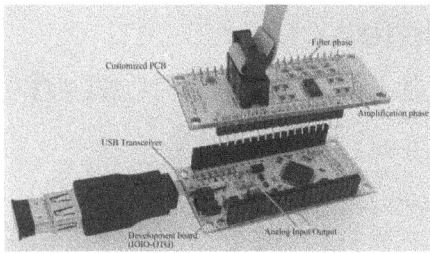

Figure 1. Signal acquisition, processing and data transmission hardware interface.

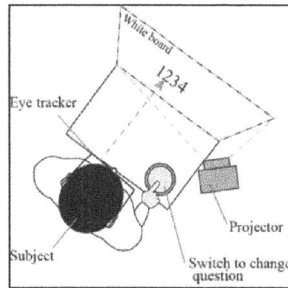

Figure 4. Experiment protocol. While wearing eye tracker conduct workload test. Sequence: 6 minutes test 2 minutes apply NASA-TLX Repeat sequence for 1 hour.

Subject A WWL =	65.4 + 6.58 × (# trials) + 19.8 × (lower left) -0.006 × (eye movement amount)
Subject B WWL =	75.5-2.13 × (multiple eye blink) -0.546 × (blink freq)
Subject C WWL =	34.1 + 6.13 × (# trials)
Subject D WWL =	No correlation
Subject E WWL =	37.1 + 6.65 × (# trial) + 0.951 × (multiple eyeblink)

Figure 3. The correlation between WWL and LOS information is described by these equations. 3 out of 5 subject showed correlation LOS Information - Weight Work Load (WWL)

the output voltage of the solar cells, due to its low power consumption it can be used for the long term. Because these type of devices are needed in workplaces and should not induce additional stress, natural eye movement detection is important [3]. Figure 1 (A) shows the device and design, (B) and (C) describes the working principle. Figure 2 shows the hardware set up.

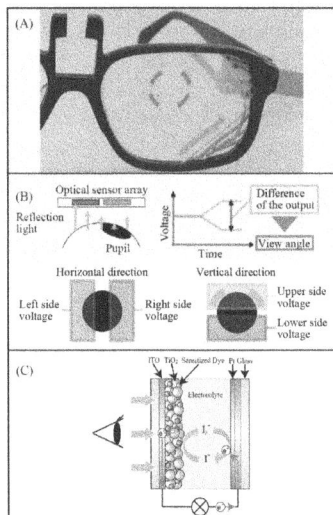

Figure 2. (A) Non-invasive wearable unobtrusive transparent optical sensor device. (B) The output of the sensor. Reflected light from the pupil is smaller than white of the pupil. The difference between the output is calculated to the view angle. (C) DSSC working principle. When light is incident, the electrolyte transports the charge between Titanium dioxide (TiO2) and Platinum (Pt) electrodes.

EXPERIMENT

Calibration

An initial calibration is carried out while the subject is wearing our system, The subject are instructed to gaze a series of six marks on a whiteboard in horizontal and vertical axes, and we record the output, also blink calibration is done similarly in order to get subject's view angle information.

MENTAL STRESS ASSESSMENT

NASA-TLX experiment is conducted with five subjects. The experiment is performed in six series of six minutes arithmetic problems (emulating mental stressful condition) and two minutes rating (applying NASA-TLX test). The experiment procedure takes one hour in total. Then the workload is calculated based on the subjects subscale rating and weight it to obtain the mean weighted workload (WWL) as shown in Figure 3.

The physical factors involved include the total amount of eye movement events, the location of LOS, the eye blinks number, multiple eye blink number (immediately back to back) and the number of trials. By eliminating the variables that does not affect the regression analysis equation we found out, a correlation between LOS, time and WWL was confirmed for subjects A and E, LOS and WWL have correlation for subject B, while no correlation was observed between LOS and WWL on subjects C and D, as shown in Figure 4.

RESULTS AND DISCUSSION

We developed a hardware and software system of a non-invasive and unobtrusive LOS sensor for workload assessment and proved a correlation between eye behavior and mental state. We also have proven that with our design is possible to perform real-time workload assessment as well as other mental state assessments such as health monitoring.

REFERENCES

1. S. G. Hart, L. E. Staveland. 1988. Development of NASA-TLX (Task Load Index): Results of Empirical and Theoretical Research. *In P. A. Hancock and N. Meshkati (Eds.) Human Mental Workload. Amsterdam: North Holland Press*

2. A. Bulling, H. Gellersen, J. Turner, M. Vidal. 2012. Wearable eye tracking for mental health monitoring. *Computer Communications* 35, 11: 1306-1311.

3. C. Cortes, N. Miki, M. Ogawa, A. Oikawa, M. Ozawa, K. Sampei. 2014. Wearable line-of-sight detection system using micro-fabricated transparent optical sensors on Eyeglasses. *Journal Sensors and Actuators A: Physical* 205: 208-214.

Multi-Modal Peer Discussion with RichReview on edX

Dongwook Yoon
Cornell University
Ithaca, NY 14850
dy252@cornell.edu

Piotr Mitros
edX
Cambridge, MA 02139
pmitros@edx.org

ABSTRACT

In this demo, we present RichReview, a multi-modal peer discussion system, implemented as an XBlock in the edX courseware platform. The system brings richness similar to face-to-face communication into online learning *at scale*. With this demonstration, we discuss the system's scalable back-end architecture, semantic voice editing user interface, and a future research plan for the profile based group-assignment scheme.

Author Keywords

Massive open online courses; peer discussion; multi-modal annotation; voice user interface; peer group assignment.

ACM Classification Keywords

H.5.3. Group and Organization Interfaces: Collaborative computing; H.5.2. User Interfaces: Interaction styles; H.5.1. Multimedia Information Systems: Audio input/output

INTRODUCTION

Peer discussion in classrooms can improve student learning outcomes with interactive engagement on the course concepts [1]. Massive open online course providers provide a large number of students with online peer discussion activities through discussion forums [2], video chats, and peer feedback on assignments [3]. These face a trade-off between the richness of synchronous interaction and the flexibility of asynchronous interactions.

We developed a multi-modal annotation system called RichReview [5] which brings a high level of expressivity into asynchronous document annotations through the use of student-recorded multimedia, including text, audio, and gestures. The system was originally built for the purpose of writing feedback, but was redesigned to support a range of modes of online peer discussion.

In this work, we demonstrate how integration of RichReview into a MOOC platform can potentially open an expressive discussion channel in asynchronous environments with large numbers of students. As the first step, we re-implemented the

RichReview's front-end, integrating it into Open edX. We designed a scalable back-end architecture for transmitting and storing multimedia comments created by a number of students. We partner these with a novel peer group assignment scheme that maximizes overall diversity of group composition using student profile data.

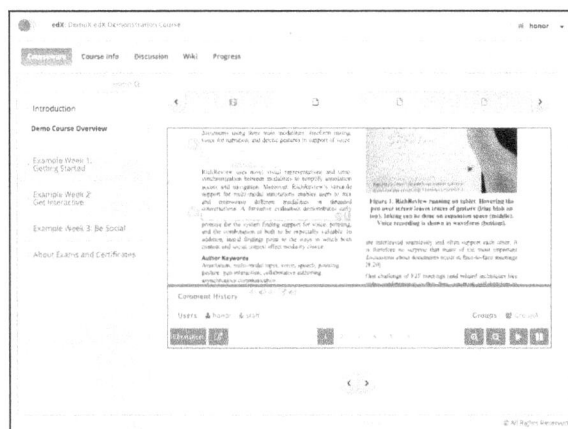

Figure 1. The RichReview XBlock running in the edX courseware.

RICHREVIEW MULTI-MODAL ANNOTATION SYSTEM

RichReview is a tablet based multi-modal annotation system for bringing richness of in-person conversation into document writing revision process. With RichReview, a commentator can record a combination of input modalities, such as pen writing and hovering, voice recording, as well as traditional modalities such as text. For example, RichReview users can verbally explain a math concept while pointing to a formula in a document and drawing a graph. Moreover, RichReview embeds the annotation thread within text lines of the annotated document, giving clear context for the comments. A prior lab study showed high potential of the system as a support tool for document-centric conversation [5].

INTEGRATION INTO EDX.ORG

Prior work demonstrated the value of RichReview in traditional classroom settings [6]. In order to more accurately measure the impact of RichReview, we would like to integrate it into a setting which supports massive numbers of learners. Open edX is a platform which support both MOOCs, with millions of learners on the edx.org web site, a large level of residential use (over 80% of MIT students use edX residentially), and over 100 open source deployments, including several deployments as part of national initiatives to improve training and education. Open edX was chosen due to the combination of support for research (including frameworks for

UIST'15 Adjunct, November 8–11, 2015, Charlotte, NC, USA.
ACM 978-1-4503-3780-9/15/11.
http://dx.doi.org/10.1145/2815585.2817809

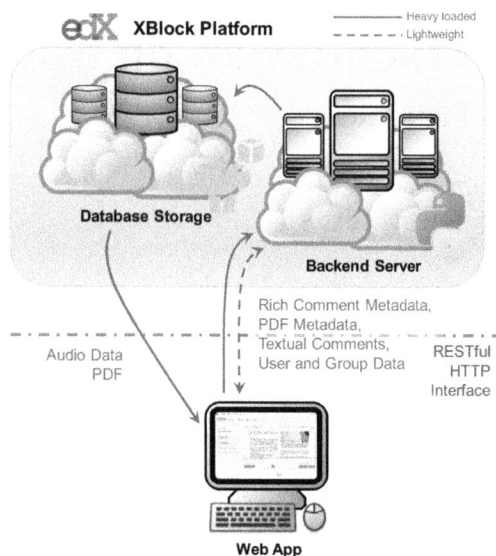

Figure 2. Scalable back-end architecture of the RichReview on edX.

randomized control trials, data collection, and frameworks for integration with novel pedagogical experiences like RichReview), anecdotal data from residential trials, and statistical evidence from MOOC trials.

A key to success is seamless integration into the edX UX, and robustly supporting tens of thousands of learners. As part of bringing RichReview to scale, we re-implemented the RichReview system as an XBlock — the components out of which Open edX courses are built. This allows the MOOC authors to include RichReview discussion sessions without managing multiple services, and for MOOC students to use RichReview seamlessly integrated into the edX interface. As can be seen in Fig. 1, the instructor can place the RichReview discussion session within the flow of the course contents. The overall architecture is shown in Fig. 2

Making the Back-end Scalable

RichReview is a media-heavy web application that exchanges large amounts of audio-visual data with the server. edX.org courses typically have tens of thousands of learners. In order to scale, we divided the data managed by RichReview into (1) high-bandwidth multimedia data (e.g. audio, PDF documents), and (2) low-bandwidth data (e.g. textual notes and metadata). The heavy-weight components are distributed through cloud file storage, which gives complete horizontal scalability. The metadata and other small data live in a conventional database. This allows queries for rapid simultaneous access to many pieces of metadata.

Semantic Voice Editing

From our prior RichReview deployment study [6], the discussant sometimes had to re-record an entire voice interaction to fix small mistakes in the middle of the recording, such as a stutter or a long pause. Recently, Rubin et al. presented an audio editing system that leverages speech transcriptions as semantic guidelines for editing voice as if it is text [4]. We are following this semantic editing approach, focusing on design

and development of live editing features, such as partial deletion or insertion. Even after having the caption-based editing system, it is a tedious repetitive task to manually trim long-pauses and 'Um's [5]. We will solve this problem by providing a batch post-processing operation that can automatically delete several such unnecessary snippets at once.

Profile Based Group Formation

We would like to explore how different peer group formations influence performances of student discussion. In MOOCs, it is an open research question to assign a large pool of students into the group composition that maximizes overall group heterogeneity or homogeneity. We will approach this problem by modeling student characteristic based on a combination of (1) the readily available profile data, such as linguistic, cultural, geographic distance, and age, and (2) the profile data inferred from a student's past RichReview discussions, such as communication styles and topic of interests. We are developing a system which minimizes or maximizes overall distance between students on the axes of those characteristic dimensions.

ACKNOWLEDGMENT

We would like to gratefully acknowledge the support from the Kwanjeong educational foundation, the course staffs who have supported the development of RichReview, as well as the students who participate by providing each other with thoughtful, meaningful feedback.

REFERENCES

1. Chi, M. T., and Wylie, R. The icap framework: Linking cognitive engagement to active learning outcomes. *Educational Psychologist 49*, 4 (2014), 219–243.

2. Mitros, P., Affidi, K., Sussman, G., Terman, C., White, J., Fischer, L., and Agarwal, A. Teaching electronic circuits online: Lessons from MITx's 6.002x on edX. In *ISCAS*, IEEE (2013), 2763–2766.

3. Mitros, P., and Paruchuri, V. An integrated framework for the grading of freeform responses. *The Sixth Conference of MIT's Learning International Networks Consortium* (2013).

4. Rubin, S., Berthouzoz, F., Mysore, G. J., Li, W., and Agrawala, M. Content-based tools for editing audio stories. In *Proceedings of the 26th annual ACM symposium on User interface software and technology*, ACM (2013), 113–122.

5. Yoon, D., Chen, N., Guimbretière, F., and Sellen, A. Richreview: blending ink, speech, and gesture to support collaborative document review. In *Proceedings of the 27th annual ACM symposium on User interface software and technology*, ACM (2014), 481–490.

6. Yoon, D., Chen, N., Randles, B., Cheatle, A., Loeckenhoff, C. E., Jackson, S. J., Sellen, A., and Guimbretière, F. Deployment of a collaborative multi-modal annotation system for instructor feedback and peer discussion. In *Proceedings of the 19th ACM Conference on Computer Supported Cooperative Work & Social Computing*, ACM (2016).

BitDrones: Towards Self-Levitating Programmable Matter Via Interactive 3D Quadcopter Displays

Calvin Rubens*, Sean Braley, Antonio Gomes,
Daniel Goc, Xujing Zhang, Juan-Pablo Carrascal and Roel Vertegaal
Human Media Lab
Queen's University, Kingston, Ontario, Canada
*j.rubens@queensu.ca, {braley, gomes, goc, xzhang, jp, roel}@cs.queensu.ca

ABSTRACT

In this paper, we present BitDrones, a platform for the construction of interactive 3D displays that utilize nano quadcopters as self-levitating tangible building blocks. Our prototype is a first step towards supporting interactive mid-air, tangible experiences with physical interaction techniques through multiple building blocks capable of physically representing interactive 3D data.

Author Keywords

Organic User Interfaces; Claytronics; Radical Atoms; Tangible User Interfaces.

ACM Classification Keywords

H.5.m. Information interfaces and presentation (e.g., HCI): Miscellaneous;

INTRODUCTION

The thought that computer interfaces might some day *physically* embody user interactions with digital data has been around for a long time. In 1965, Sutherland envisioned the "Ultimate Display" as a room in which the computer controlled the existence of matter [8]. According to Toffoli and Margolus [9], such programmable matter would consist of small, parallel, cellular automata nodes capable of geometrically shaping themselves in 3D space to create any kind of material structure. Since then, there has been a significant amount of research conducted towards this goal under various monikers, such as Claytronics [3], Organic User Interfaces [10], and Radical Atoms [4]. All of these seek, at least in part, to utilize programmable matter for user interface purposes to allow for a full two-way synchronization of bits with atoms — something the first generation of Tangible User Interfaces was not capable of [4]. While there has been progress in building hardware modules capable of various forms of self-actuation (known

as *Catoms*) [3, 7], much of the work on programmable matter has been theoretical in nature [2]. How to create a massively parallel system of Catoms capable of creating two-way immersive physical user experiences very much remains a research goal of the future. However, this lofty goal would promise virtual reality systems that would be fully physically integrated with real reality. The problem we address in this paper is that Catoms need to overcome gravity, typically via structural support by other Catoms, when building larger structures. While there has been some prior work in this area, most notably using ultrasound levitation [6], the movement of individual Catoms in threespace is typically limited. Other solutions use magnetic levitation to overcome gravity [5], again with distinct limitations on the independent motion of multiple Catoms. We propose to address the levitation problem through the use of nano quadcopter drones. While there have been explorations of swarms of quadcopters for visualization applications [1], there has been little work on fully interactive, real-time user interface applications of 3D drone displays. In this paper, we present BitDrones, an interactive 3D display that uses nano quadcopters as self-levitating voxels. Our prototype is a first step towards interactive mid-air tangible user interfaces with multiple building blocks that are capable of physically representing 3D data on the fly.

IMPLEMENTATION

In BitDrones, each drone represents a Catom that can hover anywhere inside a volume of 4m x 4m x 3m in size. Drones are safe for users, who can walk around the interaction volume and interact with each drone by touch. A drone can be used for input, for output, or for both at the same time. Simple atomic information can be displayed by a single drone, while more complex 3D data displays can be constructed using several drones, providing the rudiments for a voxel-based 3D modeling system capable of representing sparse 3D graphics in real reality.

Hardware

Figure 1 shows the 3D-printed body of a nano quadcopter of our own design. Each 8.9 cm diameter drone is equipped with quad-rotors, coreless motors, a Micro MultiWii flight controller board, a wireless Xbee point-to-point radio, and an RGB LED to provide visual feedback to the user. Each

UIST '15 Adjunct, November 08-11, 2015, Charlotte, NC, USA
ACM 978-1-4503-3780-9/15/11.
http://dx.doi.org/10.1145/2815585.2817810

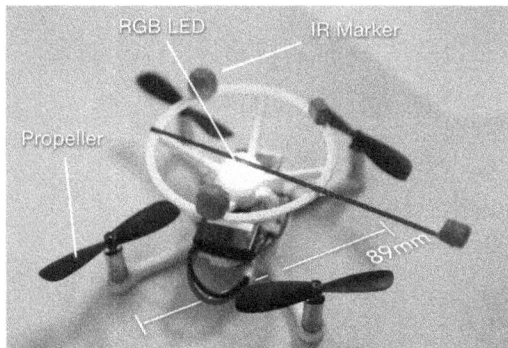

Figure 1. BitDrone with colour LED and Vicon markers.

drone also has a set of reflective markers in a unique configuration, so it can be individually tracked by a Vicon Motion Capture System [11]. An iMac provides location-based flight control information to the drones over the Xbee network.

Software

The drones run MultiWii 2.3.3 as a flight control platform. A custom C# application running on the iMac in Windows 8.1 receives drone locations from the Vicon and wirelessly sends flight and navigation control signals to the MultiWii software of each drone. A set of PID loops directs each drone's movements towards end positions based on user input and interface actions. The Vicon also tracks markers on the user's hands, allowing for gestural input. By estimating the relative positions between markers on the user's hands and on the drones, the system detects interaction primitives such as touching or dragging of individual drones across 3D space. These primitives can be combined for more complex interactions with 3D compound objects.

APPLICATION EXAMPLES

Our current implementation is limited to 3 drones, with the main limiting factor being drift due to turbulence. Drones are sufficiently stable to stay within a cube 25 cm in diameter, with some limitations on the ability to fly above one another, again due to turbulence. This means our current implementation can only be used to implement sparse 3D interfaces at present. However, we expect to be able to scale up our architecture to include at least a dozen drones in the near future. Within the limitations we designed the following application scenarios:

Interactive Representation of Real 3D Structures

Molecular modeling software allows the exploration of bonds between pairings of atoms in 3D. Our BitDrone system can represent molecular structures in 3D in mid-air, allowing users to interact with these structures in real reality. To simulate induced chemical reactions (such as electrolysis), a user can manipulate individual atoms by dragging drones in or out of a bond. LEDs on the drones represent the type of atom by colour coding.

Interactive Real-Reality InfoViz

Drones can also represent points in interactive data visualizations. For instance, the position of the drones can be determined by a mathematical expression, creating a physical representation of that expression. Manipulating one of the drones modifies some parameters of the expression, such as the curvature of a parabolic function. Other drones adjust their position accordingly, preserving the spatial relations as defined by the mathematical expression.

CONCLUSION

We presented BitDrones, an interactive, tangible 3D display that uses nano quadcopters with RGB LEDs as levitating building blocks. Our prototype is a first step towards supporting interactive mid-air tangible experiences with physical representations of 3D data.

ACKNOWLEDGMENTS

This work was supported by grants from NSERC and Immersion Inc.

REFERENCES

1. Federico Augugliaro and Raffaello D'Andrea. 2013. Admittance control for physical human-quadrocopter interaction. Control Conference (ECC), 2013 European. IEEE.
2. Seth C. Goldstein, Jason D. Campbell, Todd C. Mowry. 2005. Programmable matter. IEEE Computer. vol. 38, no. 6, 99-101.
3. Seth C. Goldstein and Todd C. Mowry. 2004. Claytronics: A scalable basis for future robots. In RoboSphere 2004.
4. Hiroshi Ishii, Dávid Lakatos, Leonardo Bonanni, and Jean-Baptiste Labrune. 2012. Radical atoms: Beyond tangible bits, toward transformable materials. Interactions 19, 1 (January 2012), 38-51.
5. Jinha Lee, Rehmi Post, and Hiroshi Ishii. 2011. ZeroN: Mid-air tangible interaction enabled by computer controlled magnetic levitation. In Proc. UIST '11. ACM, New York, NY, USA, 327-336.
6. Yoichi Ochiai, Takayuki Hoshi, and Jun Rekimoto. 2014. Pixie dust: Graphics generated by levitated and animated objects in computational acoustic-potential field. ACM Trans. Graph. 33, 4, Article 85 (July 2014), 13 pages.
7. Michael Rubenstein, Christian Ahler, and Radhika Nagpal. 2012. Kilobot: A low cost scalable robot system for collective behaviors. 2012 IEEE International Conference on Robotics and Automation (ICRA).
8. Ivan E. Sutherland. 1965. The Ultimate Display. Proceedings of IFIP 65, vol 2, pp. 506-508.
9. Tommaso Toffoli and Norman Margolus. 1991. Programmable matter: Concepts and realization. Physica D: Nonlinear Phenomena 47.1, 263-272.
10. Roel Vertegaal and Ivan Poupyrev. 2008. Organic user interfaces. Communications of the ACM 51.6 (2008): 26-30.
11. http://www.vicon.com/

Method of 3D Printing Micro-pillar Structures on Surfaces

Jifei Ou
MIT Media Lab,
Cambridge,
jifei@media.mit.e
du

Chin-Yi Cheng
MIT Architecture
Cambridge,
hajimecheng@gm
ail.com

Liang Zhou
MIT
Cambridge,
zhoul@mit.edu

Gershon Dublon
MIT Media Lab,
Cambridge,
gershon@media.
mit.edu

Hiroshi Ishii
MIT Media Lab,
Cambridge
ishii@media.mit.e
du

ABSTRACT

This work presents a method of 3D printing hair-like structures on both flat and curved surfaces. It allows a user to design and fabricate hair geometry that is smaller than 100 micron. We built a software platform to let one quickly define a hair's angle, thickness, density, and height. The ability to fabricate customized hair-like structures expands the library of 3D-printable shape. We then present several applications to show how the 3D-printed hair can be used for designing toy objects.

Author Keywords
3D Printing; Surface Texture;

ACM Classification Keywords
H.5.2. Information interfaces and presentation: User Interfaces

INTRODUCTION
3D printing is rapidly expanding the possibilities for how physical objects are fabricated [1]. Its Layer-By-Layer fabrication process has tremendous potential to enable the fabrication of physical objects not previously possible. Recently, high-resolution 3D printer is getting more and more available and affordable. This enables micron-scale structures to be fabricated. In this paper we present a bottom-up printing pipeline to fully utilize the capability of current high-resolution photopolymer 3D printers. This allows us to generate large amount of fine hair on 3D objects' surfaces. We introduce method for the fabrication of *Cilllia*. We then show examples of using *Cilllia* for toy design.

PRINTING HAIR-LIKE STRUCTURE
All the test and examples showing in this paper are printed on a commercially available Digital Light Processing (DLP) 3D printer (Autodesk Ember Printer). The DLP printer takes stacks of bitmap images from the CAD

UIST '15 Adjunct, November 08-11, 2015, Charlotte, NC, USA
ACM 978-1-4503-3780-9/15/11.

http://dx.doi.org/10.1145/2815585.2817812

models, and direct project the image to the liquid resin layer by layer. This approach allows us to construct 3D object with 2D images. It also permits overhang structure within 60 degrees during printing. The printer has the feature resolution of 50 μm on X and Y axis, and 25 μm on Z axis. The build volume is 64 by 40 by 150 mm. The used print material is near UV light photopolymer (Available on //spark.autodesk.com/ember/shop).

Challenges
Although the resolution of recent 3d printer has been improving, it is still considered impractical to directly print fine hair array on object's surface. This is due to the lack of efficient digital representation of CAD model with fine surface texture [2]. Most of the current commercially available 3D printer takes a Layer-By-Layer method to deposit/solidify materials into shapes that are designed in the CAD. It follows a Top-Down pipeline, where user creates digital 3D model, and then a program slices the model into layers for printer to print. In the field of Computer Graphics, the standard way to represent surface texture is through lofting bitmaps on the CAD model to create an optical illusion. It is not an actual 3-dimensional structure. If we were to create thousands or even more small hairs with conventional CAD system with real geometry, we will find it difficult or impractical to do: The data for describing the total geometry becomes extremely large and displaying such complex structure also takes a great deal of time

Figure 1. (a) Computer simulation of printed hair; (b) close view of actual printed hair; (c) SEM photo of the (b).

We propose a Bottom-Up 3D printing approach to design and fabricate hair-like structures without making 3D CAD models, where user directly generate printing layers that contains hair structure information for the 3D printer. Comparing to other surfaces texture such as wrinkle, hair is relatively simpler to generalize mathematically. It is usually a high aspect ratio cone that is vertical/angled to the surface. The height, thickness and profile might vary from one to another. As we know, the diameter of cone continuously decreases from the base to the tip. This method allows us to control hair printing from three aspects: 1. Single hair's geometry (1D): height, thickness, angle and profile; 2. Hair array on flat surfaces (2D): varying single hair geometry across the array on a 2D surface; 3. Hair array on curved surfaces (3D): generating hair array on any given curved surfaces.

We successfully printed a series of sample surfaces with oriented hair. Figure 1 shows that our printed geometry matches the computer simulation.

Applications

To show the capability of our printing method, we create three types of possible application for designers.

Objects with fine surface texture

As we can generate hair on any curved surfaces, we can now 3D print flowers and animals with such feature. We can also vary the thickness of the hair to control its stiffness. Figure 3 shows a hedgehog that has thicker hair (6 by 6 pixels on the base), and a bunny that has thinner one (3 by 3 pixels on the base). The hair of the latter one curls after dry due to its softness.

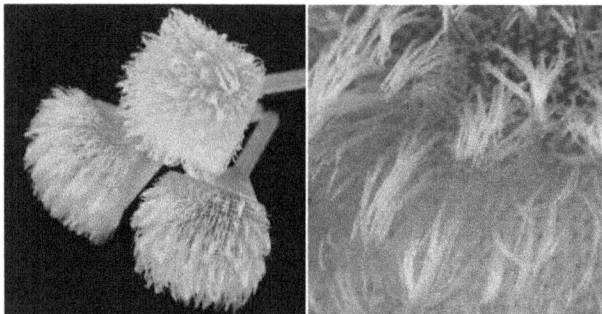

Figure 2. Successful printed hair arrays on curved surface.

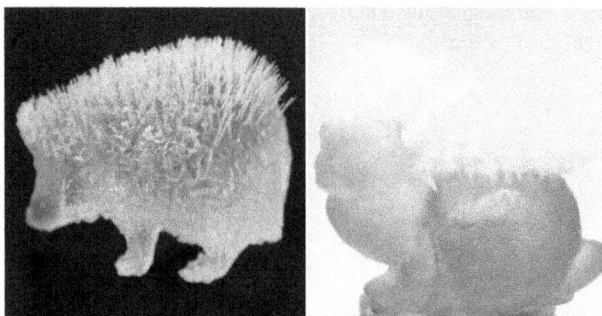

Figure 3. 3D printed figures with controllable hair stiffness.

Customized Brushes

We can also directly 3D print brushes with customized texture. Figure 4 shows four brushes with different density. With the color mapping method, one could create more complex shape of a brush for artistic expression.

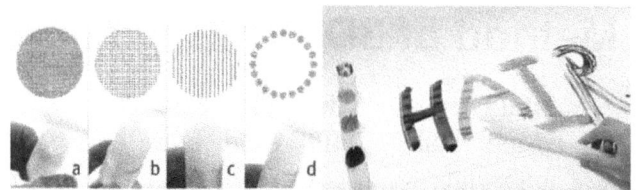

Figure 4. Printed brushes with different density.

Mechanical Adhesion

One interesting phenomenon we found during our exploration is that two panels with dense hair can tightly stick to each other when pressed their hair together. This might be because the large amount of contact surface on the hair that creates high friction. Figure 5 shows the details of the print.

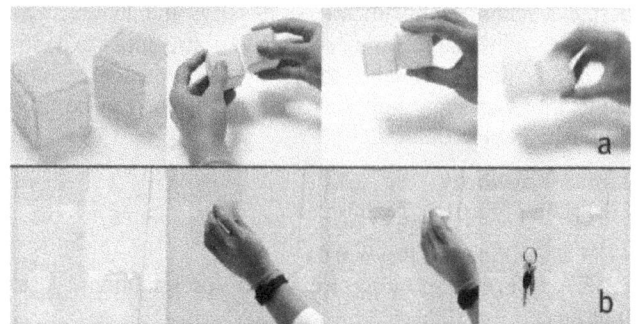

Figure 5. Printed flat surface with Cillia with mechanical adhesion property.

CONCLUSION

We present a method of 3D printing hair-like structures on both flat and curved surfaces. It allows a user to design and fabricate hair geometry at the resolution of 50 um. We built a software platform to let one quickly define a hair's angle, thickness, density, and height. The ability to fabricate customized hair-like structures not only expands the library of 3D-printable shape, but also enables us to design alternative mechanical adhesion structures.

REFERENCES

1. Karl Willis, Eric Brockmeyer, Scott Hudson, and Ivan Poupyrev. 2012. Printed optics: 3D printing of embedded optical elements for interactive devices. In Proceedings of the 25th annual ACM symposium on User interface software and technology (UIST '12). ACM, New York, NY, USA, 589-598.

2. N. Hopkinson, R.J.M. Hague, P.M. Dickens. Rapid Manufacturing, An Industrial Revolution For The Digital Age. 2006, Wiley Publication.

Dranimate: Rapid Real-time Gestural Rigging and Control of Animation

Ali Momeni and Zach Rispoli
Carnegie Mellon University
5000 Forbes Avenue, Pittsburgh, PA 15213
momeni@cmu.edu, zjrispol@andrew.cmu.edu

ABSTRACT

Dranimate is an interactive animation system that allows users to rapidly and intuitively rig and control animations based on a still image or drawing, using hand gestures. Dranimate combines two complementary methods of shape manipulation: bone-joint-based physics simulation, and the as-rigid-as-possible deformation algorithm. Dranimate also introduces a number of designed interactions that focus the users attention on the animated content, as opposed to computer keyboard or mouse.

Author Keywords

Animation, gestural control, puppetry

ACM Classification Keywords

H.5.1 Animations; H.5.2 User-centered Design; I.3.6 Interaction techniques;

INTRODUCTION

In traditional linear animation, the animator is responsible for devising and designing the intelligence and behavioral modeling of the animated character. This process is often collaboratively accomplished by a team of writers, designers and artists and requires a high level of expertise. In interactive animation, much of the intelligence and behavior modeling is moved out of the animation team' s head and performed by a machine [4]. Contemporary applications of interactive animation include motion-capture driven animation, physically based animation, live speech driven lip-sync, among others. Common among these approaches to animation is the integration of an external control system that computationally controls animated elements based on motion capture data and/or simulated physics. While interactive systems are extensively used in the motion graphics, game design and special effects industries, it also offers significant

UIST'15 Adjunct, November 8–11, 2015, Charlotte, NC, USA.
ACM ISBN 978-1-4503-3780-9/15/11.
http://dx.doi.org/10.1145/2815585.2817815.

advantages in making complex animation processes available to a much wider audience.

Dranimate is an interactive animation system that allows novice users to create complex animations by starting with a single still image (e.g. photo, drawing, etc.) and using gesture to systematically deform this still image in real-time. Dranimate implements a mixed-shape deformation algorithm that combines as-rigid-as-possible [2] with a skeletal join system animation engine ([1], [5], [3]). More importantly, Dranimate integrates a series of designed user interactions into the creation and real-time control of animated puppets that render the creation and control of an animated character intuitive and rapid.

IMPLEMENTATION

Hardware Design

Our system employs a laptop with custom software, coupled with a camera for capturing live image feeds and a Leap Motion controller for extracting hand poses. Figure 1 shows the overview of the hardware design:

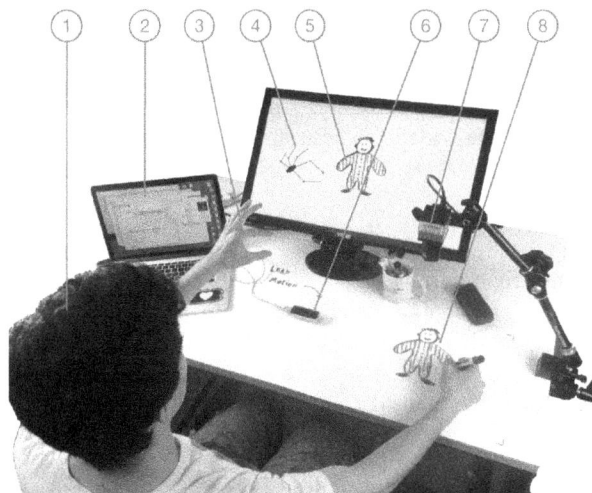

Figure 1. Hardware Overview: 1) User, 2) Laptop, 3) Gesturing hand, 4) Visualization of gesturing hand, 5) animated puppet from live drawing, 6) Leap Motion Controller, 7) Firewire Camera, 8) Drawing

Software Design

The Dranimate software is implemented in C++ using *openFrameworks*[1], an open source C++ toolkit for creative coding. This environment allows developers to effectively integrate efficient generative graphics with graphical user interfaces and gestural control from an external hardware sensor. The *openFrameworks* environment supports a growing list of *addons*[2] that offer additional functionality. In Dranimate, we employ the following addons: *ofxButterfly* and *ofxTriangleMesh* (mesh generation, ofxCV (machine vision), *ofxLeapMotion* and ofxLeapMotionGestures (gestural control), *ofxClickDownMenu* (GUI) and *ofxPuppet* (animation).

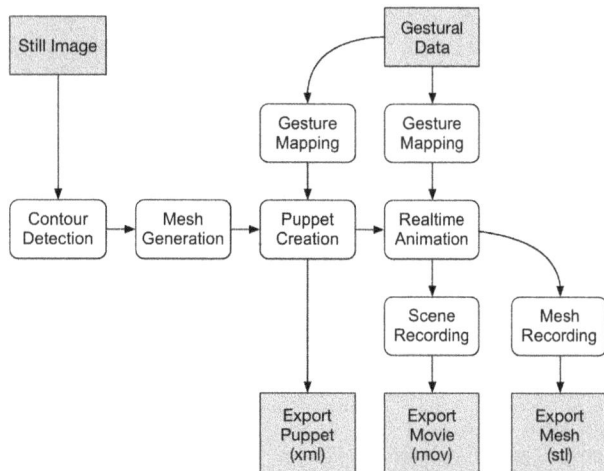

Figure 2. Software Architecture block diagram: Gray blocks at the top and bottom of the diagram represent inputs to and outputs from the system; white inside blocks represent software modules within Dranimate

APPLICATION

Our demo includes six applications represented in separate sections of the video. These applications are described below.

Still Image to animation

This application demonstrates the workflow for creating an animated figure from a still image. The source image is processed by a contour detector and passed to an automatic triangular mesh generator. The user then defines a number of expressive zones that serve as control points for the as-rigid-as-possible shape deformation engine.

Gestural control of animation

This application demonstrates the user interaction in creating and controlling a puppet gesturally. First, the user defines a series of expressive zones and assigns each to a specific finger by pointing to a mesh vertex with the left index finger, and wiggling the desired control finger on the right hand. The user then calibrates the gesture recognition

---

[1] http://openframeworks.cc
[2] http://www.ofxaddons.com/categories

by holding the right hand in a desired starting pose that will correspond with the non-deformed state of the still image. Subsequent changes in the right hand's pose animate the still image in real-time.

Drawing to Gesturally-Controlled Animation

This application demonstrates the complete workflow for starting with a drawing and creating a gesturally controlled animated character.

Complex Scene Composition

This application demonstrates the recording and layering capabilities of the Dranimate application through the incremental composition of a complex animated scene. This rapid process is executed collaboratively by an artist who draws, and a puppeteer who sequentially rigs and animates a recorded palindrome loop for each.

Collaborative Puppeteering

This application demonstrates a collaborative drawing and puppeteering scenario where two users work together to create a gesturally controlled animated dance. Each user draws a figure and rigs it using our gestural control interface.

Dranimate at Life-Scale

This application demonstrates a scenario where the projected animation as well as the interface for real-time control function at life scale. In this example, we utilize a Microsoft Kinect in place of the Leap Motion controller in order to extract body-scale gestural information.

CONCLUSION

Dranimate exploits a range of software, hardware and interaction designs to render the creation of gesturally controlled animated characters easy, fast and intuitive. In addition to obvious applications within animation and special effects, we propose that this approach to intuitive real-time animation holds promise within education, storytelling, information visualization and participatory art installations and performance.

REFERENCES

1. Burtnyk, N., & Wein, M. (1976). Interactive skeleton techniques for enhancing motion dynamics in key frame animation. *Communications of the ACM.*
2. Igarashi, T., Moscovich, T., & Hughes, J. F. (2005). As-rigid-as-possible shape manipulation. *ACM Transactions on Graphics*, *24*(3), 1134–1141.
3. Multon, F., France, L., Cani-Gascuel, M. P., & Debunne, G. (1999). Computer animation of human walking: a survey. *Journal of Visualization and Computer Animation*, *10*(1), 39–54.
4. Tomlinson, B. (2005). From linear to interactive animation. *Computers in Entertainment*, *3*(1), 5.
5. Tost, D., & Pueyo, X. (1988). Human body animation: a survey. *The Visual Computer ()*, *3*(5), 254–264.

Elastic Cursor and Elastic Edge - Applying Simulated Resistance to Interface Elements for Seamless Edge-scroll

Jinha Lee
Samsung VD Interaction Group
Suwon, Korea
lee.jinha@samsung.com

Seungcheon Baek
Samsung VD Interaction Group
Suwon, Korea
sci.baek@samsung.com

ABSTRACT

We present elastic cursor and elastic edge, new interaction techniques for seamless edge-scroll. Through the use of light-weight physical simulations of elastic behavior on interface elements, we can improve precision, usability, and cueing on the use of edge-scroll in scrollable windows or screens, and make experiences more playful and easier to learn.

Author Keywords

Pseudo-haptic simulation; physics simulation; scroll; cursor

ACM Classification Keywords

H.5.m. Information interfaces and presentation (e.g., HCI):

INTRODUCTION AND RELATED WORKS

Scrolling is a commonly used method for viewing or selecting an item from lists that do not fit in a screen or in a window. In a cursor-based environment, having to switch from select mode to scroll mode introduces additional complexities in user experience. To create a seamless experience of scroll-navigation and selection experience, several techniques have been proposed and deployed in many industrial applications. The most popular technique has been auto-scroll, or edge-scroll, where users can simply keep pushing the cursor to the border of the screen or locating the cursor near the border of a window to activate the scroll. This technique is widely used in many consumer electronics devices, namely WebOS TV and MacOS' drag-and drop interaction. However, using the edge-scroll technique poses the following challenges.

Problems of the modeless edge-scroll

First, it is hard to control the scroll-speed. The edge-scroll method employs time-based acceleration: the longer the user locates the cursor at the border, the scroll speed continues to accelerate. Once the cursor hits the edge, there is no longer a relationship between the user's motion and the speed of scrolling. Often, the user cannot decelerate in time and overshoots their target in the scrolling list.

Challenges of edge-scroll in a window

The edge-scroll method becomes particularly challenging when the user is scrolling in an area smaller than the full screen, such that a very thin margin around the scrollable area is the only edge-scrolling activation area, which the user

UIST '15 Adjunct, November 08-11, 2015, Charlotte, NC, USA
ACM 978-1-4503-3780-9/15/11.
http://dx.doi.org/10.1145/2815585.2828995

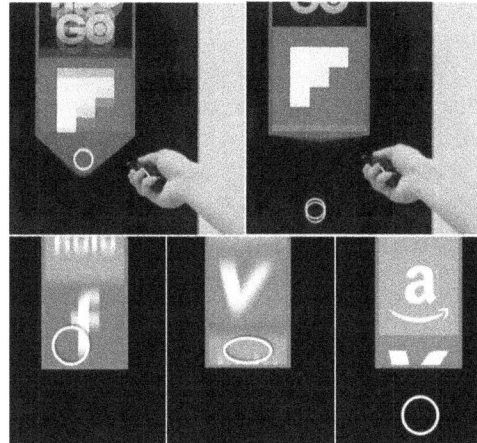

Figure 1. Elastic Edge (top) and Elastic Cursor (bottom)

will likely overshoot and leave the scrollable area with the cursor. The user's attention will be drawn away from primary selection tasks and into the problem of preventing the cursor from leaving the small scroll-activation area near the edge of the window. One possible solution, increasing the edge-scroll activation area, creates ambiguities of action between scrolling and selection of the items near the border. Problems with edge-scroll above become particularly more severe when used with a pointing device. We think solving these challenges is the key to make the edge scroll technique more usable and broadly applicable.

In this demo, we present two scrolling interaction patterns based on the metaphor of elasticity, in an attempt to give users easier and more precise control than with the previous edge-scroll techniques. Our solution is to turn a cursor and windows elastic, so that they can physically interact with one another. As a result, users can have much more visceral control over their scrolling speed, and comfortably perform edge-scroll even in an area smaller than the full screen. There have been projects looking into applying physics to virtual desktops. They explore how adding physically realistic behaviors to graphics can improve the usability and precision of controls [1][4]. While they primarily explored interaction with realistic 3D shapes, there has been research about applying such dynamism to broader graphical UIs by creating pseudo haptic visual feedback [2][3]. In our research, we explore how to reappropriate these principles in order to solve the long discussed problems of edge-scroll.

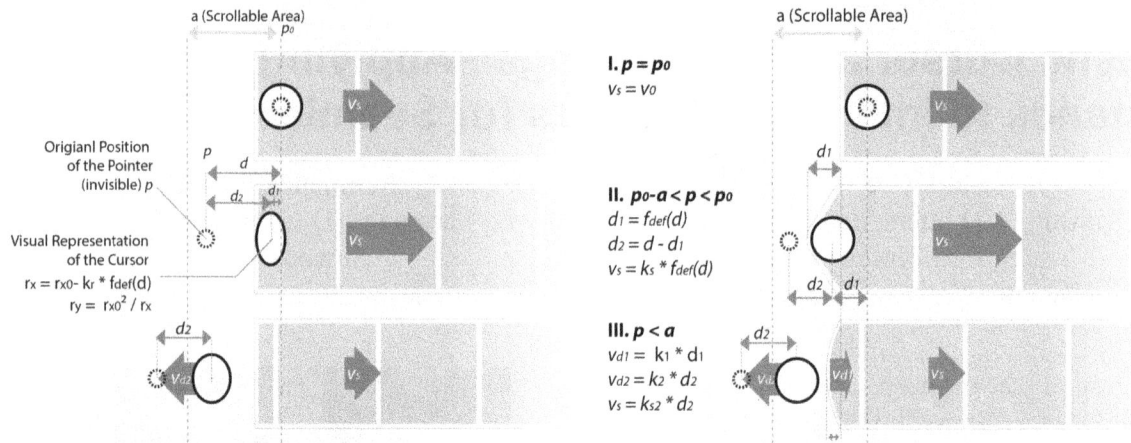

Figure 2. A mechanism for cursor-edge interactions. Left: Elastic cursor, Right: Elastic edge. k_1, k_2, k_s are constants.

ELASTIC CURSOR

It does not take the user long to understand how the elastic cursor works. The cursor looks and moves like other normal circular cursors, but when the user accidentally hits the physical edge of the screen, he will see it being squeezed, behaving as if it was made up of rubber. When the user pushes the cursor at the border of a scrollable list, the list starts moving. The more he pushes, the more the cursor gets deformed and the scroll speed increases accordingly. Simulated sensation of tension lets the user control the speed instantaneously as he scrolls through the list of items.

Edge-cursor interaction

With the Elastic Cursor, users can comfortably perform edge-scroll even in an area smaller than the full screen. When the user edge-scrolls through a list in a window, she will first feel resistance as if it is a physical border, because the cursor sticks inside the edge and distorts as if squashing against it (Figure 2. Left-II). However, if she keeps pressing it towards the edge further than a certain degree, the cursor escapes the border and the scroll speed quickly decelerates to zero, while the squeezed cursor animates back to its original circular shape (Figure 2. Left-III). In this way, the user can let the cursor escape the window to access the area outside of it when he intends to, while being able to comfortably push the cursor to the edge for scrolling.

Elastic edge

Another similar approach is to make the edge of the window elastic, enabling a similar interaction. In this case, as the user keeps pushing the undistorted, solid cursor towards the edge of the window, which will bend around the cursor itself until it snaps back when the actual pointer position crosses a predefined scroll area (Figure 2. Right).

IMPLEMENTATION

The core technique of our system is rendering the graphical cursor at a position different than the 'actual' pointer position, and mapping their distance to the scroll-speed. As the cursor touches the edge of the window (Figure 2. I), scrolling starts with a low initial velocity ($v_s = v_0$). When the user pushes the cursor further towards the edge (Figure 2.II), the radius of the cursor (r_x, r_y) changes according to the deformation variable ($f_{def}(d)$), while maintaining its size. The

deformation variable is approximately linear - or potentially sqrt, cubic, arctan, gaussian etc - to the amount of displacement (d) between the current position of the invisible, real pointer and the inner threshold of the edge-scroll area. The scroll velocity (v_s) changes according to the displacement (d). When the user pushes the cursor further beyond the outer threshold of the scroll area (Figure 2.III), the graphical cursor quickly moves back to the real pointer position and the scroll speed accordingly decelerates to zero. The same principle can be applied to Elastic edge.

INITIAL OBSERVATION

Ten participants were recruited to perform simple edge-scrolling tasks with an elastic cursor, and with a conventional cursor with time-based scroll acceleration in a full-screen situation first, then in a window smaller than the full screen. Questionnaire responses (5-point Likert scale) indicate that the elastic cursor is more comfortable to use (4.0 vs 3.8), accurate (4.2 vs 3.7) and fun to use (4.3 vs 3.1) than the baseline. Participants found edge scroll with elastic cursor particularly more comfortable to use (4.2 vs 3.1) and accurate (4.5 vs 3.4) than the baseline when used with a window smaller than the full screen. Two participants commented that selecting a target outside the window is challenging when elastic cursor is on.

CONCLUSION

We presented interactive cursor behaviors for seamless edge-scroll experience. Initial observation reveals that Elastic Cursor improves the precision of scrolling, and particularly enhances the scrolling experience in a window smaller than full screen size. We believe this approach has a potential to change the way we use cursors by not having to switch between selection mode and scroll mode.

REFERENCES

1. Agarawala, A., and Balakrishnan, R., Keepin' it real: pushing the desktop metaphor with physics, piles and the pen. In Proc. of CHI '06, 1283-1292.
2. Lécuyer, A., Burkhardt, J., and Etienne., L., Feeling Bumps and Holes without a Haptic Interface: the Perception of Pseudo-Haptic Textures In *Proc.* CHI '04, 239-246.
3. Masui, T., Kashiwagi, K., Borden, G.IV, Elastic graphical interfaces to precise data manipulation. In *Conference Companion on* CHI '95, 143-144.
4. Wilson, A., Izadi, S., Hilliges, O., Mendoza, A., and Kirk, D., Bringing physics to the surface. In Proc. UIST '08, 67-76.

Hand Biometrics Using Capacitive Touchscreens

Robert Tartz
Qualcomm Technologies, Inc.
San Diego, CA 92121
rtartz@qti.qualcomm.com

Ted Gooding
Qualcomm Technologies, Inc.
San Diego, CA 92121
tgooding@qti.qualcomm.com

ABSTRACT
Biometric methods for authentication on mobile devices are becoming popular. Some methods such as face and voice biometrics are problematic in noisy mobile environments, while others such as fingerprint require specialized hardware to operate. We present a novel biometric authentication method that uses raw touch capacitance data captured from the hand touching a display. Performance results using a moderate sample size (N = 40) yielded an equal error rate (EER) of 2.5%, while a 1-month longitudinal study using a smaller sample (N = 10) yielded an EER = 2.3%. Overall, our results provide evidence for biometric uniqueness, permanence and user acceptance.

Author Keywords
Touchscreens; biometrics; touch interaction; security

INTRODUCTION
Mobile devices increasingly store and share vast amounts of personal data. Coupled with increased reports of fraud, security is quickly becoming a major concern for mobile users. While PIN, password and pattern are common authentication methods, they require recall and entry of the correct code and can be stolen via "shoulder-surfing." Biometric authentication methods on mobile devices have begun to surface as alternatives, such as face recognition, voice recognition and more recently, fingerprint.

While improvements have been made in face and voice recognition, performance still suffers when lighting is not ideal or when background noise is present, both common problems in mobile environments. Additionally, since the face and voice are not private, they can be easier to circumvent than other methods [2]. Fingerprint scanners are available primarily on premium-tier devices and require additional hardware driving up device and manufacturing costs. Additionally, since fingerprints are associated with criminality some users may have privacy concerns [2].

Touch gestures collected over time, such as slide, pinch, and scroll have been explored by a number of researchers as an unobtrusive behavioral biometric method for continuous authentication [3]. While convenient, behavioral methods generally lack the accuracy common to physical biometric

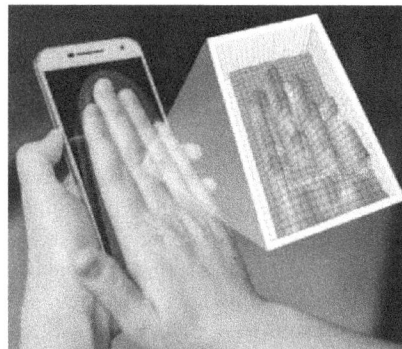

Figure 1. Scanning the hand and capturing raw touch capacitance data used for biometric matching.

methods [2, 4] and authentication can only occur after using the system over a required time period.

We first described our method in a patent application with a similar concept later described by Holz et al. [1] who used "Bodyprints" to recognize body parts and users based on raw touch capacitance data (e.g., from the ear). Holz et al. does not describe a method using the hand or fingers, which may be more accepted by users. Also, results were reported for only a small sample (N = 12) with all data collected in a single session. Thus, both biometric uniqueness and permanence as well as user acceptance, all important system parameters [2], need to be better established.

HAND BIOMETRICS USING TOUCHSCREENS
Given that hand geometry is an established and commercially accepted biometric method [2], we felt that similar features of the hand plus skin properties could be analyzed using raw touch capacitance data captured by laying the full hand or part of the hand on a touchscreen display (figure 1). To capture raw touch capacitance data we used a 7" touchscreen panel with a sensor resolution of 40 x 64 (2.4mm sensor pitch) which was connected directly to a Qualcomm DragonBoard™ for data collection. The raw data was then post-processed using the algorithm described below written in MATLAB.

Algorithm
For both studies, participants were instructed to naturally hold the touch display with their left hand and fully touch all four fingers of their right hand and top of the palm to the display using natural pressure for about 3 seconds. Data was sampled at 120Hz, then pre-processed to normalize and filter noise (figure 2). The first segmentation step averaged all 3 seconds of data, then summed the capacitance data in

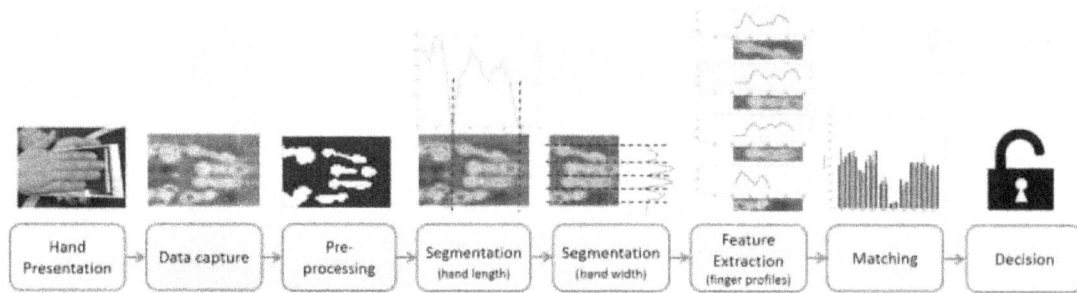

Figure 2. The hand biometric algorithm based on raw touch capacitance data.

all touch sensor rows. Finger data was then separated from palm data by first locating the tip of the longest finger via a valley in capacitance near the top of the display followed by locating the palmar digital crease via another valley in capacitance within anthropomorphic limits of the fingertip. The second segmentation step summed capacitance data in touch sensor columns of only the finger data, then separated each finger by locating the capacitance valleys between them. For each finger, the capacitance data for each row was summed, normalized via a z-score and then extracted to create a unique biometric profile for each participant.

Performance

For our first study, 40 participants were evenly sampled across gender and four age categories (ages 18 to 58). Three participants were left-handed. Eight data collection trials were collected from each participant as described above. The calculated profiles from the first 3 trials were averaged to create an enrollment template used for matching. The profiles from the next 5 trials were used as authentication attempts and compared to each of the 40 enrollment templates (8000 comparisons). The EER is the point at which the false reject rate equals the false accept rate, a benchmark for evaluating biometric systems [2]. By using normalized correlation coefficient (NCC) matching and varying the threshold for a match, results yielded an EER = 2.5% (figure 3a), establishing evidence for biometric uniqueness. Our second study sampled 5 adult males and 5 adult females with 8 trials per participant collected in 8 independent sessions over a 1-month period. The profiles from each of 61 authentication attempts were matched with each of the 10 enrollment templates (6100 comparisons). Results using NCC matching show an EER = 2.3% (figure3b), establishing evidence for biometric permanence.

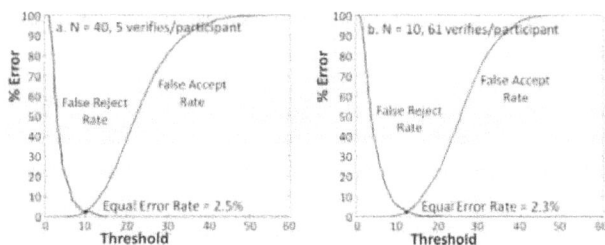

Figure 3. Performance of hand biometric authentication for a moderate sample study (a) and 1-month longitudinal study (b).

User Acceptance

Jain et al. [3] points out that acceptability of the biometric by users is a desirable parameter for biometric systems. We recruited 12 participants who briefly used a phone-based UI prototype of the hand biometric concept. When asked to rank hand biometrics on scales for ease of use and expected security level among 7 other common mobile authentication methods, hand biometrics ranked near the top on both scales. Overall, participants voiced enthusiasm for using this method on their mobile, especially on larger devices that encourage two-handed operation (e.g., tablets).

CONCLUSIONS AND FUTURE WORK

Our hand biometrics method performed well across a moderate sample of participants, with similar performance over time on a smaller sample. Participants also ranked this method as convenient and secure for authentication. These results establish evidence for biometric uniqueness, permanence and acceptability and suggest that hand biometrics with capacitive touchscreens holds promise as a simple and effective method for authentication on mobile devices that requires no additional hardware. Field studies should be conducted with larger samples over longer time periods to establish performance in actual mobile environments. Other studies could explore processing data from the full hand by using larger displays such as tablets.

ACKNOWLEDGEMENTS
This research was funded by Qualcomm Technologies, Inc.

REFERENCES
1. Holz, C., Buthpitiya, S., and Knaust, M. Bodyprint; Biometric User Identification on Mobile Devices using the Capacitive Touchscreen to Scan Body Parts. In *Proc. CHI '15*, ACM Press (2015), 3011–3014.

2. Jain, A. K., Bolle, R. and Pankanti, S., editors. *Biometrics: Personal Identification in a Networked Society*. Kluwer Academic Publishers, 1999.

3. Xu, H., Zhou, Y. and Lyu, M.R. Towards Continuous and Passive Authentication via Touch Biometrics: An Experimental Study on Smartphones. In *Proc. SOUPS*, USENIX (2014).

4. Yampolskiy, R.V. and Govindaraju, V. Behavioural Biometrics: A Survey and Classification. *Int'l J of Biometrics 1, 1* (2008), 81-113.

A Study on Grasp Recognition Independent of Users' Situations Using Built-in Sensors of Smartphones

Chanho Park
Graduate School of
Engineering,
The University of Tokyo,
7-3-1 Hongo, Bunkyo, Tokyo,
113-0033 Japan
c.park@cnl.t.u-tokyo.ac.jp

Takefumi Ogawa
Information Technology Center,
The University of Tokyo,
2-11-16 Yayoi, Bunkyo, Tokyo,
113-8658 Japan
ogawa@nc.u-tokyo.ac.jp

ABSTRACT

There are many hand postures of smartphone according to the users' situations. In order to support appropriate interface, it is important to know user's hand posture. To recognize grasp postures, which is not depend on users' situations, we consider using smartphone's touchscreen and their built-in gyroscope and accelerometer and use support vector machine (SVM). In order to evaluate our system, we described the result of the experiments when users are using the devices in the room and on the train. We knew that our system could be feasible for personal use only system by improving the information from the accelerometer. We also collected users' data when users are sitting in the room. Results showed that grasp recognition accuracy under 5 and 4 hand postures were 87.7%, 92.4% respectively when training and testing on 6 users.

Author Keywords

Grasp recognition; smartphone; accelerometer; gyroscope; touchscreen; hand posture; support vector machine;

ACM Classification Keywords

H.5.2 [Information interfaces and presentation]: User Inter faces—Input devices and strategies.

INTRODUCTION AND RELATED WORK

The rise of smartphones and tablets is changing the way users can use the devices in various works without depending on the location. We can manipulate the devices using one or two hands (Figure 1). However, hand postures of the devices depend on our situation. In some scenarios, a user's hand is occupied. So, user adopts one-handed interaction when using the devices. It is considered to be effective to

UIST'15 Adjunct, November 8–11, 2015, Charlotte, NC, USA.
ACM 978-1-4503-3780-9/15/11.
http://dx.doi.org/10.1145/2815585.2815722

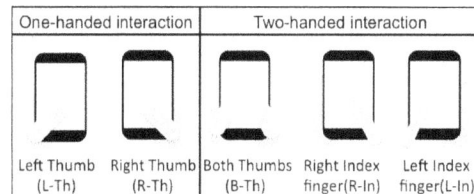

Figure 1. Grasp Recognition Set

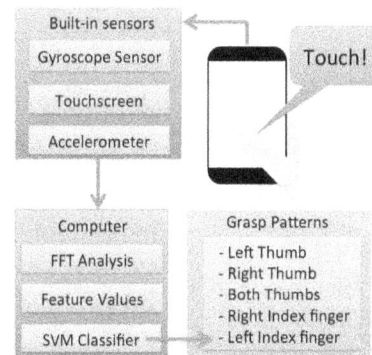

Figure 2. System Configuration

modify accordingly also interface how users are grasping the devices. Prior to our research, grasp-based interaction techniques have been researched by several works [2,3]. Goel et al. [3] detected the hand posture on mobile devices by using touchscreen and built-in gyroscope. However, the sensor data is changed by the influence of noise in users' situations. So there is a risk of low recognition accuracy. Moreover, the use of five or more consecutive touch data is difficult to recognize in a short time.

To classify hand postures independent of users' situations, we consider using touchscreen and gyroscope and we also use accelerometer, which is used to many studies on recognition of users' contexts [4]. By improving the information from the accelerometer, we have seen a potential as a system that doesn't depend on users' situations.

PROPOSED METHOD AND EVALUATION

Our system (Figure 2) requires only built-in sensors and touchscreen of smartphones to detect hand postures. Our system gets sensor data at 50Hz and touchscreen data when

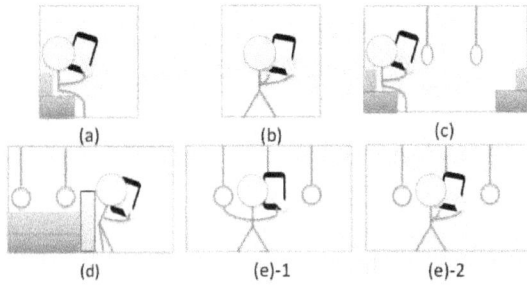

Figure 3. Using the devices: a) sit in the room (b) stand in the room (c) sit on the train (d) lean to the side of the door on the train (e) stand on the train

Feature Vector	Gyroscope	Touch Event	Acceleration	Linear acceleration
A	○	○	×	×
B	○	○	○	×
C	○	○	×	○
D	○	○	○	○

Figure 4. Feature Vector

users touch the screens as a trigger. From touchscreen, we consider touch coordinates and size as features. And we make features using 0.2 seconds of the internal sensor data before and after tapping (such as average, standard deviation, RMS, etc.). To investigate information for the movement of the devices, we adopt linear acceleration, which except for the influence of gravity. And we also leverage the amplitude of the frequency components.

In order to evaluate the differences in recognition accuracy by the feature vectors A~D, we described the result of the experiments when user was using the device in the room and on the train (Figure 4). We use LIBSVM [1], a support vector machines library, for the grasp recognition. Our application was deployed on a Samsung Galaxy Note 3 (5.7 inches). We sampled each 1000 sensor data when user taps the screen (5 postures x 5 trials x 40 targets on touchscreen) in 5 situations (Figure 3). As training data, we used another 1000 sensor data sitting in the room. Figure 5 shows the result of one user classifier. Recognition accuracies under 5 hand postures were 91.8%~95.8% when user was sitting in the room. For personal use only system, our system could be feasible. And grasp recognition accuracy increased independent of users' situations by using the features of the acceleration and linear acceleration.

We also recruited 6 participants (1 female, age 23-26) and sampled each 1000 data when they were sitting in the room. The results of 6-fold cross validation under 5 and 4 hand postures were 87.7%, 94.4% accuracy respectively using feature vector D (Figure 6, 7). In a two-handed both thumbs interaction, the movement of the device at the time of touching the screen showed a different pattern for each user. In particular, the movement of the device as user touches at the top of the screen were classified the same as 4 other hand postures.

Accuracy(%)	Feature Vectors			
Situation	A	B	C	D
(a)	91.8	95.8	93.2	95.4
(b)	89.3	75.9	90.4	79.2
(c)	80.4	87.2	86.4	88.7
(d)	81.4	87.3	82.4	86.7
(e)	82.0	82.8	84.9	83.8

Figure 5. One user recognition accuracy under 5 postures

	U1	U2	U3	U4	U5	U6	Average
5 grasp postures	79.3%	88.5%	95.1%	88.5%	94.5%	80.5%	87.7%
4 grasp postures	88%	97.6%	95.8%	96.3%	97.3%	91.4%	94.4%

Figure 6. Recognition accuracy for each user in leave-one-subject-out cross validation (feature vector D)

Grasp posture	L-Th	R-Th	R-In	L-In	Accuracy
L-Th	1162	12	6	20	96.8%
R-Th	9	1177	8	6	98.1%
R-In	1	16	1105	78	92.1%
L-In	15	10	89	1086	90.5%

Figure 7. Confusion matrix of subject-independent cross validation under 4 postures

CONCLUSION AND FUTUER WORK

We demonstrated that our system could be feasible for personal use only system independent of user's situation by improving the information from the accelerometer. In the future, we plan to analyze the feature from accelerometer to investigate its effectiveness. And we will involve extensive comparison to existing situations, which might construct an independent system for users' situations.

ACKNOWLEDGEMENTS
This research was supported in part by a Grant-in-Aid for Scientific Research (C) numbered 25330227 by the Japan Society for the Promotion of Science (JSPS).

REFERENCES

1. Chang, C.-C., and Lin, C.-J. Libsvm: A library for support vector machines. ACM Transactions on Intelligent Systems and Technology, Vol. 2, No. 3, pp.27:1-27:27, 2011.

2. Cheng, L.-P., Lee, M.-H., Wu, C.-Y., Hsiao, F.-i., Liu, Y.-t., Liang, H.-s., Chiu, Y.-C., Lee, M.-S., and Chen, M.-Y. iRotateGrasp: Automatic Screen Rotation based on Grasp of Mobile Devices. In Proc. CHI'13, ACM, 2013.

3. Goel, M., Wobbrock, J.-O., and Patel, S.-N. GripSense: Using Built-in Sensors to Detect Hand Posture and Pressure on Commodity Mobile Phones. In Proc. UIST'12, ACM, 2012.

4. Van Laerhoven, K., and Cakmakci, O. What shall we teach our pants? Wearable Computers, The Fourth International Symposium, pp77-83, 2000.

TMotion:Embedded 3D Mobile Input using Magnetic Sensing Technique

Sang Ho Yoon, Ke Huo, Karthik Ramani
C-Design Lab, School of Mechanical Engineering
Purdue University, West Lafayette, IN, USA
{yoon87, khuo, ramani}@purdue.edu

ABSTRACT

We present TMotion, a self-contained 3D input that enables spatial interactions around mobile using a magnetic sensing technique. Using a single magnetometer from the mobile device, we can track the 3D position of the permanent magnet embedded in the prototype along with an inertial measurement unit. By numerically solving non-linear magnetic field equations with known orientation from inertial measurement unit (IMU), we attain a tracking rate greater than 30Hz based solely on the mobile device computation. We describe the working principle of TMotion and example applications illustrating its capability.

Author Keywords

3D Input; Embedded Interaction; Magnetic Sensing; Mobile Interaction; Sensor Fusion

ACM Classification Keywords

H.5.2. [Information Interfaces and Presentation]: User Interfaces. — Input devices and strategies

INTRODUCTION

Recent developments in smartphone displays and sensors have resulted in enhanced visual experiences such as mobile augmented (AR) and virtual reality (VR). To support these 3D interfaces, it would be helpful to provide natural correspondence such as human motion in 3D space from the input device. Current 2D input modalities cannot fully reflect the user's intent in a 3D space. Moreover, using 3D input offers a more intuitive and quicker way to interact with 3D context interfaces. Our prototype provides a real-time 3D position tracking which utilizes fine-grain information for seamless interaction with physical environment [3].

Acquiring input data from 3D mobile space has been investigated through vision and magnet-based techniques. Occlusion and lighting conditions still limit the use of vision-based techniques in mobile environments. On the other hand, the magnetic sensing techniques which are free from occlusion

UIST'15 Adjunct, November 8–11, 2015, Charlotte, NC, USA.
ACM 978-1-4503-3780-9/15/11.
http://dx.doi.org/10.1145/2815585.2815723

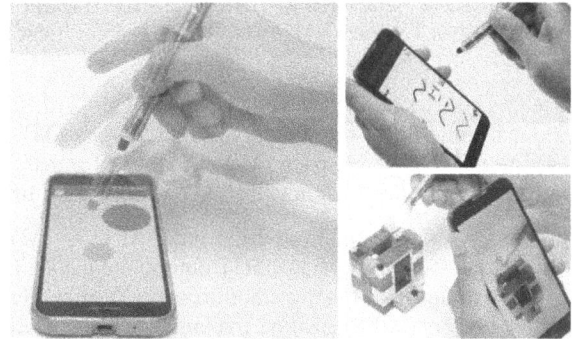

Figure 1. TMotion enables a real-time 3D position tracking using embedded permanent magnet and IMU with mobile device.

and light conditions have been also investigated [1, 4]. These works show high 2D/3D tracking accuracy in real-time operation, but they require either a desktop computation, or extensive modifications on the mobile device.

In our work, TMotion enables mobile to track an input device embedded with a magnet and an IMU. Specifically, the algorithm calculates the magnets position relative to the mobile using the magnetic field vector and the orientation of the embedded magnet. We achieve a 3D position tracking rate greater than 30Hz possibly with an unmodified device. As a 3D mobile input, TMotion provides rich interactions in above/behind device spaces.

TRACKING PRINCIPLE

2D and 3D position tracking using multiple magnetic sensors have been explored [2]. However, they require either hardware modification on the mobile device or processing through a desktop PC to overcome the lack of sensing capability or the computational load. From theory of the magnetism, 3D position of the permanent magnet in the mobile's magnetic sensor oriented space ($\mathcal{F}_{mobile}$) can be computed using Eq.(1)

$$\mathbf{H}(\mathbf{r}) = \frac{K}{r^3}\left[\frac{3\mathbf{r}(\mathbf{m}\cdot\mathbf{r})}{r^2} - m\right], r = |\mathbf{r}|, K = \frac{M}{4\pi} \qquad (1)$$

Here, H refers to the magnetic field vectors, M denotes for the magnetic moment, $\mathbf{m}$ is the directional vector of the magnet, and $\mathbf{r}$ is the location vector of magnet relative to the sensor. Given known $\mathbf{m}$, M, and H, $\mathbf{r}$ can be solved.

We assume magnet is located at (x, y, z) resulting in $\mathbf{r}$ to be $(-x, -y, -z)$. The directional unit vector of magnet is $(\mathbf{M}_x, \mathbf{M}_y, \mathbf{M}_z)$. We perform space transformation from IMU

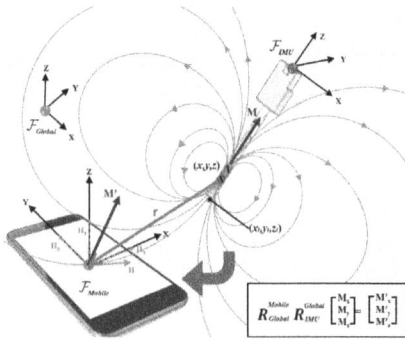

Figure 2. Magnetic vector (H) is generated by magnet. Magnetic directional vector from TMotion (M) is transformed to mobile's frame (M').

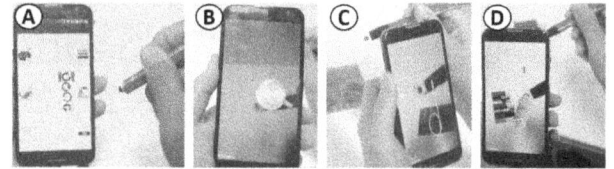

Figure 4. Example Applications: (a) Multi-level menu interface and spatial interactions including (b) 3D manipulation, (c) 3D sketching, and (d) 3D modeling in mobile AR

space ($\mathcal{F}_{IMU}$) to mobile space ($\mathcal{F}_{mobile}$). Figure 2 illustrates the transformation of the directional unit vectors (M) from TMotion to the mobile space (M'). Additional transformation has been applied to denote the 3D position of the tip.

By taking known orientations from attached IMU (M) and 3-axis magnetometer readings (H) from mobile device as inputs, we employ Newton's method to solve nonlinear equations. We observe that position tracking succeeds when the prototype operates within $160mm \times 160mm \times 200mm$ volume around the mobile device. Our approach enables a real-time computation by iterating the numerical analysis once with known orientation from IMU.

SYSTEM OVERVIEW
Figure 3 illustrates our prototype in detail. It holds multiple form factors embedded with magnets of various orientations. To avoid the magnetometer saturation, we configure the sensor stick and the embedded magnet in distinct locations (>5cm) in our prototype. With the streamed mobile's magnetometer data (75Hz), we update the tip position from the latest computation. We subtract average magnetometer readings before the prototype gets into the interaction volume to compensate geomagnetic field. For capacitive sensing, we inkjet-printed a sheet of electrodes using *AgIC* ink.

EXAMPLE APPLICATIONS
Multi-level menu interface: Users pop up a designated menu placed along the edge by hovering around the device. This is followed by moving along the z-axis for choosing sub-level menu. Final selection is confirmed with changing the grip. We utilize find-grained 3D input around the mobile device to augment traditional 2D UI capability. By taking same

approach, we can improve user experience with other 2D UI applications. This also demonstrates richer interactions using discrete spatial zones around the mobile device.

Spatial interaction for mobile AR: We demonstrate four tasks in mobile AR environment: 1) 3D model manipulation, 2) physical environment referenced 3D sketching, 3) sweeping sketch in 3D path, and 4) superimposition of the virtual creation over a physical object. We use capacitive sensing as an interaction delimiter to shift between different input modes including 'Translation' to/from 'Rotation', and the start & end of the modeling or sketching operations. Through this application, we showcase the possibility of providing rich spatial interactions behind the device.

CONCLUSION
In this paper, we present an embedded 3D mobile input using magnetic sensing technique. With the known orientations from 9DOF-IMU, we explicitly solve the position of the embedded magnet through numerical solver. We achieve a real-time position tracking without altering the hardware setup. With capacitive sensing based interaction delimiter, we utilize TMotion for a seamless embedded interaction. As 3D mobile interfaces develop, the needs for better methods to handle and exploit richer user inputs also increases. We demonstrate that TMotion potentially fulfills these requirements by presenting a real-time 3D input.

ACKNOWLEDGMENT
This work was partially supported by the NSF under grants CMMI-EDI 1235232 and IGERT 1144842. The contents of this manuscript do not necessarily reflect the views or opinions of the funding agency.

REFERENCES
1. Chen, K.-Y., Lyons, K., White, S., and Patel, S. utrack: 3d input using two magnetic sensors. In *Proc. of UIST'13*, 237–244.

2. Han, X., Seki, H., Kamiya, Y., and Hikizu, M. Wearable handwriting input device using magnetic field: Geomagnetism cancellation in position calculation. *Precision engineering 33*, 1 (2009), 37–43.

3. Ishii, H., and Ullmer, B. Tangible bits: towards seamless interfaces between people, bits and atoms. In *Proc. of CHI'97*, 234–241.

4. Liang, R.-H., Cheng, K.-Y., Su, C.-H., Weng, C.-T., Chen, B.-Y., and Yang, D.-N. Gausssense: attachable stylus sensing using magnetic sensor grid. In *Proc. of UIST'12*, 319–326.

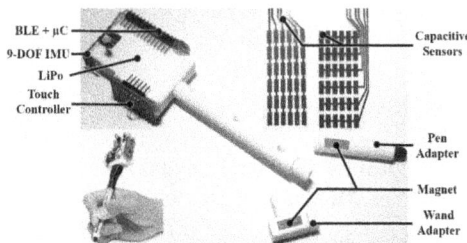

Figure 3. TMotion prototype and breakdown of its components. Permanent magnet and 9DOF-IMU are embedded for 3D position tracking.

EMG Sensor-based Two-Hand Smart Watch Interaction

Yoonsik Yang, Seungho Chae, Jinwook Shim, Tack-Don Han
Media System Lab, Yonsei University
Seoul, Republic of Korea
{yoonsikyang, seungho.chae, jin99foryou, hantack}@msl.yonsei.ac.kr

ABSTRACT

These days, smart watches have drawn more attention of users, and many smart watch products have been launched (Samsung Gear series, apple watch and etc.). Since a smart watch is put on the wrist, the device should be small and unobtrusive. Because of these features, display of the smart watch is small and there is a limitation to interaction. To overcome the limitation, many studies are conducted. In this paper, we propose a two-hand interaction technique that obtains posture information of a hand using electromyography (EMG) sensor attached to the arm and to make input interaction to a smart watch different depending on each posture. EMG sensors recognize information about a user's hand posture, and the non-dominant hand is used for smart watch inputs. In this way, different function is executed depending on postures. As a result, a smart watch that has limited input methods is given a variety of interaction functions with users.

Author Keywords

Smart watch interaction; electromyography; arm-placed devices

ACM Classification Keywords

H.5.2 [Information interfaces and presentation]: User Interfaces – Input devices and strategies.

INTRODUCTION

Wrist-worn wearable devices have been launched in a way that enabling users to wear them always as though such devices are a parts of their bodies. Wrist-worn wearable devices are designed to be small in order to improve wearability, and thus they have a small range of interaction with users and limited interaction functions. To overcome the limitation, studies on smart watch based interaction have been conducted. They can be divided into two categories.

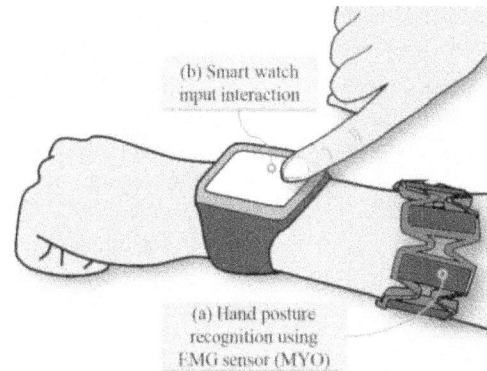

Figure 1. EMG sensor-based two-hand smart watch interaction

The first one is physical control to use specific parts of a smart watch, and the second one is input area expansion research to make interaction in areas other than display area.

Regarding studies on physical control, there is a study to make multi-touch interaction possible by attaching a pressure-sensor to the band of a smart watch [1], and [6] is smart watch based interaction to pan, zoon, navigate, and select the watch face with multi-degree-of-freedom mechanical interface. In addition, diversity of interactions via tapping the screen with a user's index finger and long finger simultaneously or sequentially was introduced [5].

With regard to studies on input area expansion, there is a study to support a various interaction through the back of a user's hand [3], and [4] is conducted to execute functions in the way of attaching a laser projector to a smart watch, printing out buttons on the arm, and pushing a relevant button. As such, many different researches have been conducted steadily to solve the issue of inconvenient input due to the limited area.

Unlike previous studies on interaction with smart watch through a user's one hand, in this paper we propose a technique of interaction with various combinations, which uses both the posture input of a user's hand with a smart watch and the input interaction of his/her non-dominant hand to the smart watch (Figure 1). In the proposed method, EMG sensors are attached to a user's hand along with a smart watch, and thus EMG information of the hand posture is obtained. It is expected that such a technique can be expanded to more various interaction methods by combining with the one handed smart watch input methods.

TWO-HAND SMART WATCH INTERACTION

System Design

This study was conducted with the idea drawn from the previous research [2] in which a user's hand posture was recognized to make different types of input interaction possible depending on each posture. In the prototype of the technique proposed in this study, a user wore MYO armband (Thalmic Labs) on the arm with a smart watch, and the user's hand posture was obtained. MYO armband used eight EMG sensors so that it was possible to obtain more stable data than using EMG sensors directly.

MYO armband supports four designated postures so far: (1) Spreading five fingers, (2) making a fist, (3) bend hand right and (4) bend hand left. For each posture, a user is able to setup a desired type of interaction by using an application. The posture information recognized through MYO armband is transmitted to a smartphone via Bluetooth. The transmitted data is then sent to a smart watch from the smart phone. In this way, the user is able to execute a different function according to posture information, while the input interaction remains the same.

Application

To verify the idea proposed in this study, we conducted two different applications including a pattern-based password unlocking application through the hand posture and touch (Fig.2), and a remote controller to control the different home appliances for each posture (Fig.3).

First, the pattern-based password unlocking application, a user took a pre- defined posture with the hand on which a smart watch was put, and input a pattern with the non-dominant hand. When the pattern was equal to the hand's posture, the password was unlocked.

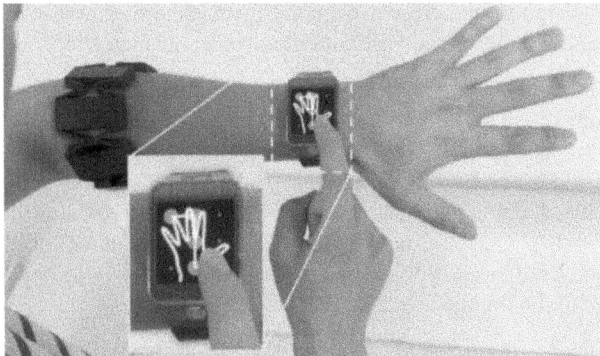

Figure 2. Pattern-based password unlocking application

Second, for the remote controller application, user had to select the home appliances such as TV and an air conditioner, with the pre-defined posture. Air conditioner is pre-defined with "spreading five fingers" posture and TV is pre-defined with "making a fist" posture. Then non-dominant hand interacts with smart watch by touch. Users can control home appliance with a smart watch, fast and conveniently by using two-hand smart watch interaction.

Figure 3. Home appliance control application: Home appliances changes depending on users' hand posture

Through the proposed interaction technique, the user was able to access the function of a smart watch in more various ways than conventional touch-based ways.

CONCLUSION AND FUTURE WORK

This paper described a technique of performing different types of interaction depending on a user's hand posture with the use of a smart watch and EMG sensors. Prototyping revealed that the proposed technique was applicable to users in more diverse ways. Up to now, for an interaction prototype of interaction function, the basic postures that MYO armband supported were used. In the follow-up research, we will study recognition of many types of user's hand posture.

ACKNOWLEDGEMENTS

This work was supported by the National Research Foundation of Korea (NRF) grant funded by the Korea government(MEST) (No.2012R1A2A2A01014499)

REFERENCES

1. Ahn, Y., Hwang, S., Yoon, H., Gim, J. and Ryu, J. H. BandSense: Pressure-sensitive Multi-touch Interaction on a Wristband. In *Proc. CHI 2015*, 251-254.

2. Argyros, A. A. and Lourakis, M. I. Vision-based interpretation of hand gestures for remote control of a computer mouse. In *Computer Vision in Human-Computer Interaction 2006*, 40-51.

3. Knibbe, J., Martinez, P. D., Bainbridge, C., Chan, C. K., Wu, J., Cable, T. and Coyle, D. Extending interaction for smart watches: enabling bimanual around device control. In *Proc. CHI 2014*, 1891-1896.

4. Laput, G., Xiao, R., Chen, X. A., Hudson, S. E. and Harrison, C. Skin buttons: cheap, small, low-powered and lickable fixed-icon laser projectors. In *Proc. UIST 2014*, 389-394.

5. Oakley, I., Lee, D., Islam, M. D. and Esteves, A. Beats: Tapping Gestures for Smart Watches. In *Proc. CHI 2015*, 1237-1246.

6. Xiao, R., Laput, G. and Harrison, C. Expanding the input expressivity of smartwatches with mechanical pan, twist, tilt and click. In *Proc. CHI 2014*, 193-196

Investigating the "Wisdom of Crowds" at Scale

Alok Shankar Mysore[*]
PES Institute of Technology
alok.shankar@pesit.pes.edu

Vikas S Yaligar[‡]
National Institute of
Technology Karnataka
vikasyaligar@ieee.org

Imanol Arrieta Ibarra
Stanford University
imanol@stanford.edu

Camelia Simoiu
Stanford University
csimoiu@stanford.edu

Sharad Goel
Stanford University
sgoel@stanford.edu

Additional Authors [*]
Various Institutions [†]

ABSTRACT

In a variety of problem domains, it has been observed that the aggregate opinions of groups are often more accurate than those of the constituent individuals, a phenomenon that has been termed the "wisdom of the crowd." Yet, perhaps surprisingly, there is still little consensus on how generally the phenomenon holds, how best to aggregate crowd judgements, and how social influence affects estimates. We investigate these questions by taking a meta wisdom of crowds approach. With a distributed team of over 100 student researchers across 17 institutions in the United States and India, we develop a large-scale online experiment to systematically study the wisdom of crowds effect for 1,000 different tasks in 50 subject domains. These tasks involve various types of knowledge (e.g., explicit knowledge, tacit knowledge, and prediction), question formats (e.g., multiple choice and point estimation), and inputs (e.g., text, audio, and video). To examine the effect of social influence, participants are randomly assigned to one of three different experiment conditions in which they see varying degrees of information on the responses of others. In this ongoing project, we are now preparing to recruit participants via Amazon's Mechanical Turk.

Author Keywords
Crowdsourcing; online experiment; crowd consensus.

ACM Classification Keywords
H.5.m. Economics: Experimentation Design

INTRODUCTION
At a 1906 county fair, the statistician Francis Galton watched as eight hundred people competed to guess the weight of an ox. He famously observed that the median of the guesses, 1,207 pounds, was, remarkably, within 1% of the true weight [1].

Simple aggregation—as in the case of Galton's ox competition, or voting in democratic elections—has been shown to be a surprisingly powerful technique for prediction, inference, and decision-making. Over the last century, there have been dozens of studies that examine this wisdom of crowds effect. For example, crowd judgements have been used to identify phishing websites [6], answer general knowledge questions [5], and forecast weather-related events [3]. In these applications, a wide variety of aggregation methods have been considered, ranging from standard measures, such as the mean and median, to more specialized, domain-specific techniques, such as those based on cognitive models of decision making [4]. However, given the diversity of experimental designs, subject pools, and analytic methods employed, it has proven difficult to compare studies and extract general principles. It is thus unclear whether these documented examples are a representative collection of a much larger space of tasks that exhibit a wisdom of crowds phenomenon, or conversely, whether they are highly specific instances of an interesting, though ultimately limited occurrence.

[*]Ramesh Arvind[*], Chiraag Sumanth [*], Arvind Srikantan[*], Bhargav HS[*], Mayank Pahadia[‡], Tushar Dobhal[‡], Atif Ahmed[‡], Mani Shankar[‡], Himani Agarwal, Rajat Agarwal, Sai Anirudh-Kondaveeti, Shashank Arun-Gokhale, Aayush Attri, Arpita Chandra, Yogitha Chilukuri, Sharath Dharmaji, Deepak Garg, Naman Gupta, Paras Gupta, Glincy Mary Jacob, Siddharth Jain, Shashank Joshi, Tarun Khajuria, Sameeksha Khillan, Sandeep Konam, Praveen Kumar-Kolla, Sahil Loomba, Rachit Madan, Akshansh Maharaja, Vidit Mathur, Bharat Munshi, Mohammed Nawazish, Venkata Neehar-Kurukunda, Venkat Nirmal-Gavarraju, Sonali Parashar, Harsh Parikh, Avinash Paritala, Amit Patil, Rahul Phatak, Mandar Pradhan, Abhilasha Ravichander, Krishna Sangeeth, Sreecharan Sankaranarayanan, Vibhor Sehgal, Ashrith Sheshan, Suprajha Shibiraj, Aditya Singh, Anjali Singh, Prashant Sinha, Pushkin Soni, Bipin Thomas, Lokesh Tuteja, Kasyap Varma-Dattada, Sukanya Venkataraman, Pulkit Verma, Ishan Yelurwar

[†]Jaypee Institute Of Information Technology; BITS; National Institute of Technology Karnataka, Indian Institute of Technology Delhi; PES Institute of Technology; International Institute of Information Technology; BMS College of Engineering; Bhagwan Parshuram Institute of Technology; Indian Institute of Technology Guwahati; College of Engineering; College of Engineering Chengannur; Bharati Vidyapeeth's College Of Engineering; Maharaja Agrasen Institute of Technology; Cluster Innovation Centre; Rajiv Gandhi University of Knowledge Technologies; Indraprastha Institute of Information Technology

EXPERIMENT DESIGN

To systematically investigate the wisdom of crowds, we developed a modular online experiment that presents participants with 1,000 questions drawn from 50 domains. Each domain includes 20 questions on a specific topic. For example, one domain tests individuals' knowledge of geography, and asks them to identify 20 countries from their silhouettes.

Domains include: tests of explicit knowledge, such as, general knowledge, spatial reasoning, and popular culture; tacit knowledge, including emotional intelligence, knowledge of cultural norms, and foreign language skills ; and prediction ability, as prediction of election outcomes, upcoming movies' box office earnings and sport scores.These domains span across four different types of media (text, image, video and audio) and four question types (point estimate, binary, multiple choice, and ranking).

When participants begin a new domain, they are asked to estimate their ability relative to the crowd, "Out of 100 people answering these questions, where do you think you will place? We also ask participants to report their level of confidence (on a 5-point scale) on each question (see Figure 1). With this information, we seek to more efficiently aggregate answers by accounting for self-assessed expertise.

If participants receive information about the guesses of others, that might plausibly yield far better answers than those obtained via independent responses. But there is also a worry that such social influence would result in herding behavior, which in turn could decrease collective performance [5]. To investigate the effects of social influence, participants are randomly assigned to one of three experimental conditions. In the first group, participants are shown the previous five answers to the question; in the second group, they see the previous five answers with the highest self-reported confidence. The third group is the control, in which participants do not receive any information about others' responses.

To encourage participation and engagement, we incorporate two competitive elements into the design of the platform. A timer is included which is set to expire in 30-45 seconds (depending on the question type). Second, we adopt a theme for the platform that lends a social and collaborative feel to the experiment. Namely, participants progress through a series of bee-like-avatars as they complete domains, ultimately becoming the "queen bee" if they complete all the questions.

COLLABORATIVE DESIGN & IMPLEMENTATION

Given the scale of the experiment, its design and implementation was conducted collaboratively by a group of approximately 100 undergraduate students in India led by two graduate students at Stanford, as part of Stanford's Aspiring Researchers Challenge (`http://aspiringresearchers.soe.ucsc.edu`). 54 of these students are listed as co-authors on this submission based on their contribution to the project. This unconventional approach—in which we leveraged the wisdom of crowds to study the wisdom of crowds—allowed us to analyse a much larger and more diverse set of tasks than would be possible with traditional methods.

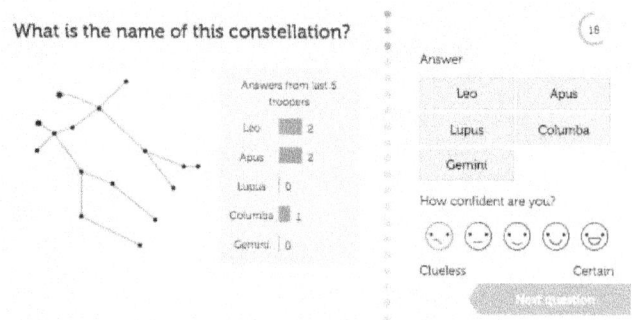

Figure 1. Sample multiple choice question with social condition.

We started by conducting a collaborative literature review, finding and summarizing over 100 related papers on the subject. We then collectively brainstormed nearly 200 ideas for question categories, of which 50 were ultimately selected to be included in the experiment. Creating a domain requires finding a suitable corpus of questions, and, for certain domains, creating and editing the necessary movies, audio, and images. We accomplished these tasks by splitting into 23 smaller teams of 2-5 students. Finally, the experiment platform was fully implemented by two specialized teams of students who focused on front-end [*] and back-end design [‡].

PROJECT STATUS & FUTURE WORK

A preliminary version of the experiment is available at `http://wisdomofcrowds.stanford.edu`. Having completed this first phase of the project, we are now working to integrate the platform with Amazon's Mechanical Turk in order to recruit participants. After running a series of pilot studies, we expect to launch a large-scale version of the experiment, with a goal of eliciting 100 responses for each of 1,000 questions in three different social information conditions, for a total of 300,000 responses.

REFERENCES

1. Galton, F. Vox populi (the wisdom of crowds). *Nature 75* (1907), 450–451.

2. Goldstein, D. G., McAfee, R. P., and Suri, S. The wisdom of smaller, smarter crowds. In *Proceedings of the fifteenth ACM conference on Economics and computation*, ACM (2014), 471–488.

3. Hueffer, K., Fonseca, M. A., Leiserowitz, A., and Taylor, K. M. The wisdom of crowds: Predicting a weather and climate-related event. *Judgment and Decision Making 8*, 2 (2013), 91–105.

4. Lee, M. D., Zhang, S., and Shi, J. The wisdom of the crowd playing the price is right. *Memory & cognition 39*, 5 (2011), 914–923.

5. Lorenz, J., Rauhut, H., Schweitzer, F., and Helbing, D. How social influence can undermine the wisdom of crowd effect. *Proceedings of the National Academy of Sciences 108*, 22 (2011), 9020–9025.

6. Moore, T., and Clayton, R. Evaluating the wisdom of crowds in assessing phishing websites. In *Financial Cryptography and Data Security*. Springer, 2008, 16–30.

Effective Interactions for Personalizing Spatial Visualizations of Collections

Kenneth C. Arnold
Harvard SEAS
kcarnold@seas.harvard.edu

Krzysztof Z. Gajos
Harvard SEAS
kgajos@eecs.harvard.edu

ABSTRACT

Interactive spatial visualizations powered by machine learning will help us explore and understand large collections in meaningful ways, but little is yet known about the design space of interactions. We ran a pilot user study to compare two different interaction techniques: a "grouping" interaction adapted from interactive clustering, and an existing "positioning" interaction. We identified three important dimensions of the interaction design space that inform future design of more intuitive and expressive interactions.

Author Keywords

interactive spatial visualization; mixed-initiative interfaces

INTRODUCTION

Today we have access to an unprecedented diversity of large and multifaceted collections. Search and recommendation technologies help retrieve specific items when we already know appropriate keywords or exemplars. However, for synthesis tasks like writing a "Related Work" section or summarizing customer feedback, a visual overview of the whole collection would be helpful. Moreover, many overviews are possible, emphasizing different relationships: research papers can share technical approach or evaluation area, or customer feedback can be about a similar product component or arise in a similar context of use. Users may not know what relationships are important to them a priori, so synthesis can involve a process of discovery through exploring many overviews.

Tools for generating overviews have traditionally been limited to explicitly defined metadata such as dates or keywords, required expert knowledge about how to control a visualization by setting parameters, or required manual placement or annotation of many items. Recent advances in interactive visualization have begun to use interactive machine learning to help people generate overviews more easily by allowing direct manipulation of a small number of items, inferring their organizational intent, and applying that intent to the full collection[3, 2]. Reducing the friction of generating one overview will enable people to explore multiple possible overviews more quickly, increasing the likelihood of meaningful discovery.

UIST '15 Adjunct, November 08-11, 2015, Charlotte, NC, USA
ACM 978-1-4503-3780-9/15/11.
http://dx.doi.org/10.1145/2815585.2815727

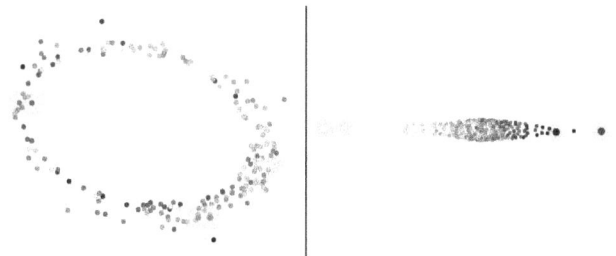

Figure 1. Two visualizations produced with our system, using two different interactions. Left: grouping two reds separately from two blues (represented by grey boxes) organizes colors by hue. Right: placing light colors on the left and dark colors on the right organizes by lightness.

Applying machine learning in overview visualization presents new design challenges: what kinds of manipulations can users perform, and how can the system respond effectively and intelligibly? For example, one line of prior work (which we denote "positions") has users manipulate an automatically generated spatial layout by moving individual items; the system responds by inferring what features are important to the user and rearranging the remaining items accordingly [3]. Another line of prior work (which we denote "groups") has users group items into clusters and offers suggestions for how to complete the clustering [2]. But there has so far been no systematic characterization of the *design space* of possible interactions.

To identify important dimensions of the design space, we built a spatial visualization system with two different interfaces (Figure 1) and ran pilot user studies to compare how people used them. We identified three new design dimensions: what entities can users compare (e.g., items or groups), what affordances does the system provide to express their observations (e.g., one or many kinds of similarity; continuous or discrete choices), and when and to what degree the system takes initiative (e.g., reorganizing after each interaction vs. offering suggestions).

INTERACTIVE SYSTEM

We built an interactive spatial visualization system that uses multidimensional scaling (MDS[1]) to semi-automatically place related items close together in a 2D spatial layout. We parameterize "relatedness" by defining the pairwise distance as a weighted sum of distances along each feature. We implemented simplified versions of two prior interactions:

For the "positions" interface, we follow Hu *et al.* 2003 [3]: the user drags items to specific places, which become position constraints. The system adjusts the feature weights to minimize the MDS cost of the items that the user has placed.

For the "groups" interface, we adapted an approach from interactive clustering [2] to spatial layouts: the user groups items, but the system positions the groups and ungrouped items. We use their weight learning approach (omitting classifier features) to learn feature weights that best distinguish the groups.

STUDY DESIGN

We conducted pilot studies with 10 participants to compare users' experience with the two different interfaces. Participants interacted with a collection of fonts annotated with crowdsourced attributes [4] and were tasked with preparing a summary highlighting different kinds of designs that fonts in the collection might support. Each participant attempted the same task twice, once with each of the interfaces. In a semi-structured interview, we asked participants to compare their experiences with the two interfaces.

FINDINGS

Our observations led us to identify the following design dimensions for interactive spatial visualization systems.

What entities get compared?

One design dimension is what kinds of entities the system encourages the user to compare. While both interfaces afforded comparing items to each other, the "groups" interface encouraged comparing an item to an emerging group.

Different kinds of comparisons enabled people to make different kinds of observations. Most participants focused on superficial characteristics of the fonts like thickness or curviness, but a few were able to identify cross-cutting characteristics like what kind of design the font would be appropriate for (as the task encouraged them to do). We observed those participants comparing items not just with each other but with a *group* or *spatial region* that they were in the process of constructing. One participant noted that the "groups" interaction was more conducive to this kind of comparison.

Participants expressed desires to make comparisons beyond what the interface afforded, e.g., comparing an item to the entire collection (in saying that an item is "unique") or comparing regions or groups with each other (by moving groups closer or farther apart to express similarity or dissimilarity).

Affordances for expressing observations

Another design dimension is what affordances the system provides people to express their observations: what kinds of observations can be expressed, and how are those observations encoded?

Both interfaces allowed people to express observations about similarity, but both limited those observations to similarity along one kind of criterion at a time. In practice, participants picked a certain kind of similarity criterion early on and refined it; to support exploration, an interface may need to allow people to express multiple types of similarity judgments simultaneously.

All participants readily explained their interactions verbally in terms of names for features, groups of items, or relationships among items, suggesting that semantic names might be useful to express. Since neither interface afforded expressing these

semantic rationales and structures, participants sometimes forgot why they put an item in a particular place or group, and some participants feared that the system might disturb a meaningful structure that they were creating.

How the observation is encoded is also important. In the "positions" interface, people encode similarity via relative placement, which participants generally found easy. But the "groups" interface requires encoding similarity observations into mutually-exclusive group membership decisions, which may explain why participants reported greater cognitive load in that interface.

User vs. system initiative

Since both the user and the system can manipulate the visualization, balance of user and system initiative is an important design dimension: when and to what extent should the system manipulate the visualization? In both interfaces we studied, the system refined the visualization after every interaction of any kind. Consequently, iterative refinement of emerging groups was smooth, but several participants reported fear of "losing" an observation that they had not yet been able to express or apprehension about the results of adding an item to a group. Other design choices are possible: the system might only offer suggestions (like iCluster [2]), respond after only certain kinds of interactions, or respond in more limited ways (such as only partially rearranging the visualization).

CONCLUSION

Interactive spatialization systems are promising for supporting synthesis and exploratory organization, but fulfilling that promise requires designing effective interactions. Designers should consider what entities to make easy to compare, what affordances to provide for expressing observations, and when and to what extent to have the system take initiative. Further exploration along these design dimensions will lead to more expressive interfaces that will enable more insightful discovery.

Acknowledgments Thanks to Ofra Amir, Pao Siangliulue, and others in Harvard IIS for helpful feedback, and to our pilot study participants.

REFERENCES

1. Ingwer Borg and Patrick Groenen. 1997. *Modern Multidimensional Scaling: Theory and Applications.* Springer New York, New York, NY.

2. Steven M. Drucker, Danyel Fisher, and Sumit Basu. 2011. Helping users sort faster with adaptive machine learning recommendations. *Lecture Notes in Computer Science* 6948 LNCS (2011), 187–203.

3. Xinran Hu, Lauren Bradel, Dipayan Maiti, Leanna House, Chris North, and Scotland Leman. 2013. Semantics of directly manipulating spatializations. *IEEE Transactions on Visualization and Computer Graphics* 19, 12 (2013), 2052–2059.

4. Peter O'Donovan, Jānis Lībeks, Aseem Agarwala, and Aaron Hertzmann. 2014. Exploratory font selection using crowdsourced attributes. *ACM Transactions on Graphics* 33, 4 (2014).

Fix and Slide: Caret Navigation with Movable Background

Kenji Suzuki, Kazumasa Okabe, Ryuki Sakamoto
Yahoo Japan Cooperation
[kensuzuk | kokabe | ryusakam]@yahoo-corp.jp

Daisuke Sakamoto
The University of Tokyo
sakamoto@is.s.u-tokyo.ac.jp

ABSTRACT

We present a "Fix and Slide" technique, which is a concept to use a movable background to place a caret insertion point and to select text on a mobile device. Standard approach to select text on mobile devices is touching to the text where a user wants to select, and sometimes pop-up menu is displayed and they choose "select" mode and then start to specify an area to be selected. A big problem is that the user's finger hides the area to select; this is called a *"fat finger problem."* We use the movable background to navigate a caret. First a user places a caret by tapping on a screen and then moves the background by touching and dragging on a screen. In this situation, the caret is fixed on the screen so that the user can move the background to navigate the caret where the user wants to move the caret. We implement the Fix and Slide technique on iOS device (iPhone) to demonstrate the impact of this text selection technique on small mobile devices.

Author Keywords

Caret; movable background; text selection; pointing; touch interaction; mobile device.

ACM Classification Keywords

H.5.2. Information interfaces and presentation (e.g., HCI): Interaction styles (e.g., commands, menus, forms, direct manipulation).

INTRODUCTION

Pointing on a screen and selecting text is a fundamental operation to use computing devices. We usually use mouse, trackball, and/or touchpad to make these operations in the desktop computing environment. These indirect manipulation methods had been replaced to the direct touch manipulation in the mobile devices; we directly touch to the screen of mobile devices to select an object. This method is better in terms of we can directly touch to the object on the screen, however this generates a new problem, which is, user's fingers hide an object on the screen. This is the popular issue in mobile computing research and we call it as the fat finger problem (Figure 1; left). This makes the user to point and/or select objects on the mobile device

UIST '15 Adjunct, November 08-11, 2015, Charlotte, NC, USA
ACM 978-1-4503-3780-9/15/11.
http://dx.doi.org/10.1145/2815585.2815728

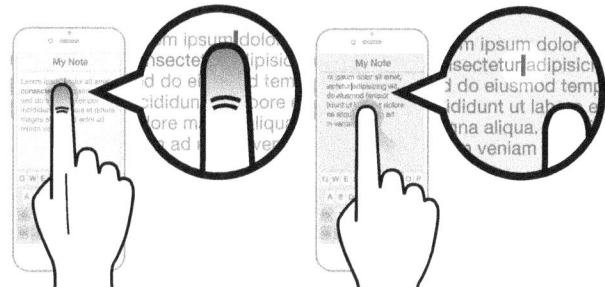

Figure 1: Standard caret navigation (left) and "Fix and Slide" technique (right): User moves the background text to navigate a caret instead of moving caret itself.

difficult, and frustrate the user to operate device precisely.

This will be a problem to select a text as well. In case of text selection, users need to move a caret to specify a starting point and destination of text to select. Standard user interface on mobile devices require users to touch a starting point to place a caret, but usually precise operation is necessary and difficult to move a caret to where the user want to start to select with small font text. And then the users drag their finger on the screen to select destination and again the precise operation is required. All in all, pointing and selecting text on mobile devices, like smartphones or related wearable devices, is more difficult than the desktop computing environment.

We present a caret navigation (or we can say "placing a text insertion point") technique using an idea of movable background, that is, the user first fixes the caret on the text and slides the background to where the user wants to place the caret (Figure 1; right). We name this approach "Fix and Slide" technique. We implement a working prototype to understand the usability of the Fix and Slide technique and demonstrate the effectivity of it.

FIX AND SLIDE TECHNIQUE

Fat finger problem is a well-know problem in mobile computing devices, and various approaches had been presented Shift is one of the famous interfaces to solve this problem [3]; occluded screen content is displayed in a call-out above the finger. We can see this technique in the iOS devices. TapTap is another approach to show a popup, which displays magnified view where a user wants to zoom in [1]. There is another approach to use an offset cursor for touch device, however it was slower than direct touch [2]. Overall, standard method requires moving a caret where to select by dragging users' finger on the screen.

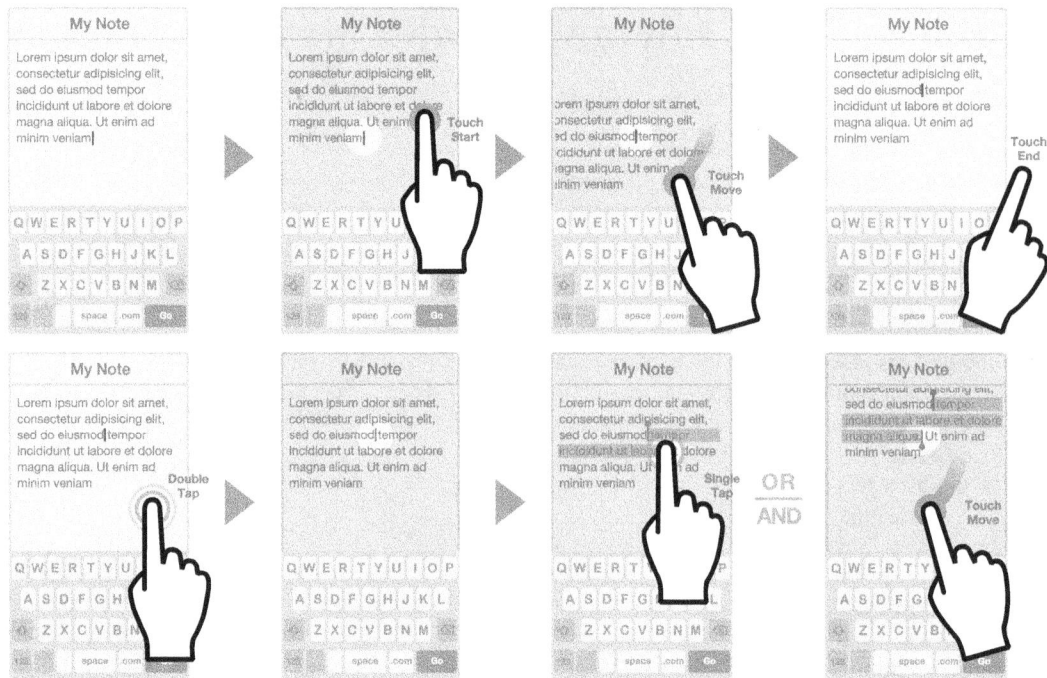

Figure 2: Overview of "Fix and Slide" technique.

Instead, we fix the caret first by tapping on a screen and then slide the background where the text on the surface. This makes not to hide the area of point and/or select, and avoid the fat finger problem when we use our fingers for tapping on the mobile devices. We implement prototype system on iPhone 6 with iOS 8.2. The display size is 4.7 inches with 1,334 x 750 resolution.

Caret Navigation

Problem of placing the caret precisely on text in small devices, people first taps on a text but the caret is usually appeared on incorrect place where near to the target so that they need to slide their finger on the screen but the target is usually under the finger. In case of Shift [1], or related technique is employed for text selection, a call-out is displayed just above the finger and enables the user to see the text, but usually the text is small and hard to move their finger slightly. We can say this is a problem of direct manipulation.

Instead, we use the indirect manipulation method (Figure 2; top). Users just tap on the screen to place the caret (Fix), and touch and move anywhere on the screen (Slide) to manipulate the background to set the caret on the target. Usually, users might tap on near the target, but due to the problem we mentioned above (hard to place the caret precisely), they need to adjust the place.

Text Selection

After the users placed the caret on the target, they can select the text (Figure 2; bottom). A double tap is a command to change mode from placing caret to the text selection mode.

They can select text by taping on the screen and move background to move the caret to the target (end of the text selection). This text selection operation is recognized as "two caret navigation with changing mode by double tapping." "Two finger touch and scroll" allows the users to scroll up and down on the document to select long area beyond the screen space.

CONCLUSION

We presented the "Fix and Slide" technique to place a text insertion point (e.g., caret) and select text on the mobile devices. As for the next step, we are planning to conduct a formal experiment comparing with existing caret navigation and text selection methods on mobile device (e.g., iOS and Android), to validate the concept. iOS and Android has a different caret navigation and text selection technique so that we consider that comparing our technique with both interaction technique is necessary for the formal experiment.

REFERENCES

1. Anne Roudaut, Stéphane Huot, and Eric Lecolinet. 2008. TapTap and MagStick: improving one-handed target acquisition on small touch-screens. In *Proc. AVI '08*, ACM, 146-153.

2. Andrew Sears and Ben Shneiderman. 1991. High precision touchscreens: design strategies and comparisons with a mouse. *Int. J. Man-Mach. Stud* 34, 4: 593-613.

3. Daniel Vogel and Patrick Baudisch. 2007. Shift: a technique for operating pen-based interfaces using touch. In *Proc. CHI '07*, ACM, 657-666.

LegionTools: A Toolkit + UI for Recruiting and Routing Crowds to Synchronous Real-Time Tasks

Mitchell Gordon
Computer Science Department
University of Rochester
m.gordon@rochester.edu

Jeffrey P. Bigham
HCI and LT Institutes
Carnegie Mellon University
jbigham@cs.cmu.edu

Walter S. Lasecki
Department of EECS
University of Michigan
wlasecki@umich.edu

ABSTRACT

We introduce LegionTools, a toolkit and interface for managing large, synchronous crowds of online workers for experiments. This poster contributes the design and implementation of a state-of-the-art crowd management tool, along with a publicly-available, open-source toolkit that future system builders can use to coordinate synchronous crowds of online workers for their systems and studies.

We describe the toolkit itself, along with the underlying design rationale, in order to make it clear to the community of system builders at UIST when and how this tool may be beneficial to their project. We also describe initial deployments of the system in which workers were synchronously recruited to support real-time crowdsourcing systems, including the largest synchronous recruitment and routing of workers from Mechanical Turk that we are aware of. While the version of LegionTools discussed here focuses on Amazon's Mechanical Turk platform, it can be easily extended to other platforms as APIs become available.

Author Keywords

Crowdsourcing; Real-Time; Human Computation; Tools

INTRODUCTION AND BACKGROUND

Human computation is the process of using people as part of a computational process, often to solve problems that fully-automated approaches cannot yet solve. Crowdsourcing is the process of making an open call to a group of potential workers. Combined, these provide a powerful method for bringing human intelligence to bear on hard problems on demand.

Recently, synchronous crowdsourcing has been used to create systems capable of responding in real time [4]. However, these tasks require extensive coordination, which adds a challenging hurdle to the process, especially for practitioners in other fields. Bernstein et al. introduced the *retainer model* for pre-recruiting workers in order to reliably have access to human intelligence in less than two seconds for real-time tasks [1]. However, no tools for this process are widely available.

UIST '15 Adjunct, November 08-11, 2015, Charlotte, NC, USA
ACM 978-1-4503-3780-9/15/11.
http://dx.doi.org/10.1145/2815585.2815729

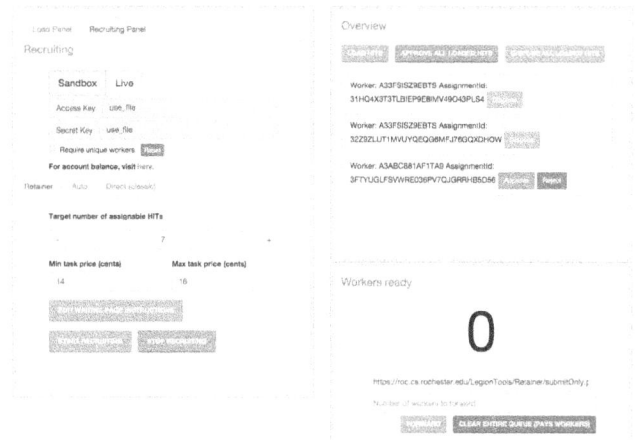

Figure 1. The main LegionTools web interface. Users can easily recruit workers and manage completed tasks all with an easy-to-use interface.

In this poster paper, we introduce LegionTools to provide a publicly-available tool for recruiting and routing workers quickly and efficiently to tasks, with more fine-grain control than has been previously possible. Unlike the standard retainer model, LegionTools routes a user-specified number of workers to a given task, even if more are currently in the retainer pool. This not only allows for more controlled execution parameters for the system using LegionTools, but also improves the average speed of response by filtering for the *fastest N workers in a set of K*.

SYSTEM

This section explains the design and implementation of LegionTools, as well as an easy-to-use GUI interface to the toolkit.

Managing Experiments

LegionTools provides an account system so that multiple researchers or groups of researchers may use a single installation. Users log in using their unique Mechanical Turk credentials. These keys are hashed on the client side, and are never stored or transmitted to the server as plain text.

Each account in LegionTools has its own set of experiments. An experiment represents a single task type. Logging in provides access to all past experiments and allows the user to create new ones, either by entering custom information or duplicating an prior example. Users can switch between experiments on the fly, allowing them to easily manage multiple experiments simultaneously. For instance, on a single instance of LegionTools, multiple researchers could each be actively maintaining multiple retainer pools simultaneously without effecting each others efforts. The idea of being able to easily manage HITs for multiple experiments being conducted on a single set of Mechanical Turk keys as though they are separate is a key contribution of LegionTools.

Recruiting Workers

LegionTools makes it easy to recruit a desired number of workers with the press of a single button. It uses a form of search engine optimization to recruit a desired number of workers quickly by leveraging how Mechanical Turk displays HITs to make tasks more visible to workers by frequently re-posting not-yet-accepted tasks (similar to quikTurkit [2]).

LegionTools makes it very easy to employ the retainer model in a user's experiments. The retainer model allows the user to pool a desired number of workers and in real-time send them to begin a task all at the same time. LegionTools shows a counter with the number of workers who are actively waiting in real time, and the user forwards the desired number of users to a given URL. LegionTools will stop recruiting new workers once the desired retainer size has been reached, and will resume if workers choose to leave the retainer. This automatic maintenance of the retainer pool reduces the attention that requesters must pay to recruiting workers.

Managing Completed HITs

LegionTools allows users to easily accept, reject, and dispose completed or expired HITs. Using the Overview panel at the top left, the user with a single click can view a list of all HITs for their given experiment, and either manually review them or choose to accept them all.

EXAMPLE INTERACTION

To demonstrate LegionTools' flexibility in supporting a variety of use cases, lets take the hypothetical researcher Maria. Maria's lab all shares a single Mechanical Turk account, and they conduct multiple experiments simultaneously. Maria is currently conducting one experiment, and would like to begin another. She opens LegionTools in her web browser, logs in with her Mechanical Turk keys, and creates a new experiment: filling in the HIT title, description, etc. Maria would like all workers to arrive at her task at the exact same time, so she uses the retainer mode. She enters a retainer size of 10, and clicks 'start recruiting.' A moment later, the live counter shows that there are 13 workers waiting. She enters her task's URL and forwards 10 of the workers. To repeat this, Maria need not do anything; workers will continue to be recruited into the retainer and she can forward them as needed. Once Maria is done, she simply clicks 'Stop recruiting,' causing the HIT cleanup process to automatically complete. Once all workers have finished Maria's task, she clicks 'Load HITs' in the Overview panel and clicks 'Accept All.'

At any time, Maria can close LegionTools in her browser and easily come back to right where she was in the process. Maria has completed all of this without effecting any other of the lab's experiments.

REPRESENTATIVE DEPLOYMENTS

LegionTools has made several of our research projects possible. We have used it to recruit and direct workers from thousands of HITs. Several research groups at multiple universities have used also LegionTools as a key part of their projects.

As an example, consider Glance [3], a system that uses the crowd to quickly and accurately code behavioral events in video. It used LegionTools during its evaluation to recruit thousands of workers. LegionTools was left in 'automatic' mode for several days, and constantly recruited workers and sent them to video clips. LegionTools allowed us to continually re-post tasks to prevent them going ignored, while ensuring that only unique workers completed the test (a checkbox in the UI). This sped up completion, and would have previously required a one-off solution.

Another Glance experiment performed a speed test that required all workers to begin analyzing video simultaneously. This required using the retainer mode to recruit workers for just under 20 minutes to reach a pool of over 70 workers. All workers were then forwarded to a single task. 85% of workers began the task within 5 seconds of prompting. To our knowledge, this is the largest ever synchronous workforce recruited from a crowd platform to date.

Another example use was during a workshop with roughly 20 participants grouped into teams of 3-4. Each team was working on creating a small interactive crowd task, and most were unfamiliar with recruiting workers from online crowd platforms. To make it easy to facilitate their task creation, Ether-Pad was used to create a simple 'live' task, and LegionTools was used by one of the organizers to route workers immediately to tasks once workshop participants' tasks were ready. Over the course of 2 hours, 5 teams requested over 40 workers be directed to tasks, in specified sized groups of between 2 and 5. All workers arrived at their tasks within approximately 5 seconds.

CONCLUSIONS AND FUTURE WORK

LegionTools provides a key resource for systems builders who want to focus on creating new real-time crowdsourcing systems, without needing to build new layers atop crowdsourcing platforms. In on-going work, we are creating an API that will allow systems to create their own predictive allocation algorithms to better automatically control the routing of workers to tasks where their input is needed.

REFERENCES

1. Bernstein, M. S., Brandt, J., Miller, R. C., and Karger, D. R. Crowds in two seconds: Enabling realtime crowd-powered interfaces. In *Proc. of UIST* (2011).

2. Bigham et al., J. P. Vizwiz: Nearly real-time answers to visual questions. In *Proc. of UIST* (2010).

3. Lasecki, W. S., Gordon, M., Koutra, D., Jung, M. F., Dow, S. P., and Bigham, J. P. Glance: Rapidly coding behavioral video with the crowd. In *Proc. of UIST* (2014).

4. Lasecki, W. S., Murray, K. I., White, S., Miller, R. C., and Bigham, J. P. Real-time crowd control of existing interfaces. In *Proc. of UIST* (2011).

KickSoul: A Wearable System for Feet Interactions with Digital Devices

Xavier Benavides
MIT Media Lab
Cambridge, USA
xavib@media.mit.edu

Chang Long Zhu
MIT Media Lab
Cambridge, USA
changzj@media.mit.edu

Pattie Maes
MIT Media Lab
Cambridge, USA
pattie@media.mit.edu

Joseph A. Paradiso
MIT Media Lab
Cambridge, USA
joep@media.mit.edu

ABSTRACT

In this paper we present a wearable device that maps natural feet movements into inputs for digital devices. KickSoul consists of an insole with sensors embedded that tracks movements and triggers actions in devices that surround us. We present a novel approach to use our feet as input devices in mobile situations when our hands are busy. We analyze natural feet's movements and their meaning before activating an action. This paper discusses different applications for this technology as well as the implementation of our prototype.

Author Keywords

DIY; gesture recognition; wearable electronics.

ACM Classification Keywords

H.5.2 [Information Interfaces and Presentation].

INTRODUCTION

We are surrounded by a large number of devices in almost every context of our life. We use computers, TVs, phones and wearable devices that offer the possibility of performing daily activities faster and more effectively than ever before. Most of these devices have visual interfaces that rely on hand gestures and touch interaction, as they are easy and natural for us. However, there are occasions when our hands are busy or it is not acceptable to make use of them, preventing us from interacting with our devices.

This same problem also occurs in other situations of our life, and we tend to use our feet as a substitute. With our feet we can perform easy actions while our hands are focused on other tasks. As an example, we use them to open and close doors or move objects that are on the floor. These actions can be divided in two main groups; actions where we move objects closer in order to use them and actions where we kick an object that we no longer need and want to move it further away. In this paper we want to connect these natural feet interactions with actions in our digital

UIST '15 Adjunct, November 08-11, 2015, Charlotte, NC, USA
ACM 978-1-4503-3780-9/15/11.
http://dx.doi.org/10.1145/2815585.2815730

devices, for example, so that we can kick our foot to delete a file from the computer, or perform the opposite gesture (pulling our foot towards us) to save a document.

KickSoul is a wearable device in the form of an insole. It has sensors embedded to track the user's movements, understand the intended actions, and transmit this information to devices around us. The work contributes in (1) mapping real-world feet interactions to our devices, (2) the development of the software and hardware, and (3) implementation of a set of applications.

RELATED WORK

There is research that uses feet movements to interact with devices [4]. One closely related project is Kick [1], which captures the kick gesture of the foot with a Kinect in order to enable interaction with mobile devices. Kickables [2] is another related project that introduces tangible objects that users manipulate with their feet to interact with digital content projected on the floor. A project by Paelke [3] proves that the rear camera of a smartphone can be used to capture feet movements that can be used in phone games.

Our project differs from previous work by (1) offering a mobile and portable solution, (2) being based in natural interactions rather than creating a new language of interaction, and (3) showing a set of compelling applications.

INTERACTIONS SUPPORTED

The system supports two types of interactions: "move closer" and "move away" (Figure 3). An action is triggered when the system detects one of these gestures. The system maps the outcome of these gestures to actions that can be performed with our digital devices. Some examples that may be triggered with the "move closer" while working in a computer are zooming in or saving a document. On the other hand, when the "move away" gesture is detected, we could zoom out or delete a file.

IMPLEMENTATION

In order to develop the system, we sewed electronic components onto an insole placed inside of a shoe. To endow the insole with data collection capabilities, we embedded a 6-axis IMU (gyroscope and accelerometer) that tracks the movements of the foot. The data is collected by a

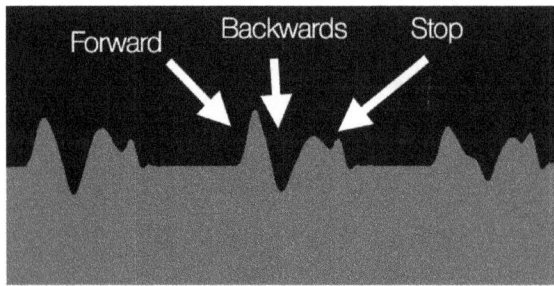

Figure 1. Data obtained from the accelerometer after applying the LPF. We can distinguish three stages while walking: walking forward, backward and stop movement.

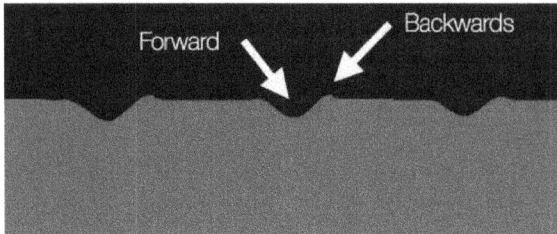

Figure 2. Data obtained from the gyroscope, where we can see the forward and backward movement.

microcontroller that analyzes and transmits the information over Bluetooth to a smartphone application. The smartphone is used as a bridge between the actions performed by the user and the nearest device that surround us.

In order to detect gestures and avoid errors in the system, we applied a low-pass filter to the raw data collected from the accelerometer (Figure 1). After that, we combine the information from the gyroscope (Figure 2) and accelerometer. Finally, an algorithm analyzes the resulting data and detects the movement performed using predefined patterns.

USAGE SCENARIOS

KickSoul enables users to interact with smart devices using our feet. As an example, sometimes we arrive home carrying bags from the supermarket, which makes difficult to turn on a light. With our system, we just need to be close enough to the light and perform the "move closer" gesture with our foot to turn on the light.

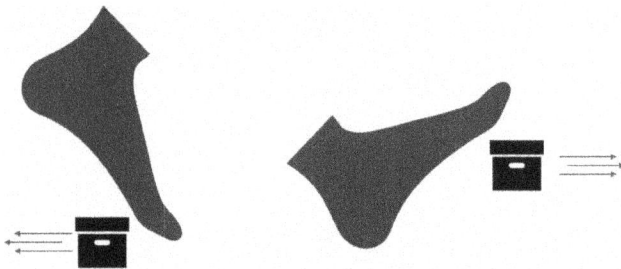

Figure 3. "Move closer" and "Move away" gesture.

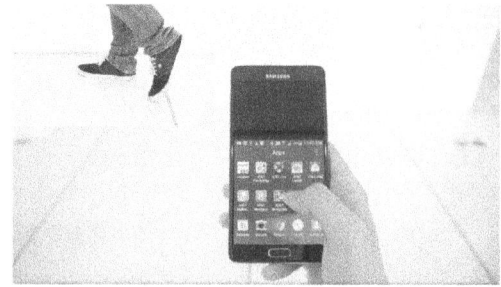

Figure 4. The user is moving his foot backwards to make the screen of the phone move accordingly.

Another application is related with *phones with big screens*. As a consequence, it is becoming difficult to interact with them using just one hand. However, we can use our foot gesture to move the screen up/down and right/left, so that we are able to hold the phone and interact with it using only one hand (Figure 4).

The system can be used to reject *phone calls* when it is not possible to use our hands, or we are using them for other tasks.

Finally, we can use the feet movements as *shortcuts* while interacting with a computer. In a map application, we can zoom in and out by performing the "move closer" and "move away" gesture. If we are writing a document, we can use our foot to save or delete the file.

CONCLUSIONS

We demonstrated an easy to deploy technology and described usage scenarios to interact with digital devices when our hands are busy. Most of these interactions are short in time and not very complex. As a consequence, feet become a suitable substitute or complement to hands, as they tend to be free when our hands are not.

REFERENCES

1. Han, T., Alexander, J., Karnik, A., Irani, P., & Subramanian, S. (2011, August). Kick: investigating the use of kick gestures for mobile interactions. In *Proceedings of the 13th International Conference on Human Computer Interaction with Mobile Devices and Services* (pp. 29-32). ACM.

2. Schmidt, D., Ramakers, R., Pedersen, E. W., Jasper, J., Köhler, S., Pohl, A., ... & Baudisch, P. (2014, April). Kickables: Tangibles for feet. In *Proceedings of the SIGCHI Conference on Human Factors in Computing Systems* (pp. 3143-3152). ACM.

3. Paelke, V., Reimann, C., & Stichling, D. (2004, September). Foot-based mobile interaction with games. In *Proceedings of the 2004 ACM SIGCHI International Conference on Advances in computer entertainment technology* (pp. 321-324). ACM.

4. Paradiso, J. A., Hsiao, K. Y., Benbasat, A. Y., & Teegarden, Z. (2000). Design and implementation of expressive footwear. *IBM systems journal*, *39*(3.4), 511-529.

Capacitive Blocks: A Block System that Connects the Physical with the Virtual using Changes of Capacitance

Arika Yoshida, Buntarou Shizuki, Jiro Tanaka
University of Tsukuba, Japan
Tennoudai 1-1-1, Tsukuba, Ibaraki, Japan 305-8571
{yoshida,shizuki,jiro}@iplab.cs.tsukuba.ac.jp

ABSTRACT

We propose a block-stacking system based on capacitance. The system, called Capacitive Blocks, allows users to build 3D models in a virtual space by stacking physical blocks. The construction of the block-stacking system is simple, and fundamental components including physical blocks can be made with a 3D printer. The block is a capacitor that consists of two layers made of conductive plastic filament and between them a layer made of non-conductive plastic filament. In this paper, we present a prototype of this block-stacking system and the mechanism that detects the height of blocks (i.e., the number of stacked blocks) by measuring the capacitance of the stacked blocks, which changes in accordance with the number of stacked blocks.

Author Keywords

Capacitive block; tangible; building block; stacking; 3D printing; computational crafts; interactive devices

ACM Classification Keywords

H.5.2. Information Interfaces and Presentation (e.g. HCI): User Interfaces.

INTRODUCTION

Many people enjoy playing with toys, such as building blocks and fusible beads, that are made by combining parts using their hands. Motivated by and based on such toys, we developed a block-shaped capacitor that can be printed with a 3D printer. We also developed a block-stacking system, which we call Capacitive Blocks. It allows users to build 3D models in a virtual space by stacking physical blocks, where the system counts the stacked physical blocks by measuring the capacitance and renders them as 3D models in a virtual space. There have been a number of researches on interfaces based on block stacking. Most of those blocks contain electronic devices in the block or need external cameras to recognize how many blocks are stacked. In contrast, our block-stacking

UIST '15 Adjunct, November 08-11, 2015, Charlotte, NC, USA.
ACM 978-1-4503-3780-9/15/11.
http://dx.doi.org/10.1145/2815585.2815731

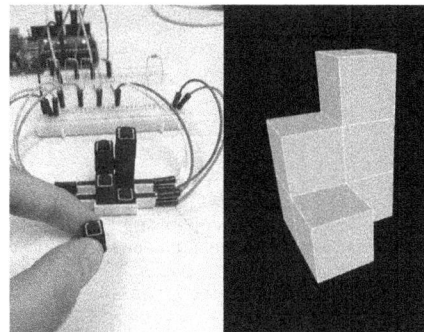

Figure 1: Overview of Capacitive Block system. (Left) Prototype of Capacitive Blocks system. (Right) An application using left mechanism.

system can detect the number of stacked blocks without embedding electronic devices in the blocks and without using external cameras, making the construction of the block-stacking system simple.

RELATED WORK

There are many researches that provide interfaces based on detecting the height of blocks. Chan et al. [4] developed blocks whose surface and contact area were connected electrically. Ando et al. [1] developed blocks that could detect the three-dimensional shape using infrared LEDs and phototransistors spread all over the blocks surfaces. Baudisch et al. [3] developed blocks whose heights were detected using an under-the-desk camera with a fiberglass bundle and a marker in a block. However, these block systems need embedded electronic devices or external cameras, making the system's construction more complicated.

CAPACITIVE BLOCKS

We designed a $7.8 \times 7.8 \times 11.4$ mm block whose shape is based on a 1×1 LEGO brick. The block consists of three parts (Figures 2a-2c): two layers (the block's outside and core) made of conductive plastic filament (Proto-Plant Inc.) and between them a layer made of non-conductive plastic filament (Figure 2b). When a user stacks some blocks on a connector of a connection system (Figure 3), the system recognizes the number of blocks on the connector and renders the blocks as 3D models in a virtual space. Recognizing the number of blocks on a connector is based on measurement of the block's capacitance. We used Arduino UNO and Processing 2.0 to measure the capacitance, recognize the number of blocks, and render the 3D models.

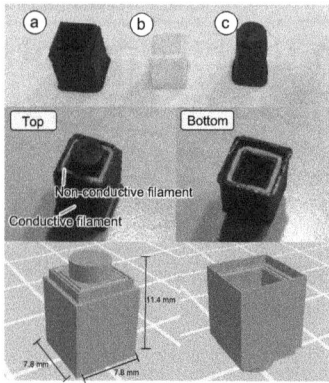

Figure 2: Block of Capacitive Blocks system.

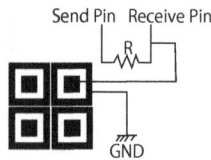

Figure 3: Connection system consisting of 2×2 connectors and its circuit diagram.

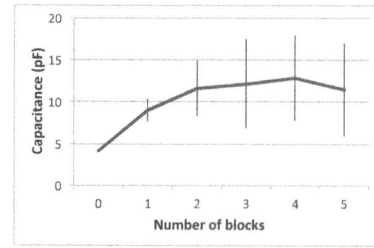

Figure 4: Capacitance averages with standard error bars.

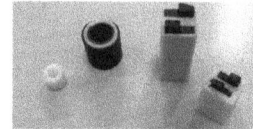

Figure 5: Other shapes of Capacitive Blocks.

Changes in stacked capacitance

To recognize the number of blocks, changes in capacitance are used. Fundamentally, a capacitor has at least two conductors that can store electrical charges by using the electrical potential difference between the conductors. Also, we know that the capacitance of n equivalent capacitors C connected in parallel is nC. Using these fundamentals, we designed and printed the blocks shown in Figure 2 using a 3D printer. A block was found to have a capacitance of 5 pF - 15 pF (mostly around 10 pF). Also, we connected the circuit for measuring the capacitance [2] under each connector. Our current implementation uses a 1 MΩ resistor as R in Figure 3.

Measurement of capacitance

To test how our approach described in the previous section works, we placed 0–5 blocks on a connector and measured the capacitance of blocks including the connection with an LCR meter (DER EE Electrical Instrument, DE-5000). We did this 10 times (i.e., 10 trials) for each number of blocks. We show all the results in Table 1 and the average capacitance with its standard error in Figure 4.

As Figure 4 shows, because the standard error becomes large when the number of blocks is equal to or greater than three,

recognizing the number of blocks is error-prone. We consider that these results are due to individual differences in the capacitance of the blocks and looseness in the connections of the blocks. To solve these problems, it is necessary to redesign the block so that it has a precise capacitance and a good connection with other blocks.

Other Shapes

Two conductors placed in parallel form a capacitor; therefore, we believe our system can use or even recognize various kinds of blocks (e.g., by using different capacitances as IDs), so we are currently exploring other shapes of Capacitive Blocks such as beads as shown in Figure 5.

CONCLUSION AND FUTURE WORK

We presented a block-stacking system called Capacitive Blocks, which allows users to build 3D models in a virtual space by stacking physical blocks. We also presented the system that detects the height of blocks (i.e., the number of blocks) by measuring the capacitance, which changes in accordance with the number of stacked blocks. In future, we plan to redesign the block so that it has a precise capacitance and a good connection with other blocks to improve the accuracy in recognizing the number of stacked blocks. In addition, as future challenges, we plan to study other block shapes and implement a large-scale connection system, e.g., 8×8 (our current connection system is 2×2), and evaluate the system.

REFERENCES

1. Ando, M., Itoh, Y., Hosoi, T., Takashima, K., Nakajima, K., and Kitamura, Y. StackBlock: Block-shaped interface for flexible stacking. In *UIST'14 Adjunct* (2014), 41–42.

2. Capacitive Sensing Library. http://playground.arduino.cc/Main/CapacitiveSensor?from=Main.CapSense.

3. Baudisch, P., Becker, T., and Rudeck, F. Lumino: Tangible blocks for tabletop computers based on glass fiber bundles. In *CHI '10* (2010), 1165–1174.

4. Chan, L., Müller, S., Roudaut, A., and Baudisch, P. CapStones and ZebraWidgets: Sensing stacks of building blocks, dials and sliders on capacitive touch screens. In *CHI '12* (2012), 2189–2192.

	Number of blocks					
	0	1	2	3	4	5
1	4.1	6.75	7.13	7.51	10.69	8.89
2	4.09	10.72	17.24	21.46	21.95	22.41
3	4.15	8.57	10.28	12.22	11.58	10.42
4	4.08	8.67	8.80	9.16	9.34	8.44
5	4.14	10.43	15.84	20.43	20.69	20.57
6	4.1	7.67	10.66	8.27	8.88	9.69
7	4.15	9.63	11.27	12.33	12.96	11.57
8	4.18	9.27	11.65	15.09	15.73	8.66
9	4.1	10.31	14.38	7.69	7.81	8.26
10	4.19	7.58	8.70	7.33	8.61	5.72

Table 1: Measurement of capacitance.

Haptic-enabled Active Bone-Conducted Sound Sensing

Yuya Okawa
Tokai University
4-1-1 Kitakaname, Hiratsuka-shi, Kanagawa,
259-1292, Japan
5bdrm002@mail.u-tokai.ac.jp

Kentaro Takemura
Tokai University
4-1-1 Kitakaname, Hiratsuka-shi, Kanagawa,
259-1292, Japan
takemura@tokai.ac.jp

ABSTRACT

In this study, we propose active bone-conducted sound sensing for estimating a joint angle of a finger and simultaneous use as a haptic interface. For estimating the joint angle, an unnoticeable vibration is input to the finger, and a perceptible vibration is additionally input to the finger for providing haptic feedback. The joint angle is estimated by switching the estimation model depending on the haptic feedback and the average error of the estimation is within about seven degree.

Author Keywords

Active Sensing; Finger Joint Angle; Vibration; Haptic Interface;

ACM Classification Keywords

H.5.2. User Interfaces: Input devices and strategies;
B.4.2. Input/Output Devices: Channels and controllers

INTRODUCTION

Intuitive interfaces have been studied for VR and AR environments in previous researches. A glove-type system such as Cyberglove can estimate the joint angle of the hand using optical fibers, and operation can be realized using gesture information. Additionally, haptic feedback is achieved using a vibration actuator attached on the finger[1]. However, it is essential for wearable interfaces to develop compact devices, so we have previously proposed active bone-conducted sound sensing for estimating the joint angle[2]. We found that the transmitted vibration depends on the joint angle, and we successfully estimated the joint angle of the elbow using sound inputs. In the present study, we improve upon our previous study and propose a method using vibration sensing and actuation for estimating the joint angle and simultaneously providing haptic feedback based on the human perceptual capability.

HAPTICE-ENABLED ACTIVE BONE-CONDUCTED SOUND SENSING

Active bone-conducted sound sensing is a method used for estimating the joint angle using actively inputted sound. The

UIST'15 Adjunct, November 8-11, 2015, Charlotte, NC, USA
ACM 978-1-4503-3780-9/15/11.
DOI: http://dx.doi.org/10.1145/2815585.2815732

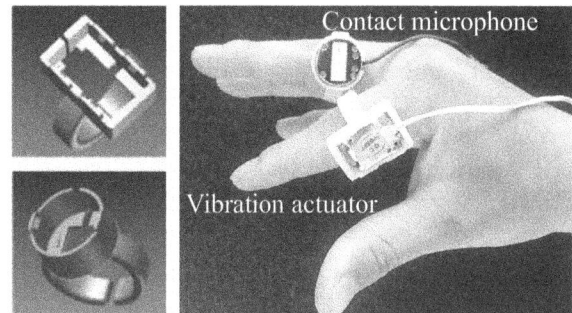

Figure 1. Ring-type sensing devices consists of a vibration actuator (Surface Transducer Small COM-10917, SparkFun Electronics) and a contact microphone (CM-01B, Measurement Specialties). Each case is printed using a 3D printer.

sensing device consists of a vibration actuator and a contact microphone as a shown in Figure 1.

Frequency for estimating joint angle

When the joint angle is estimated, we have to use an unnoticeable vibration as input signal because many receptors are distributed on the fingers. Therefore, we experimentally confirmed all receptors can sense vibration of up to approximately 800 Hz. As a result, the vibration frequency for estimating the joint angle is set higher than 1000 Hz.

When the measurement object is the MP joint angle of the finger, we have to choose the optimal vibration. Therefore, we input six sine curves from 1000 to 2000 Hz to the index finger, and Figure 2 shows the relationship between the vibration amplitude and the MP joint angle. When we employ a vibration over 1400 Hz as an input signal, the variation pattern does not increase monotonically. On the other hand, the vibrations which are under 1200 Hz increase monotonically; additionally, the amplitude and angle show a linear correlation. Frequencies of 1000 and 1200 Hz are considered suitable as input signals for this trial subject, because monotonic increase is observed concurrently. However, bone sizes have individual difference. Therefore, in order to estimate the joint angle, it is advisable to execute calibration every time.

The Vibration pattern for estimating joint angle with haptic feedback

The Pacinian corpuscles are one of the four dominant receptors distributed in the palms; it is a rapidly adapting receptor. Its optimal sensitivity is approximately 200 Hz[3], and therefore, we employ this frequency as the vibration for haptic

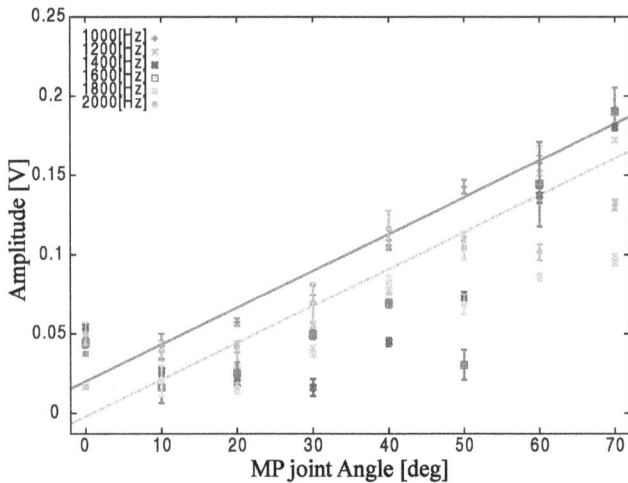

Figure 2. Relationship between vibration amplitude and angle of MP joint when subject flexes MP joint of index finger.

feedback. Providing haptic feedback and estimating the joint angle can be performed simultaneously by inputting synthesized vibration which includes unnoticeable and perceptible vibrations. When synthesized vibration is input, the estimation model has to be switched for estimating joint angle accurately.

Estimating MP joint angle and providing haptic feedback

The vibration amplitude is recorded for creating two estimation models. First, when a sine curve is input for estimating the joint angle, the propagated vibration is recorded several times at $0°$ and $70°$. Next, when a synthesized vibration is input for providing haptic feedback, the propagated vibration is also recorded at same angles. We apply linear approximation to these data for creating two calibrated models. A bandpass filter is applied for extracting vibration which is used for estimating a joint angle. Then, the joint angle can be estimated using these models.

In order to confirm the feasibility of the proposed method, we designed and implemented a gripper controller in virtual environment as shown in Figure 3. We employ Open Dynamics Engine as a physics engine to detect collisions. The finger of gripper was controlled using the estimated MP joint angle. Normally, sine curve was input to the finger for estimating joint angle, and the synthesized curve was input when the gripper grasped a ball as shown in Figure 3.

EXPERIMENTS

We experimentally estimated the MP joint angle to evaluate the accuracy of our proposed method. In this experiment, we employed sine curves of 1000 and 200 Hz for the estimation and haptic feedback, respectively. Three subjects flexed the MP joint of the index finger. We measured the vibration amplitude to estimate the angle of the MP joint every $10°$. The estimated accuracy was computed as shown in Figure 4, and the average error of the estimated angle is under $7°$. Accordingly, we confirmed that the joint angle can be estimated when haptic feedback is provided.

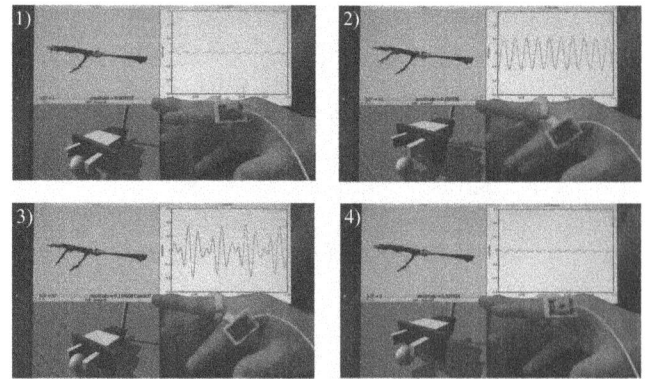

Figure 3. Snapshots of haptic feedback using simulation. The gripper did not touch the object in photos 1–2, and therefore, a simple sine curve is input to the index finger as a vibration. On the other hand, the gripper touched the object in photos 3, and therefore, the synthesized curve is input for haptic feedback.

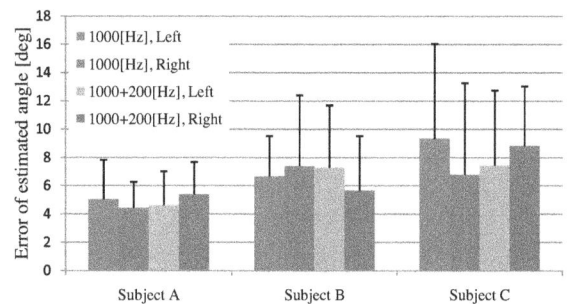

Figure 4. Accuracy of estimating MP joint angle. The index fingers of each subject's left and right hands are used in the experiment.

CONCLUSION

In this study, we have proposed active bone-conducted sound sensing that enables haptic feedback using perceptible and unnoticeable vibrations, and we experimentally confirmed the feasibility of our proposed method through experiments.

Currently, joint angle during flexion is estimated using the model, and therefore, we will create the other model for estimating MP joint angle completely during extension as future work. Additionally, we will realize appropriate feedback for tactile sensation using various vibration patterns.

ACKNOWLEDGEMENT

This work was supported by JSPS KAKENHI Grant Number 15K00285.

REFERENCES

1. K. Minamizawa et al. Ghostglove: Haptic existence of the virtual world. In *ACM SIGGRAPH 2008 new tech demos*, ACM Press (2008), 18.

2. K. Takemura et al. Active bone-conducted sound sensing for wearable interfaces. In *Proc. of the 24th annual ACM symposium adjunct on User interface software and technology* ,ACM Press (2011), 53–54.

3. G.M.Shepherd. *Neurobiology*. Oxford University Press.

Perspective-dependent Indirect Touch Input for 3D Polygon Extrusion

Henri Palleis
University of Munich (LMU)
Munich, Germany
henri.palleis@ifi.lmu.de

Julie Wagner
University of Munich (LMU)
Munich, Germany
julie.wagner@ifi.lmu.de

Heinrich Hussmann
University of Munich (LMU)
Munich, Germany
hussmann@ifi.lmu.de

ABSTRACT

We present a two-handed indirect touch interaction technique for the extrusion of polygons within a 3D modeling tool that we have built for a horizontal/vertical dual touch screen setup. In particular, we introduce perspective-dependent touch gestures: using several graphical input areas on the horizontal display, the non-dominant hand navigates the virtual camera and thus continuously updates the spatial frame of reference within which the dominant hand performs extrusions with dragging gestures.

Author Keywords

3D polygon modeling; extrusion; bimanual interaction; perspective-dependent gestures;

ACM Classification Keywords

H.5.m. Information Interfaces and Presentation (e.g. HCI): Miscellaneous

INTRODUCTION AND RELATED WORK

Extrusion in conventional 3D authoring tools (e.g. Blender) requires users to frequently switch modes resulting in a sequential workflow of alternating selection, extrusion, transformation as well as navigation commands. While in WIMP environments these commands are invoked by selecting menu items, applying keyboard shortcuts or operating graphical handles, multi-touch input for 3D interaction faces fundamental challenges: apart from fatigue effects, touch imprecision and occlusion issues [1], the mismatching *degree of integration* [2] has inspired different approaches for basic 3D object manipulation (e.g. [5, 4]) and navigation (e.g. [3]).

We approach these challenges by exploring indirect touch input techniques in a horizontal/vertical dual touch-display setup. In this context, we have developed a 3D polygon modeling tool called FAD (Finger-Aided Design) that includes a novel approach towards polygon extrusion. Our main design goal was to reduce activation costs [2] and encourage bimanual operation: we consider the horizontal display as a *tool*

UIST '15, November 08–11, 2015, Charlotte, NC, USA
ACM 978-1-4503-3780-9/15/11. http://dx.doi.org/10.1145/2815585.2815733

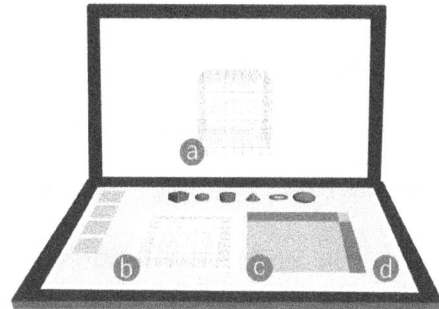

Figure 1. Our notion of the horizontal display as *tool space*: graphical input areas (b-d) with direct mappings to operations allow spatial activation and encourage two-handed interaction.

space that can display several spatially multiplexed and task-dependent UI elements and input areas with direct mappings to task functions. In our extrusion tool, the non-dominant hand controls the camera viewpoint and frames the scope of potential extrusions performed with the dominant hand using dedicated *graphical input areas* (see figure 1). Further, the spatial multiplexing also allows to operate tools simultaneously, e.g. enabling the extrusion of bent shapes through concurrent extrusion and scene navigation.

In general, we see the following benefits of our approach: (1) indirect touch improves ergonomics, precision and occlusion, (2) the spatial multiplexing of graphical input areas allows a restriction to simple one- and two-finger gestures instead of introducing complex gesture sets and (3) our design encourages but does not enforce bimanual input, allowing flexible hand/task-relationships.

PERSPECTIVE-DEPENDENT EXTRUSION WITH FAD

Figure 1 gives an overview of FAD's *tool space* for the extrusion task: (a) the scene object, (b) the polygon selection tool, (c) the extrusion touch pad, and (d) the base layer for scene navigation.

Basics. One-finger touch gestures on the base layer (d) orbit the camera around the selected object (a), two-finger pinch gestures control the zoom level.

Selecting Surfaces and Polygons. Users select a surface of the scene object on the vertical screen (a) via direct touch. Then, the *polygon selection tool* (b) displays an animated virtual camera motion towards the selected surface (point-of-interest, similar to Navidget [3]). Inside the polygon selection tool, users can select and deselect single polygons of the object by tapping and dragging.

Perspective-dependent Polygon Extrusion. Once a set of polygons of an object is selected, the selection can be extruded up, down, left or right via dragging gestures on the extrusion touch pad (c) with the dominant hand. The interpretation of the gestures depends on the orientation of the scene controlled with the non-dominant hand on the *tool space's* base layer (d).

The extrusion touch pad consists of a square area containing a horizontal and a vertical bar. Gestures within the horizontal and vertical bar extrude the selection along the respective surface normal in a constrained manner depending on the scene camera's orientation: for example, figure 2 (1) shows the interpretation of the rightward gesture in a side-view: visual feedback shows alternative selection areas on the up- and down-side of the extruded end indicating how a subsequent up- or down-ward gesture would be interpreted in the current camera orientation. The visual feed is continuously updated with the manipulation of the camera viewpoint (see figure 2 (3) to (4)).

Gestures outside the constraining bars also extrude the selection along the respective axis. However, an additional translation is applied by considering both translation deltas from the touch input. The additional translation vector is also dependent on the camera perspective and is parallel to the surface normals of the polygons contained in the alternative selections.

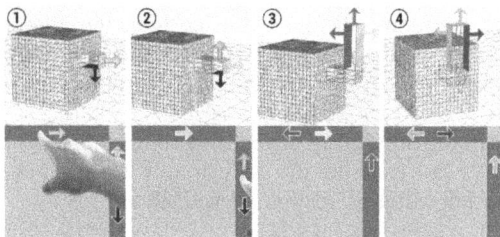

Figure 2. Extrusion workflow: arrows in the diagram indicate perspective-dependent polygon selections and the according gestures on the extrusion touch pad. (3) and (4): polygon selections flip when the view is rotated.

Implementation of the Extrusion

The extrusion logic is handled by an event handler that divides touch events on the extrusion pad in three phases: During the first phase (100 ms), touch deltas are summed up to determine the direction of the extrusion (up, down, left or right). Then, the extrusion is executed once (new geometry is created) and finally, the continuing touch input controls the translation of the newly created polygons. This results in a fluent movement, that enables users to extrude selected polygons by simple one-finger dragging gestures. Implementation details and code are made available at http://www.medien.ifi.lmu.de/fadextrusion.

After each extrusion movement and after each change of the camera viewpoint, all newly created polygons are assigned to one of the following directions: left, right, up or down. This is done by constructing local coordinate axes of the camera and calculating angles between them and the polygons' surface normals.

The initial extrusion of polygons selected in the polygon selection tool is a special case in FAD, as there are no other polygons facing in other directions that can be extruded yet. In this case, the touch input of the extrusion pad is used to insert the new geometry into the mesh and to translate the new polygons in the manner described above.

Bent Extrusion with Scene Navigation

We also explored a more integral way of extruding bent shapes compared to existing tools that allow to specify a path and then extrude along that path. Building upon the two-handed control of extrusion and navigation, our workflow allows to create bends and twists by rotating the camera with the non-dominant hand while extruding polygons with the dominant hand. Figure 3 illustrates the interaction technique: while the right hand extrudes to the left, the left hand performs a camera rotation around the object's Y-axis. During the camera movement the right hand continues the extrusion movement.

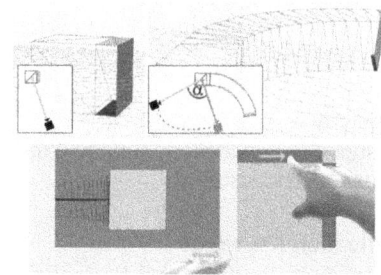

Figure 3. Creating bent shapes with simultaneous extrusion and camera control. α is the angle of camera rotation and corresponds to the sum of rotation angles of the automatically extruded polygons.

FUTURE WORK

We plan the evaluation of our technique regarding the general usability, the required learning for bimanual operation as well as its influence on the exploration of 3D shapes during modeling. Further, we will enhance our technique with the ability to immediately rotate and scale extruded polygons with two-finger gestures.

REFERENCES

1. Albinsson, P.-A., and Zhai, S. High precision touch screen interaction. In *Proc. of SIGCHI'03*, 105–112.

2. Beaudouin-Lafon, M. Instrumental interaction: An interaction model for designing post-wimp user interfaces. In *Proc. of SIGCHI'00*, 446–453.

3. Hachet, M., Decle, F., Knödel, S., and Guitton, P. Navidget for 3d interaction: Camera positioning and further uses. *Int. J. Hum.-Comput. Stud. 67*, 3 (Mar. 2009), 225–236.

4. Hancock, M., Carpendale, S., and Cockburn, A. Shallow-depth 3d interaction: Design and evaluation of one-, two- and three-touch techniques. In *Proc. of CHI'07*, 1147–1156.

5. Reisman, J. L., Davidson, P. L., and Han, J. Y. A screen-space formulation for 2d and 3d direct manipulation. In *Proc. of UIST '09*, 69–78.

FoldMecha: Design for Linkage-Based Paper Toys

Hyunjoo Oh
ATLAS Institute
University of Colorado Boulder
430 UCB, Boulder, CO 80309
hyunjoo.oh@colorado.edu

Mark D. Gross
ATLAS, Computer Science
University of Colorado Boulder
430 UCB, Boulder, CO 80309
mdgross@colorado.edu

Michael Eisenberg
Computer Science
University of Colorado Boulder
430 UCB, Boulder, CO 80309
duck@cs.colorado.edu

ABSTRACT
We present *FoldMecha*, a computational tool to help non-experts design and build paper mechanical toys. By customizing templates a user can experiment with basic mechanisms, design their own model, print and cut out a folding net to construct the toy. We used the tool to build two kinds of paper automata models: walkers and flowers.

Author Keywords
Computational design tool; papercraft; paper automata

ACM Classification Keywords
H.5.m. Information interfaces and presentation (e.g., HCI): Miscellaneous.

INTRODUCTION AND RELATED WORK
Papercraft invites a diverse range of people to investigate art, craft and mechanics through hands-on making in varied forms. One example is a paper mechanical automaton toy–a field that itself has a long history [3]. Whereas many earlier automata models are associated with the history of clockwork and timepieces, contemporary models tend to be employed as a kinetic art medium (e.g. Cabaret Mechanical Theatre: http://www.cabaret.co.uk) or a playful learning medium. Because building a moving craft artifact encourages the acquisition of skills in mechanical construction, handcraft, and storytelling, it has been used as a popular educational medium for children. Rob Ives (http://www.robives.com) books and website invite educators and children to download printed kits, for example, the "Flying Pig".

To efficiently design a paper automaton model, one must understand fundamental structures whereby mechanisms and physical forms combine to generate a movement. Here, inspired by Theo Jansen's Strandbeest (http://www.strandbeest.com/) and Matthew Gardiner's

Oribotics (http://www.oribotics.net/), we set out to make paper walkers and flowers–a linkage-based walking mechanism and an opening and closing mechanism. A mechanical linkage is an assembly of connected bodies to manage movement. Within linkage-based mechanisms, we wanted to experiment with changing the dimensions and proportions of mechanisms, but we found that each variation required a tedious process of trial-and-error. Therefore we built a parametrized simulator to visualize designs and their behavior.

Computational tools to unfold virtual modeling to assist building physical papercraft [2, 5] and designing and fabricating mechanical characters have been built. In [6] users design automata by selecting from a parameterized set of mechanisms. In [1] users design and fabricate mechanical characters based on a motion library to identify appropriate mechanisms. ChaCra [4] supports rapid crafting of planar mechanical characters. We likewise support designing and building animatronics but focus on modeling part not mechanism.

Our system, FoldMecha, helps novice designers experiment with diverse forms, design their own models, and construct the physical prototype through the system-generated folding net (see Figure 1). We describe our use of this tool in building a paper walker and a paper flower.

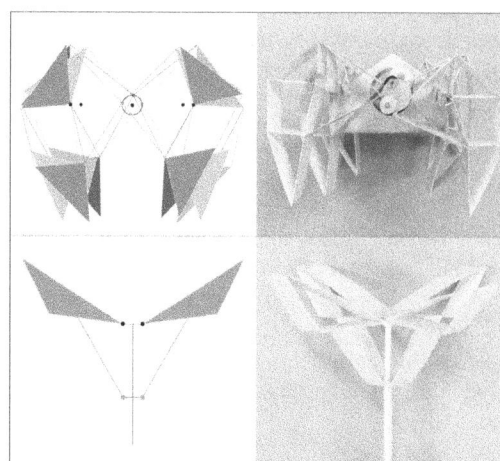

Figure 1. Simulation of the mechanical structures in FoldMecha (left) and paper prototypes via the folding nets generated by the system (right)

UIST '15 Adjunct, November 08-11, 2015, Charlotte, NC, USA
ACM 978-1-4503-3780-9/15/11.
http://dx.doi.org/10.1145/2815585.2815734

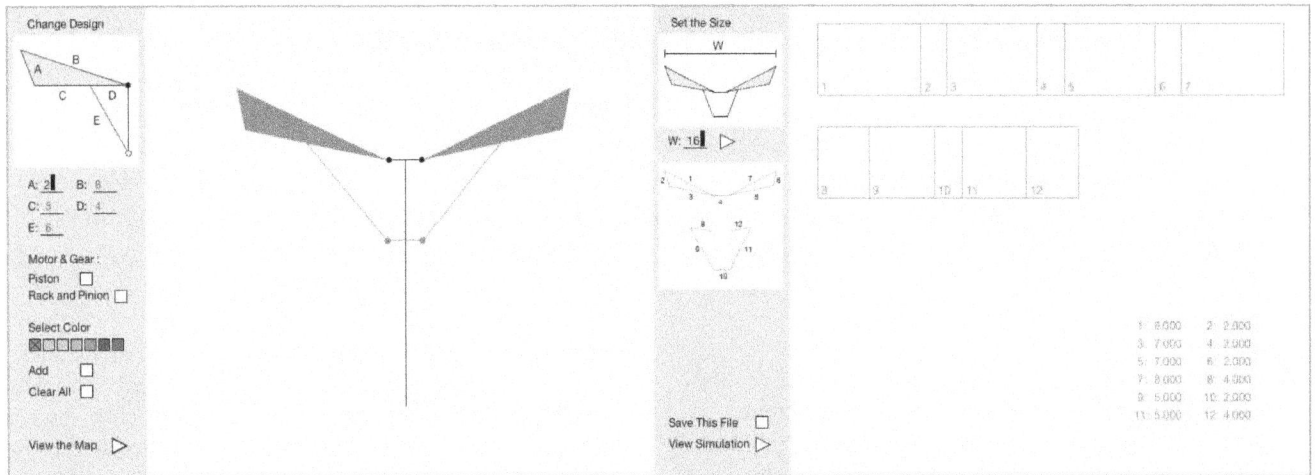

Figure 2. Sequential screen snapshots of FoldMecha: a user can design a model with the simulation and select a mechanism to apply (left), then download the folding net as a PDF format to print, cut, and build the paper model (right).

FOLDMECHA: COMPUTATIONAL DESIGN SYSTEM FOR LINKAGE-BASED PAPER AUTOMATA

Figure 2 shows sequential screen snapshots of FoldMecha simulating the opening and closing of a paper flower. Along with animating mechanisms integrated with forms, FoldMecha supports additional functions for hands-on learning and designing.

A user begins with a default model to see how the mechanism works. Then the user modifies key design parameters (top left panel) and observes how this changes the movement. The simulation helps users understand how form and mechanical behavior are integrated and enables them to design their own working models by varying template parameters. After setting the design parameters, a user selects a mechanism (in building flowers: either "Rack and Pinion" or "Piston") to generate the movement, and then "View the Map" navigates to the next page, which displays folding nets of the parts in the selected color with default dimensions. The default size is 15-16 cm, but one can scale the width; the software changes the dimensions on the screen accordingly. The user can save and print the file in a PDF format, and build models by following the folding instruction on the left panel.

Customization using templates

Building a device with mechanical movement requires accurate structures, which in turn requires understanding both the physical forms and the mechanisms. Designing different models, not from scratch but by modifying parameters in a template, can lower the entry bar for novice users. Simple interactions—entering parameters, selecting colors, adding models, etc.—support users customizing the "look and feel" of a variety of forms within the working structure.

Simplified prototyping with paper strips

We simplified the design and construction process to support novices to reduce trial-and-error. Our system generates paper folding nets as paper strips with marked folding locations; after cutting, users fold the strips following the printed instructions to build the design.

FUTURE WORK

We plan to add other models for users to create and build a wide spectrum of mechanical toys. With FoldMecha we aim to lower the entry bar and to extend the design space of paper craft automata.

ACKNOWLEDGMENTS

This material is based upon work supported by the National Science Foundation under Grant No. IS1451463.

REFERENCES

1. Coros, S.; Thomaszewski, B.; Noris, G.; Sueda, S.; Forberg, M.; Sumner, R. W.; Matusik, W.; and Bickel, B. 2013. Computational design of mechanical characters. *ACM Trans. Graph.* 32: 4, Article 83 (July 2013), 12 pages.

2. Eisenberg, M. and Nishioka, A, 1997. Creating polyhedral models by computer. *J. Comput. Math. Sci. Teach.* 16, 4 (November 1997), 477-511.

3. Hiller, M. (1988) Automata and Mechanical Toys. London: Bloomsbury Books

4. Megaro, V.; Thomaszewski, B.; Gauge, D.; Grinspun, E.; Coros, S.; and Gross, M. 2014. Chacra: An Interactive Design System for Rapid Character Crafting.

5. Mitani, M. and Suzuki, H. 2004. Making papercraft toys from meshes using strip-based approximate unfolding. *ACM Transactions on Graphics* 23:3 (August 2004), 259-263.

6. Zhu, L.; Xu, W.; Snyder, J.; Liu, Y.; Wang, G.; and Guo, B. 2012. Motion-guided mechanical toy modeling. *ACM Trans. Graph.* 31, 6, Article 127 (November 2012), 10 pages.

Juggling the Effects of Latency: Software Approaches to Minimizing Latency in Dynamic Projector-Camera Systems

Jarrod Knibbe[1,2], Hrvoje Benko[1], Andrew D. Wilson[1]

[1] Microsoft Research, Redmond, USA
{benko,awilson}@microsoft.com

[2] University of Bristol, UK
Jarrod.Knibbe@bristol.ac.uk

Figure 1. The Juggling Display; projection alignment on fast-moving objects through software-based latency reduction.

ABSTRACT

Projector-camera (pro-cam) systems afford a wide range of interactive possibilities, combining both natural and mixed-reality 3D interaction. However, the latency inherent within these systems can cause the projection to 'slip' from any moving target, so pro-cam systems have typically shied away from truly dynamic scenarios. We explore software-only techniques to reduce latency; considering the best achievable results with widely adopted commodity devices (e.g. 30Hz depth cameras and 60Hz projectors). We achieve 50% projection alignment on objects in free flight (a 34% improvement) and 69% alignment on dynamic human movement (a 40% improvement).

Author Keywords

Projector-camera systems; latency; prediction

INTRODUCTION

Latency in projector-camera (pro-cam) systems can easily result in projection 'slipping' from a moving target. As a result of this, the use of pro-cams in truly active scenarios has been avoided. Previous work exploring latency reduction has primarily focused on advanced hardware-based approaches (e.g. [5]). This approach is at odds with the lightweight, commodity-hardware based development style favored by both the research and enthusiast communities (i.e. 30Hz depth-cameras with 60Hz projectors, as in [1, 6] for example). We explore software only approaches to latency reduction that can be applied to

UIST '15 Adjunct, November 08-11, 2015, Charlotte, NC, USA
ACM 978-1-4503-3780-9/15/11.
http://dx.doi.org/10.1145/2815585.2815735

any hardware configuration, in order to facilitate pro-cam usage in dynamic settings. We report on a preliminary investigation of projection on both objects under free flight and on-the-body of fast moving users.

RELATED WORK

Pro-cam systems have long been a popular tool for the HCI community (e.g. [1, 6]). However, latency is a problem for the experience; constraining movement speeds [6] or resulting in image misalignment, as can be seen in the video for [1]. As a result of latency effects, research has considered hardware-based solutions, such as high-speed cameras [5] and multi-camera setups [4]. For example, Lumospheres projects on balls in free flight [4]. Using 6 cameras operating at 120Hz, Lumospheres tracks and predicts the balls' future position. With this technique, Lumospheres achieves on-object projection in all frames, with 80% projection accuracy. We employ similar principles using only one commodity 30Hz depth-camera to explore achievable projection accuracy.

Other works have considered software-based motion modelling across a range of domains, such as projectile motion in sports tracking [3]. We draw upon this as one further motivation for our work.

MOTION PREDICTION FOR LATENCY REDUCTION

In order to reduce the effects of latency and increase projection alignment we use motion prediction to model and calculate the future states of objects (similarly to [4].)

In our work we consider two different scenarios for latency reduction. In the first, we explore *projection on objects under free flight*. In the second, we explore *projection on bodies in dynamic motion*. Our system uses a Kinect camera, a commodity 60Hz projector and a Windows 7 laptop. We measured the latency of 9 different projectors when paired with a 30Hz Kinect and calculated an average latency of 102.5ms (+/- 6ms std. dev). Alongside latency effects, other sources of projection slip also exist in pro-cam systems, such as camera calibration errors and rolling shutter effects (see [2] for a discussion) and pro-cam synchronization errors.

Objects in Free Flight – Predictable Motion

We developed a *Juggling Display*. In standard 3 ball juggling the balls can easily exceed 4m/s, resulting in 40cm of projection slip given ~100ms of system latency. At the zenith of the ball's flight, as speeds decrease, fleeting alignment occurs, resulting in only ~14% of the balls' flight being illuminated without latency correction.

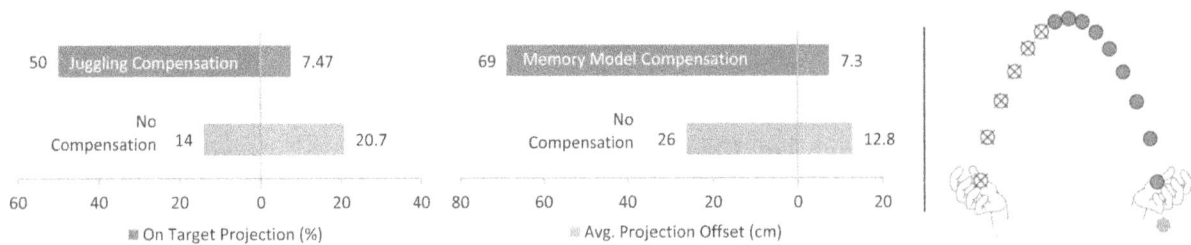

Figure 2. Left: Objects in free flight evaluation results. Mid: On-body projection evaluation results. Right: Blue balls indicate frames available for projection alignment (after Kalman filter initialization, 3 frames, and 100ms prediction step, 3 frames).

As the balls' location at any time during flight can be calculated based on a set of physical laws, we term this *Predictable Motion*. We fit a projectile motion model to a Kalman filter to smooth our tracking values (from the depth camera) and predict the balls location into the future (to account for latency). We specify low values for process noise, but high uncertainty for observation (to account for the rolling shutter and calibration inaccuracy in our camera).

Preliminary Evaluation

Three jugglers performed 'standard' 3-ball cascade juggling for 2 minutes under no latency correction (condition 1) and full latency correction (condition 2). The juggler's used softballs (9.7cm diameter) and stood 2.5m from the pro-cam unit. We provide 2 accuracy measurements; average projection offset captured automatically using image processing, and a binary projection 'aligned vs. missed' measure based on all frames with an estimated >10% projection alignment.

With no latency correction, we found that 14% of balls in flight are projected upon and that the average projection offset is 20.7cm (Figure 2). With latency correction, we achieve 50% projection accuracy and an average offset of 7.47cm.

On-body Projection – Semi-Predictable Motion

Human motion includes a wide range of patterns and repetition, for example in walking, dancing and athletic performance (e.g. the basic performance of different shots in tennis) [7], thus we term this *Semi-Predictable Motion*.

In order to predict bodily motion, we train a motion lookup model based on a person's previous movements. After a brief training window (20secs), our lookup model can take into account the intricacies of personal performance, such as acceleration patterns, maximal reach and personal style. The performer's ongoing movement details continue to further train the model for ongoing prediction.

Preliminary Evaluation

Three participants performed up-down and circular hand movements at 1.5m/s, as guided by the system. Each participant performed each movement for 15s. A 10cm graphic was projected onto the hand's location, as tracked through the Kinect Skeletal tracker.

With no latency correction, only 26.3% of projected frames fall on target (with an average offset of 12.8cm.) With our motion model approach, 69% of frames fell on target, with an average offset of 7.3cm.

DISCUSSION AND CONCLUSION

At 50% alignment for objects in free-flight and 69% alignment for on-body projection, our results demonstrate an improvement in projection alignment of 34% and 40% respectively. These results are constrained by a couple of key challenges. Firstly, a Kalman filter requires a few frames of data to initialize and smooth sensor values, and combined with a prediction step of 100ms (per system latency), this results in approximately 6 or 7 frames of missed projection in a 15 frame ball flight (observed average) – suggesting an achievable maximum of 60% with our approach. We are keen to explore further machine learning techniques to reduce the initial missed frames and increase the achievable maximum projection. Secondly, at 4m/s a juggling ball travels 13.2cm between (non-linearly sampled) camera frames and measures only 22 pixels across in camera space (at 2.5m) – resulting in position measurement noise that detracts from projection alignment. Similarly in the on-body scenario, at speeds greater than 1m/s the Kinect skeletal tracker becomes increasingly inaccurate, effecting our on-body projection alignment.

When combined with the effects of visual motion blur, we believe our results are compelling and we encourage the reader to view our associated video. Although these results still fall short of the projection accuracy achievable through hardware augmentation (such as an estimated average offset of 2.91cm, derived from [4]), we believe they form a good launch point for further exploration in this area and hope this will motivate further work on software-only approaches to latency reduction.

REFERENCES

1. Harrison, C. et al. OmniTouch: Wearable Multitouch Interaction Everywhere. *UIST '11*, ACM (2011).
2. Khoshelham, K. Accuracy analysis of kinect depth data, in archive of ISPRS, (2011), 133–138.
3. Kitani, K. et al. BallCam!: Dynamic View Synthesis from Spinning Cameras. *UIST Adjunct '12*, ACM (2012), 87–88.
4. Koike, H. et al. LumoSpheres: Real-time Tracking of Flying Objects and Image Projection for a Volumetric Display. *AH '15*, ACM (2015), 93–96.
5. Okumura, K. et al. Lumipen: Projection-Based Mixed Reality for Dynamic Objects. (2012), 699–704.
6. Sodhi, R. et al. LightGuide: Projected Visualizations for Hand Movement Guidance. *CHI '12*, ACM (2012).
7. Coupled Oscillators and Biological Synchronization. http://www.scientificamerican.com/article/coupled-oscillators-and-biological/.

Color Sommelier

KyoungHee Son, Seo Young Oh, Yongkwan Kim, Hayan Choi, Seok-Hyung Bae, Ganguk Hwang[*]

Department of Industrial Design & Department of Mathematical Sciences[*], KAIST

kyounghee.son | seoyoung.oh | yongkwan.kim | hayan.choi | seokhyung.bae | guhwang @ kaist.ac.kr

ABSTRACT

We present Color Sommelier, an interactive color recommendation system based on community-generated color palettes that helps users to choose harmonious colors on the fly. We used an item-based collaborative filtering technique with Adobe Color CC palettes in order to take advantage of their ratings that reflect the general public's color harmony preferences. Every time a user chooses a color(s), Color Sommelier calculates how harmonious each of the remaining colors is with the chosen color(s). This interactive recommendation enables users to choose colors iteratively until they are satisfied. To illustrate the usefulness of the algorithm, we implemented a coloring application with a specially designed color chooser. With the chooser, users can intuitively recognize the harmony score of each color based on its bubble size and use the recommendations at their discretion. The Color Sommelier algorithm is flexible enough to be applicable to any color chooser in any software package and is easy to implement.

Author Keywords

Interactive color recommendation; collaborative filtering.

INTRODUCTION

With the emergence of various types of digital authoring software, even non-designers have become able to produce digital content in daily life, such as documents and presentation slides. When authoring digital content, they often need to choose colors, which significantly influence to the resulting quality. However, for most people with insufficient knowledge and experience regarding color theory, it is not an easy task to choose harmonious colors that will produce a pleasing affective response [1].

To ease this situation, online communities such as Color CC (formerly Kuler) and COLOURLovers have emerged. In such communities, users generate, share, and rate color palettes. Color palettes with high ratings can be considered harmonious, qualified by the preferences of the general public.

However, users still have difficulties in applying color palettes from such communities to their work at hand. They have to explore a vast set of color palettes and decide on one even before starting their work. They are also challenged when trying to add more colors to a chosen palette with a fixed number of colors (typically 5) and to make partial changes to the palette, inevitably resulting in harmony degradation.

Thus, we present *Color Sommelier*, an interactive color recommendation system based on community-generated color palettes (Figure 1). Color Sommelier enables users to easily choose harmonious colors for their workflow at their discretion, while utilizing the online community's collective knowledge of color harmony.

Figure 1. A screenshot of an interactive coloring application with a color chooser implementing Color Sommelier.

COLOR RECOMMENDATION ALGORITHM

In order to recommend harmonious colors, we paid attention to algorithms that are frequently used by e-commerce web sites such as Amazon.com to recommend products to each customer. However, we did not aim at personalized preference modeling that they commonly use because modeling the inexperienced color-choosing schemes of non-experts would reproduce similar unskilled results. Thus, instead of modeling general *user-item* relations [4], we set up qualified *color-palette* relations in order to recommend harmonious colors to both non-experts and experts.

Our algorithm consists of color-palette relation prediction and interactive recommendation. In the prediction stage, we first built a sparse color-palette matrix with community ratings of palettes, each of which composed of only 5 colors. We then estimated all unknown color-palette relations using collaborative filtering. In the recommendation stage, for user-selected colors, Color Sommelier calculates the harmony scores of the remaining colors in real time based on the pre-calculated full color-palette matrix.

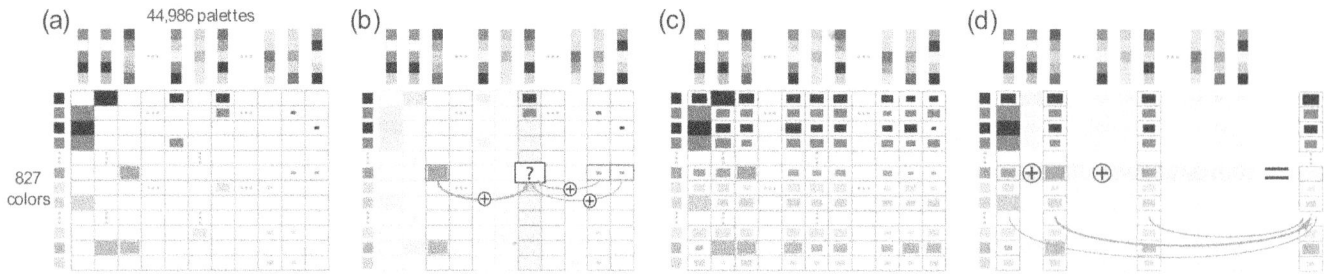

Figure 2. Conceptual overview of the Color Sommelier algorithm: (a) an initial sparse color-palette matrix built from quantized Color CC palettes, (b) prediction of color-palette relations using collaborative filtering, (c) the resulting full matrix, and (d) calculation of the harmony scores of the remaining colors for a chosen color (highlighted).

Predicting Color-Palette Relation by Collaborative Filtering

We used the 44,986 Color CC palettes with their community ratings, which were publicized by O'Donovan and Hertzmann [3]. We first discretized color space into a finite number of color buckets (we chose 827 for our color chooser implemented in Figure 1, right) evenly distributed in the perceptually uniform $CIEL^*a^*b^*$ color space ($\Delta L^*=\Delta a^*=\Delta b^*=10$). We then set up a color-palette matrix (827×44,986 in our case) in which each row corresponds to a color, each column to a palette, and each element to the community rating of each palette (Figure 2a). Because a Color CC palette has 5 colors, each column initially has only 5 non-empty elements.

To fill empty elements of the matrix, we used an item-based collaborative filtering technique [5]. For the value of an empty element of a column, which implies how much the corresponding color is harmonious with the corresponding palette, we calculated the weighted average of the non-empty elements on the same rows of other palettes (Figure 2b), where the weight of each palette is determined by how much it is similar to the given palette having the empty element of interest. We defined palette similarity as the inverse of palette distance, a root mean squared $CIEL^*a^*b^*$ distance between two palettes with the closest-first matched color pairs. After it completes the matrix (Figure 2c), Color Sommelier is ready to make a recommendation.

Interactive Recommendation with Color-Palette Matrix

When a user chooses a color, Color Sommelier calculates the harmony score of each of the remaining colors that matches the chosen color (Figure 2d) from the matrix. The harmony scores are calculated by weighted averaging column vectors, where the weight of each column is the rating of the chosen color within that column. If multiple colors are chosen, the weight is the sum of the ratings. Each time the user chooses different color(s), Color Sommelier updates the harmony scores. This interactive recommendation enables users to iteratively choose colors until they are satisfied.

INTERACTIVE COLORING APPLICATION

To show the usefulness of Color Sommelier, we built a coloring application (Figure 1). A user picks a color on the color chooser on the right, and applies the color to the outlined image on the left by clicking an area to fill. Used colors are added to the user palette at the bottom for later use.

The user can reuse one of them by clicking on it in the palette, and remove one from the palette by flicking it away.

For the coloring application, we designed a special color chooser similar to Microsoft's hexagonal color chooser [2] to help users see all colors at a glance without having to navigate 3D color space, allowing them to find their desired colors quickly (Figure 1, right). We split chromatic colors into six hue groups and located each on a triangular area of the hexagonal grid in such a way that lightness decreases radially. We positioned grays separately under the hexagon.

Our color chooser provides an unobtrusive recommendation; the more harmonious a color is with a chosen color(s), the bigger the bubble that is displayed (Figure 1, right). Users can intuitively recognize a recommendation and use it at their discretion (they may even ignore it).

CONCLUSION AND FUTURE WORK

In this paper, we suggested a novel method of interactive color recommendation utilizing collective knowledge on color harmony. The Color Sommelier algorithm is flexible enough to be applicable to any color chooser in any software and is easy to implement. We look forward to seeing Color Sommelier help users orchestrate color harmony in a wide range of application areas that go beyond drawing and coloring, including creating documents and charts.

ACKNOWLEDGEMENT

This project was supported by Brain Korea 21 Plus and the National Research Foundation of Korea (2011-0014806).

REFERENCES

1. Burchett, K. E. (2002). Color harmony. *Color Research & Application*, 27(1), 28-31.
2. Busch, B., Ho, R., Keller, M., Ruescher, H., Wilfrid, E., & Harris, C. (1999). *U.S. Patent No. 5,903,255.* Washington, DC: U.S. Patent and Trademark Office.
3. O'Donovan, P., & Hertzmann, A. (2011). Color compatibility from large datasets. In *Proc. SIGGRAPH '11*.
4. O'Donovan, P., Agarwala, A., & Hertzmann, A. (2014). Collaborative filtering of color aesthetics. In *Proc. CAe '14*, 33–40.
5. Sarwar, B., Karypis, G., Konstan, J., & Riedl, J. (2001). Item-based collaborative filtering recommendation algorithms. In *Proc. WWW '01*, 285-295.

AirFlip-Undo: Quick Undo using a Double Crossing In-Air Gesture in Hover Zone

Keigo Shima, Ryosuke Takada, Kazusa Onishi, Takuya Adachi, Buntarou Shizuki, Jiro Tanaka
University of Tsukuba, Japan
Tennoudai 1-1-1, Tsukuba, Ibaraki, Japan 305-8571
{keigo,rtakada,onishi,adachi,shizuki,jiro}@iplab.cs.tsukuba.ac.jp

ABSTRACT

In this work, we use AirFlip to undo text input on mobile touchscreen devices. AirFlip involves a quick double crossing in-air gesture in the boundary surfaces of hover zone of devices that have hover sensing capability. To evaluate the effectiveness of undoing text input with AirFlip, we implemented two QWERTY soft keyboards (AirFlip keyboard and Typical keyboard). With these keyboards, we conducted a user study to investigate the users' workload and to collect subjective opinions. The results show that there is no significant difference in workload between keyboards.

Author Keywords

In-air gesture; hover gesture; touch panel; double crossing gesture; one handed.

ACM Classification Keywords

H.5.2. Information Interfaces and Presentation (e.g. HCI): Interaction styles; Input devices and strategies.

INTRODUCTION

Hover sensing capability is available on several smartphones and provides richer interaction. For example, it allows users to unlock a pattern lock without touching the touchscreen of their smartphone. Users can do so securely because fingerprints are not left on the touchscreen. In our previous work, we used this capability to design a quick double crossing in-air gesture for mobile devices, called AirFlip [2]. We have applied AirFlip to rotating a map in map applications and switching tabs in Web browsers. In this paper, we apply Air-Flip to undoing text input. In addition, we investigated users' workload and collected subjective opinions on this application as a preliminary user study.

AIRFLIP

AirFlip is a quick double crossing gesture made within the boundary surfaces of the hover zone AirFlip is performed

UIST '15 Adjunct, November 08-11, 2015, Charlotte, NC, USA
ACM 978-1-4503-3780-9/15/11.
http://dx.doi.org/10.1145/2815585.2815737

only with the thumb of the hand holding the smartphone. Figure 1 shows how to use AirFlip. Users move their thumb into the hover zone from the side and then move it out of the zone quickly.

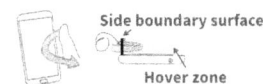

Figure 1. Overview of AirFlip.

While in-air gestures currently available on mobile devices with hover sensing capability require keeping or moving the finger within the hover zone, AirFlip utilizes motion that crosses the boundary surfaces of the hover zone. To avoid conflict with these existing operations, finger movement that satisfies two conditions is recognized as AirFlip: 1) The moving distance of a users' finger in the hover zone is 300 pixels and over; and 2) The hovering time of users' finger in the hover zone is between 350 ms and 1000 ms. In this paper, we apply AirFlip to undoing text input. We call this gesture AirFlip-Undo. Figure 2 shows a use case. Suppose that a user was going to type "just like it says on the can good," but has typed "just like it sdys" (Figure 2a). In this case, she must undo the typing of "sdys" (Figure 2b) and type "says" (Figure 2c). AirFlip-Undo allows her to do this with only five controls, i.e., one AirFlip-Undo and typing "s," "a," "y," and "s," while using the conventional backspace key requires six controls, i.e., pressing the backspace key three times to delete "s," "y," and "d," and typing "a," "y," and "d."

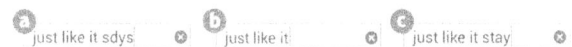

Figure 2. Modifying text input by using AirFlip-Undo. a: Wrong text. b: Undo typing of "sdys." c: Typing correct text.

PRELIMINARY USER STUDY

To evaluate AirFlip-Undo, we conducted a user study to investigate the users' workload and to collect subjective opinions on AirFlip-Undo.

Participants and Apparatus

The participants were eight volunteer university undergraduates/graduates (21-24 years old, $M = 21.75$). Everyone used a smartphone on a daily basis. They had been using mobile devices for 14 to 73 months ($M = 45.25$) The study was conducted on a Galaxy S4 SC-04E (Android 4.2.2, 5-inch screen, 1920 px × 1080 px resolution). For comparison, we implemented two QWERTY soft keyboards (AirFlip keyboard and

Typical keyboard). AirFlip-Undo was implemented on only AirFlip keyboard. While the participants' fingers were within the hover zone, AirFlip keyboard vibrated the smartphone to provide feedback. Before the task started, each participant was free to practice with AirFlip keyboard until becaming familiar with AirFlip-Undo.

Task

Each participant used Google Web Search to search phrases that were presented by the experimenter. A trial of the task involved searching a phrase chosen at random from a set of 500 phrases that MacKenzie et al. [4] chose. A session consisted of five trials. Each participant carried out five sessions in succession for each keyboard. In total, the participants conducted 50 trials (5 trials × 5 sessions × 2 keyboards). The participants took a break for one minute between sessions. To counterbalance, four participants (P1–P4) used AirFlip keyboard first; the others (P5–P8) used Typical keyboard first. Each time the five sessions were completed, the participants filled out a NASA-TLX [3] questionnaire. We used a Japanese version of NASA-TLX [1] because all participants were Japanese. After the experiment, the participants filled out a questionnaire used to collect opinions on AirFlip-Undo. The experiment took about 70 minutes per participant, including the prior explanation and answering the questionnaires.

Results and Discussion

Figure 3 shows the NASA-TLX score. Table 1 shows the mean of the weights given for the six NASA-TLX scales. Those shown in the table are the averaged results of the eight participants.

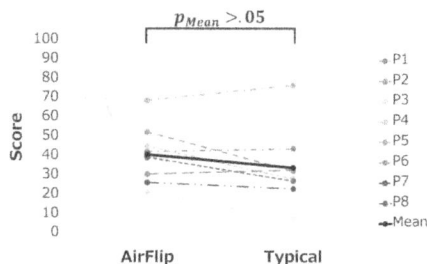

Figure 3. NASA-TLX scores.

	AirFlip keyboard	Typical keyboard	p
Mental Demand (MD)	3.00 (1.12)	3.25 (0.97)	0.56
Physical Demand (PD)	2.38 (1.58)	2.13 (1.27)	0.68
Temporal Demand (TD)	1.88 (1.27)	2.13 (1.76)	0.71
Own Performance (OP)	2.38 (0.99)	2.38 (1.49)	1
Effort (EF)	2.50 (1.94)	2.38 (1.73)	0.78
Frustration (FR)	2.88 (2.09)	2.75 (2.05)	0.84

Table 1. Weights given for six NASA-TLX scales (0–5 scale, low to high). Results in table are averaged results of the eight participants.

According to Table 1, the score of AirFlip keyboard was higher than that of Typical keyboard for three fields: Physical Demand (PD), Effort (EF), and Frustration (FR). Each result is due to the following reasons. First, the PD of AirFlip was higher because the participants were not familiar with AirFlip. Moreover, the participants using AirFlip had to move their thumb outside of the hover zone once, i.e., requiring the participants to move their thumb exaggerated motion, thus it increased the participants' load. Second, the EF

of AirFlip was higher because AirFlip is an in-air gesture. The participants using AirFlip had to move their thumb in the hover zone without touching the display. Therefore, the participants had to be careful not to touch the display. Finally, the FR of AirFlip was higher because the vibrational feedback produced by AirFlip was too strong. That is, while a participants' thumb was in the hover zone, AirFlip keyboard kept vibrating the smartphone to provide feedback, frustrating the participants'. In the participants' opinions, P1 and P2 commented, "I was bothered by the smartphone continuing to vibrate." P6 and P8 commented, "I felt my hand was tired." Therefore, it is necessary to redesign the feedback in the future. In comparison, the score of AirFlip was lower than that of Typical for two fields: Mental Demand (MD) and Temporal Demand (TD). The opinions supported this result. P1, P2, and P8 commented, "AirFlip is intuitive." P3, P4, and P5 commented, "AirFlip may be quick." From these opinions, redesigning the feedback would make AirFlip a gesture that can be performed naturally.

While the score of AirFlip keyboard was higher, as shown in Figure 3, there was no significant difference between the two keyboards' workload. In other words, although the AirFlip keyboard was frustrating because of the vibration feedback, using AirFlip to undo typing may be useful for users. As a hint for future improvement, one opinion we got was "I want visual feedback" from P4. Therefore, we plan to design visual feedback as well as redesign haptic feedback.

CONCLUSION

We showed AirFlip-Undo, which uses AirFlip to undo text input on mobile touchscreen devices. The results of our user study showed that there was no significant difference between the workloads with AirFlip keyboard and with Typical keyboard. For future work, we plan to design visual feedback as well as to redesign haptic feedback in order to lower the workload of AirFlip-Undo. Furthermore, we also plan to implement undo–possible applications with AirFlip other than those that use text input.

REFERENCES

1. Haga, S., and Mizugami, N. Japanese version of NASA Task Load Index: Sensitivity of its workload score to difficulty of three different laboratory tasks. *The Japanese journal of ergonomics 32*, 2 (1996), 71–79. (in Japanese).

2. Hakoda, H., Kuribara, T., Shima, K., Shizuki, B., and Tanaka, J. AirFlip: A double crossing in-air gesture using boundary surfaces of hover zone for mobile devices. In *Proceedings of the 17th international conference on Human-computer interaction*, HCII '15 (2015). (to appear).

3. Hart, S. G., and Staveland, L. E. Development of NASA-TLX (Task Load Index): Results of Empirical and Theoretical Research. In *Human Mental Workload*, vol. 52. North-Holland, 1988, 139 – 183.

4. MacKenzie, I. S., and Soukoreff, R. W. Phrase sets for evaluating text entry techniques. In *CHI EA '03* (2003), 754–755.

Remot-IO: a System for Reaching into the Environment of a Remote Collaborator

Xavier Benavides *
MIT Media Lab
Cambridge, USA
xavib@media.mit.edu

Judith Amores *
MIT Media Lab
Cambridge, USA
amores@media.mit.edu

Pattie Maes
MIT Media Lab
Cambridge, USA
pattie@media.mit.edu

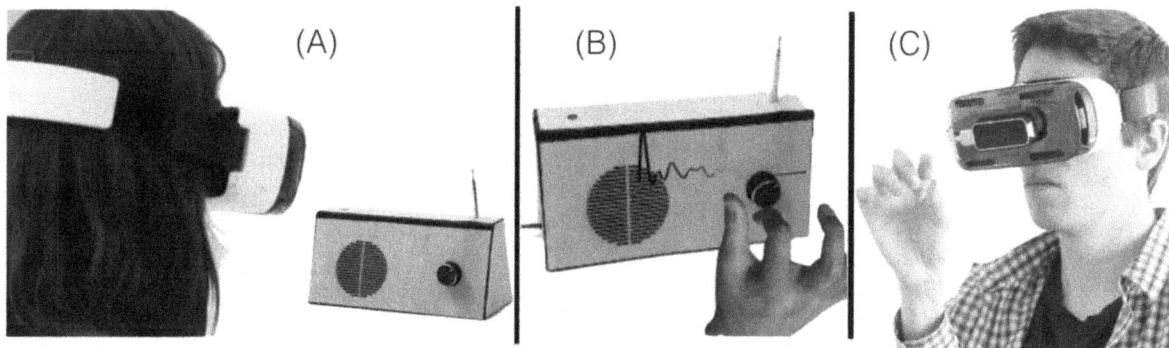

Figure 1. A novice user (A) shares her point of view and can see (B) the overlaid virtual real-time hand gestures of the remote expert and visualize, interact and modify properties of sound waves in real time by using hand gestures. The expert can remotely control the knobs and buttons of the radio and thus change the behavior of the radio using commonly used gestures (C).

ABSTRACT

In this paper we present Remot-IO, a system for mobile collaboration and remote assistance around Internet connected devices. The system uses two Head Mounted Displays, cameras and depth sensors to enable a remote expert to be immersed in a local user's point of view and control devices in that user's environment. The remote expert can provide guidance through the use of hand gestures that appear in real-time in the local user's field of view as superimposed 3D hands. In addition, the remote expert is able to operate devices in the novice's environment and bring about physical changes by using the same hand gestures the novice would use. We describe a smart radio where the knobs of the radio can be controlled by local and remote user alike. Moreover, the user can visualize, interact and modify properties of sound waves in real time by using intuitive hand gestures.

Author Keywords

Remote collaboration; Shared experiences; Telepresence;

UIST '15 Adjunct, November 08-11, 2015, Charlotte, NC, USA
ACM 978-1-4503-3780-9/15/11.
http://dx.doi.org/10.1145/2815585.2815738

3D interaction; Augmented reality; Hands free Interaction.

ACM Classification Keywords

H.5.2 [Information Interfaces and Presentation]: User Interfaces - Training, help, and documentation;

INTRODUCTION

In the last 10 years, commercial teleconferencing systems such as Skype or Google Hangout have been increasingly used to enable communication with people that are in distant locations. Improvements in telecommunications technology have made it possible to collaborate with peers at a distance using cheap and widely available technology. However, these technologies do not support physical co-presence in the task domain and remote physical actions are not possible: a user can show a remote collaborator their environment but that collaborator cannot point at things in this environment let alone make changes or perform physical actions. For example, if a user needs help operating a device, they can call a remote expert, but the expert can only talk the user through fixing the problem, they cannot directly act upon the device.

The emergence of connected, "Internet of Things" objects and devices (IoT) makes it possible for a remote expert to do so. The Remot-IO system makes it possible for the remote expert to "reach" their hands across the Internet into the environment of the user who needs help so as to point and gesture at things as well as make actual changes to that environment simply by making hand gestures. We believe

* Both authors contributed equally to this work.

that Internet of Things technology can fill the gap between remote distance and physical presence through remotely controlled Internet devices.

However many phenomena of our smart environments are invisible for our visual sense, examples ranging from temperature, electromagnetic waves, pollution to audio and physical laws. This project visualizes hidden physical properties of the environment and allows the user to be immersed in another perception of the world, where the auditory sense and the visual sense are merged. We created a system that lets the user interact with and modify properties of sound waves in real time. We explore the usage of head mounted displays in combination with Internet connected devices in the context of a physical remote collaboration (Figure 1). We thereby enhance the possibilities of augmenting daily physical objects to visualize hidden information, enabling the user to form a better understanding of certain concepts and phenomena.

SYSTEM DESCRIPTION
The Remot-IO prototype consists of two HMDs that are connected via Wi-Fi and are used by a remote expert and a novice user respectively. Both users are immersed in the *novice's* field of view by sharing the video feed of the camera that is embedded in the *novice's* HMD (Figure 1A). The hands of the *expert* are tracked with a depth sensor and superimposed in real-time in the *novice* user's environment (Figure 1B). Both of them can see the *novice's* hands in the novice's environment as well as the virtual representation of the *expert* user's hands.

We also created a do-it-yourself radio to allow the user to investigate sound waves, radio frequencies and in general the physics behind sound. The system visualizes in real time the sound data that is collected through a network of sensors placed in the environment. We use augmented reality technology in order to recognize the pattern of the radio and display the hidden data. Moreover, the design of the radio includes a remotely controllable knob that can be either operated by the physical hand of the novice user as well as by the virtual hand of the remote user. The *expert* user can modify the behavior of the remotely located radio by performing hand gestures such as tuning the volume of the radio by placing the hand over the knob and performing a rotation gesture with the fingers. Once the system detects such a gesture, the knob button will physically move and turn according to the virtual hand gesture.

RELATED WORK
Some notable projects are inTouch [1], which is a system that creates the illusion that two people, separated by distance, are interacting within the same physical environment. Another project by Brave et al [2] presents a new approach to enhance remote collaboration based on touch and physicality. Physical Telepresence [3] presents a shape display as a shared workspace for remote collaboration. ShowMe [4] is a collaborative system where

the users wear HMDs and can communicate with one another using 2-handed gestures and voice. BeThere [5] explores the use of 3D gestures and remote spatial input without any type of HMD.

Remot-IO differs from previous work by (1) providing a portable solution using HMDs, (2) enabling the devices users collaborate around to be operated locally as well as remotely using the same gestures, (3) creating the feeling of physical co-presence by the remote user acting as a ghost and finally (4) supporting free, natural hand gestures for remote interaction with devices.

POSSIBLE APPLICATIONS
The Remot-IO system is especially useful for applications involving remote maintenance and repair. For example, a remote expert could train or assist a novice user in how to operate a complex industrial machine. Both of them wear the system so the remote user can show to the novice operator how to manipulate the smart machine.

The Remot-IO system could also be used for telepresence applications. The novice's HMD could be mounted on a tele-operated robot which would enable a user to move around a remote space and interact with things such as light switches. The local user, if any, will see a change in the light level and would see the physical position of the switch change.

The system could also support experiential learning about certain physics phenomena through observation and hands-on experimentation.

CONCLUSION
This paper describes Remot-IO, an immersive platform that uses videoconferencing, 3D hand gestures and IoT technology to offer a solution for remote collaboration around smart devices with physical interfaces that can be operated locally as well as remotely using hand gestures.

REFERENCES
1. Brave, S., & Dahley, A.. inTouch: a medium for haptic interpersonal communication. In CHI'97 EA (pp. 363-364). ACM.

2. Brave, S., Ishii, H., & Dahley, A.. Tangible interfaces for remote collaboration and communication. In Proc. of the CSCW 1998 ACM (pp. 169-178). ACM.

3. Leithinger, D., Follmer, S., Olwal, A., & Ishii, H.. Physical telepresence: shape capture and display for embodied, computer-mediated remote collaboration. In Proc. of UIST 2014 (pp. 461-470). ACM.

4. Amores, J., Benavides, X., & Maes, P.. ShowMe: A Remote Collaboration System that Supports Immersive Gestural Communication. In Proc. of CHI 2015 EA (pp. 1343-1348). ACM.

5. Sodhi, R. S., Jones, B. R., Forsyth, D., Bailey, B. P., & Maiocci, G. BeThere: 3D mobile collaboration with spatial input. In Proc. of CHI 2013 (pp. 179-188). ACM

Daemo: a Self-Governed Crowdsourcing Marketplace

Stanford Crowd Research Collective *
Stanford HCI Group
daemo@cs.stanford.edu

ABSTRACT

Crowdsourcing marketplaces provide opportunities for autonomous and collaborative professional work as well as social engagement. However, in these marketplaces, workers feel disrespected due to unreasonable rejections and low payments, whereas requesters do not trust the results they receive. The lack of trust and uneven distribution of power among workers and requesters have raised serious concerns about sustainability of these marketplaces. To address the challenges of trust and power, this paper introduces Daemo, a self-governed crowdsourcing marketplace. We propose a *prototype task* to improve the work quality and *open-governance model* to achieve equitable representation. We envisage Daemo will enable workers to build sustainable careers and provide requesters with timely, quality labor for their businesses.

Author Keywords

crowdsourcing; crowd research; crowd work.

ACM Classification Keywords

H.5.3. Group and Organization Interfaces: Computer-supported cooperative work

INTRODUCTION

Paid crowdsourcing marketplaces such as Mechanical Turk and Upwork have created opportunities for workers to supplement their income and enhance their skills, while allowing requesters to get their work completed efficiently. These marketplaces have attracted many participants globally; however, they have repeatedly failed to ensure high-quality results, fair

* This project was created via a world-wide, crowdsourced research process initiated at Stanford University: S. Gaikwad, D. Morina, R. Nistala, M. Agarwal, A. Cossette, R. Bhanu, S. Savage, V. Narwal, K. Rajpal, J. Regino, A. Mithal, A. Ginzberg, A. Nath, K. R. Ziulkoski, T. Cossette, D. Gamage, A. Richmond-Fuller, R. Suzuki, J. Herrejon, K. V. Le, C. Flores-Saviaga, H. Thilakarathne, K. Gupta, W. Dai, A. Sastry, S. Goyal, T. Rajapakshe, N. Abolhassani, A. Xie, A. Reyes, S. Ingle, V. Jaramillo, M.D. Godinez, W. Angel, M. Godinez, C. Toxtli, J. Flores, A. Gupta, V. Sethia, D. Padilla, K. Milland, K. Setyadi, N. Wajirasena, M. Batagoda, R. Cruz, J. Damon, D. Nekkanti, T. Sarma, M.H. Saleh, G. Gongora-Svartzman, S. Bateni, G. Toledo-Barrera, A. Pena, R. Compton, D. Aariff, L. Palacios, M. P. Ritter, Nisha K.K., A. Kay, J. Uhrmeister, S. Nistala, M. Esfahani, E. Bakiu, C. Diemert, L. Matsumoto, M. Singh, V. Jaramillo-Lopez, K. Patel, R. Krishna, G. Kovacs, R. Vaish, M. Bernstein

UIST '15 Adjunct, November 08-11, 2015, Charlotte, NC, USA.
ACM 978-1-4503-3780-9/15/11
http://dx.doi.org/10.1145/2815585.2815739

Figure 1. Task creation workflow for a requester: prototype task creation, initial submissions review, and hiring high quality workers for future milestones. [https://daemo.stanford.edu].
Icon courtesy Font Awesome by Dave Gandy - http://fontawesome.io

wages, respect for workers, and convenience in authoring effective tasks [1].

From our interviews with requesters, it has become clear that they struggle to trust their workers. They will rerun tasks, discard gathered data, and add increasingly complex worker filters. On the other hand, workers do not trust requesters to follow through with pay and fair treatment. In response, workers often withhold their full effort unless they have an experience with the requester.

Moreover, existing marketplaces suffer from uneven distributions of power [4]. For example, requesters have the power to deny payments for finished tasks and workers have inadequate means to contest this. Operational governance and rules have been secondary considerations on markets thus far, fitted to support the focus on the commoditizing of work. This resulted in an asymmetrical relationship between workers, requesters, and the marketplace on fronts such as parity of information access, wage negotiation, and reputation. A common complaint [3]: "We can be rejected yet the requesters still have our articles and sentences. Not Fair."

We present Daemo, a crowd-built, self-governed crowdsourcing marketplace. To increase trust, we introduce the idea of *prototype tasks*, where each new task must first launch in an intermediate feedback mode where workers can comment on the task, requesters can review the submissions and qualify a subset of workers to continue. During this phase, workers and requesters work together to refine the task description and reduce errors. Daemo also adopts a representative democratic governance model to elect a leadership board. Engaging all vested parties in the governance of the marketplace gives an opportunity to create genuine worker-requester relationships and redefine the future of work.

RELATED WORK

Feedback, wages, task decomposition, and quality control are some of the fundamental elements of a successful crowdsourcing marketplace [1]. Requesters often rely on "gold standard" tasks, i.e., questions with known answers, to evaluate the performance and quality of submissions [2]. However, this tends to still place all blame on workers rather than letting requesters share it for poor task interface design. Several venues such as Turker Nation and Dynamo Forums have been created so that workers' opinion can be heard [3, 4]. However, these venues are still outside the marketplaces, isolated from the requesters' reach. Daemo aims to embed an open-governance structure as a part of the platform's design.

DAEMO

Promoting Trust and Power in Tasks

Daemo tackles issues of trust and power by giving requesters a low-risk method for testing task quality and workers' abilities. Daemo divides all tasks into milestones. A task can have one or many milestones. For instance, a macrotask of "make a poster" could have a first milestone of "sketch the poster's layout". Or, with a microtask of labeling 1,000 images, the first milestone might be to have three workers label ten images. By executing early milestones, workers and requesters can build common ground and adjust the task description. This avoids having workers "run away" to do large amounts of work before realizing it was unnecessary, as they had not agreed on the specifics or covered all edge cases. It also facilitates discussing cost and time to do a job. Daemo requires that each task begin with a short milestone, a *prototype task*. This prototype task is a small percentage of tasks for microtasks, and a first step toward the larger goal for macrotasks. Through the prototype task, requesters can: (1) identify the most suitable workers for their task; (2) be assured that workers understand the task; and (3) directly discuss with workers how the task might be improved.

Open Governance

While the mechanisms of crowd work have evolved, the asymmetrical power dynamics of workers and employers remained unchanged. Daemo addresses the power imbalance and mitigates the inherent trust issues by introducing a representative democratic governance model that elects a leadership board composed of three workers, three requesters, and a researcher. This leadership board is empowered to make policy decisions for the platform. Including all vested parties in the governance of the platform provides an opportunity for idea transfer, transparent communication, and engagement in platform direction.

Over the course of a three-week period, we conducted an experiment within our large research cohort to rapidly prototype three organizational models to guide Daemos design and development: representative democracy, participatory democracy, and weighted democracy (participatory democracy with each vote weighted by participants' reputation within the system). The researchers within the project represent a diverse population from 26 countries with ages ranging from 17 to 48. We sought to assess various aspects of the models including: communication and responsiveness, participation levels, ease of bringing an idea to execution and transparency of information and process. We captured overall participation including unique number of participants, total voting volume,

sentiment regarding each model's effectiveness in instilling trust and power, as well as number of executed ideas. The leadership board election generated 255 votes (206 to elect representative, 49 on ideas), 31 ideas offered, and 2 actions; participatory democracy generated 52 votes, 33 ideas offered, and 1 action; weighted democracy generated 19 votes, 16 ideas offered and 0 actions. Despite possible temporal or novelty effects, the effects are quite strong. Post experiment survey results indicated that 64% of respondents identified the leadership board as the desired approach, supplemented by an open platform for idea submission and a central leadership board to facilitate research, decision, and execution of submitted ideas.

FUTURE USABILITY EVALUATION PLAN

We plan to evaluate our proposed model by recruiting requesters and workers to exercise our system. A crucial aspect of our prototype task model is that we have added an option for a feedback textbox to the task creation module. This should facilitate worker and requester collaboration towards improved task descriptions. In addition, by having workers and requesters interact early in the process, worker selection should be improved, and we anticipate increased trust between the two parties. We will test the usability of our task workflows using heuristic evaluation and direct observation. We have already performed some preliminary tests on the task creation workflow. Our subjects found some parts of the task formulation to be confusing. In the future, we will add more instructions to guide the user as they create the task.

FUTURE WORK AND CONCLUSION

Daemo envisions a future of crowd work that is built around trust rather than antagonism. We have no illusions that requesters and workers will stop maximizing their individual utility; however, we believe that targeted contributions in task design, reputation, and representation can lead users to assume better of each other, rather than markets for lemons. Our next step is to create incentive-compatible reputation systems, such that ratings become more informative (and so that not every requester and worker has 95% approval and 4.75 stars). Ultimately, we aim to inspire current crowd marketplaces to adopt alternative visions, or achieve a foothold ourselves in the crowd work ecosystem. We believe that we can achieve improved task quality and fairness with our augmented task workflow and an open governance model.

REFERENCES

1. Kittur, A., et al. The future of crowd work. In *Proc. CSCW 2013*. 2013.

2. Le, J., Edmonds, A., Hester, V., and Biewald, L. Ensuring quality in crowdsourced search relevance evaluation. In *SIGIR workshop on crowdsourcing for search eval.* 2010.

3. Martin, D., Hanrahan, B.V., O'Neill, J., and Gupta, N. Being a turker. In *Proc. CSCW 2014*. 2014.

4. Salehi, N., et al. We are dynamo: Overcoming stalling and friction in collective action for crowd workers. In *Proc. CHI 2015*. 2015.

MagPad: A Near Surface Augmented Reading System for Physical Paper and Smartphone Coupling

Ding Xu[1], Ali Momeni[1], Eric Brockmeyer[2]

[1] Carnegie Mellon University
5000 Forbes Avenue, Pittsburgh, PA 15213
dx@andrew.cmu.edu, momeni@cmu.edu

[2] Disney Research Pittsburgh
4720 Forbes Avenue, Pittsburgh, PA 15213
eric.brockmeyer@disneyresearch.com

Figure 1. A hybrid ensembles of smartphone and paper document for augmented reading. (a) spinning magnets frame and system arrangement; (b) the smartphone shows occluded content; (c) a user read reference by clicking on a citation

ABSTRACT
In this paper, we present a novel near surface augmented reading system that brings digital content to physical papers. Our system allows a collocated mobile phone to provide augmented content based on its position on top of paper. Our system utilizes built-in magnetometer of a smartphone together with six constantly spinning magnets that generate designed patterns of magnetic flux, to detect 2D location of phone and render dynamic interactive content on the smartphone screen. The proposed technique could be implemented on most of mobile platforms without external sensing hardware.

Author Keywords
Augmented reading, Smart lens, Active magnetic sensing

ACM Classification Keywords
H.5.1 Artificial, augmented, and virtual realities; H.5.2 User Interfaces - Input devices and strategies.

INTRODUCTION
Paper and mobile devices both have their advantages for reading. Physical paper offers spatial arrangement, tangibility and affordance [1-3]. It also provides a good mental representation for comprehension and memory [4]. In contrast, mobile devices excel at providing dynamic

UIST'15 Adjunct, November 8–11, 2015, Charlotte, NC, USA.
ACM 978-1-4503-3780-9/15/11.
DOI: http://dx.doi.org/10.1145/2815585.2815740

multimedia content, allowing vast storage and easy sharing; but have limitations on screen size and display resolution [2-3].

Paper and mobile devices are used in parallel in different scenarios and sometimes are complementary to each other. Research shows that close distance between smartphone and reading documents is preferred in order to create a joint focus zone in such hybrid ensembles [7]. However, most prior augmented reading systems employ computer vision technologies that require a smartphone to be some distance above the paper document in order for its camera to capture a good image [2-3], a limitation that was identified in [5]. We focus on coupling physical documents and digital content together through interactions that do not require hovering the smartphone above the paper document, in order to lower switch time between physical and digital content and to facilitate a more focused reading experience.

We propose MagPad: a near-surface interaction system of augmented reading for physical paper and smartphone coupling. The MagPad employs an optical metaphor where a lens displays the content it frames but also reveals additional information. In our system, the smartphone shows the physical content it occludes on the screen, but also responds to users' input, layers additional digital content, or directs the user to related information. Our proposed interaction shortens the time required to switch from one medium to another; reduces physical handling efforts; and provides a location-based content rendering in effort to overcome the limited screen size of smartphones.

IMPLEMENTATION
We proposed a low cost active magnetic sensing technique to predict 2D location of a smartphone using spinning magnets based on the idea proposed in [6]. Our system is comprised of a physical frame that sits beneath the paper

document and contains six DC motors around its perimeter (Figure 1a). Each DC motor spins a permanent magnet at a predefined frequency (3.5Hz, 6Hz, 8Hz, 10Hz, 12.5Hz and 15Hz) held constant with a Hall effect sensor-based feedback control system. Each spinning magnet generates a periodic sinusoidal magnetic flux throughout the reading area. As the mobile phone is moved around the reading area, the amplitude of each frequency band indicates the distance between the corresponding magnet and the smartphone.

A smartphone app samples the phone's magnetometer at 100Hz and streams the data to a laptop using the OpenSoundControl protocol [8] for signal processing and location recognition. FFT analysis of this data (128 samples, Blackman window) extracts spectral information about the magnetic flux. We construct our feature vectors from the energy in the first 32 bands of the FFT, along with statistical analysis of the FFT data (band ratio, mean, variance, maximum band amplitude and index, kurtosis). We train a SVM classifier to first predict the current quadrant (i.e. top-left, top-right, bottom-left, bottom-right); subsequently, two SVM regression models are trained and loaded to predict x and y location within the quadrant.

Finally, we use a photo or existing digital version of the physical document to dynamically render the corresponding part of the content on-screen and at scale once smartphone's location is updated (Figure 1b).

APPLICATION

References reading for academic paper
In this application, we combine the tactility, legibility and spatial arrangement of paper documents with a smartphone's ability to present dynamic content. We focus on providing extended content based on references section of an academic paper. When a user moves a smartphone over the reference section and clicks on a citation, the application displays corresponding PDF on screen (Figure 1b, 1c). This application offers an efficient way to present relevant digital content next to physical document for hybrid reading.

Translation
In this application we focus on scenarios where only physical version of document is available. A photo of physical page is captured, analyzed using optical character recognition and scaled to generate a digital version before reading. When a user comes across unfamiliar words or sentences while reading the physical text, the smartphone can be placed on that area and act as a prompt translator for selected words or sentences on screen (Figure 2a).

Social annotation
In this application we focus on collaborative social annotation (Figure 2b) where the users is able to discover, read and contribute to text annotations stored in the cloud for a given document. The smartphone is used as a digital

layer to show or hide public comments by placing or removing smartphone on certain position. This enables users to read physical document but save annotations digitally and in the cloud.

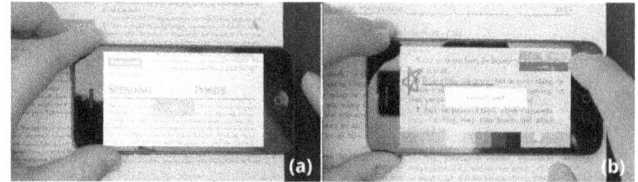

Figure 2. Demo applications (a) translation (b) social annotation

CONCLUSION
In this paper, we proposed a low cost technology and three applications for a near surface augmented reading system pairing physical documents with a smartphone. Our proposed interaction shortens the distance and lowers the switch time between physical text and digital content, and provides a responsive content display based on mobile device's location. As the development of context aware sensing technologies, we believe our system can bring much potential of bridging digital services to our physical reading with new interactions.

REFERENCES
1. Sellen, A.J. and R.H.R. Harper, The Myth of the Paperless Office. 1st ed. 2001: MIT press

2. Liao, Chunyuan, et al. Pacer: fine-grained interactive paper via camera-touch hybrid gestures on a cell phone. Proceedings of the SIGCHI Conference on Human Factors in Computing Systems. ACM, 2010.

3. Erol, Berna, Emilio Antúnez, and Jonathan J. Hull. HOTPAPER: multimedia interaction with paper using mobile phones. Proceedings of the 16th ACM international conference on Multimedia. ACM, 2008.

4. Jabr, Ferris. The reading brain in the digital age: The science of paper versus screens. Scientific American, 11 2013.

5. Sang-won Leigh, Philipp Schoessler, Felix Heibeck, Pattie Maes, and Hiroshi Ishii. THAW: Tangible Interaction with See-Through Augmentation for Smartphones on Computer Screens, TEI2015, 2015.

6. Bianchi, Andrea, and Ian Oakley. MagnID: Tracking Multiple Magnetic Tokens. Proceedings of the Ninth International Conference on Tangible, Embedded, and Embodied Interaction. ACM, 2015.

7. Heinrichs, Felix, et al. Toward a theory of interaction in mobile paper-digital ensembles. Proceedings of the SIGCHI Conference on Human Factors in Computing Systems. ACM, 2012.

8. Wright, Matthew. Open sound control 1.0 specification. Published by the Center For New Music and Audio Technology (CNMAT), UC Berkeley, 2002.

Adding Body Motion and Intonation to Instant Messaging with Animated Text

Weston Gaylord
Stanford University
Stanford, CA 94305, USA
wag@stanford.edu

Vivian Hare
Stanford University
Stanford, CA 94305, USA
vhare@stanford.edu

Ashley Ngu
Stanford University
Stanford, CA 94305, USA
ashngu@stanford.edu

ABSTRACT

Digital text communication (DTC) has transformed the way people communicate. Static typographical cues like emoticons, punctuation, letter case, and word lengthening (ie. Hellooo") are regularly employed to convey intonation and affect. However, DTC platforms like instant messaging still suffer from a lack of nonverbal communication cues. This paper introduces an Animated Text Instant Messenger (ATIM), which uses text animations to add another distinct layer of cues to existing plaintext. ATIM builds upon previous research by using kinetic typography in communication. This paper describes the design principles and features of ATIM and discusses how animated text can add more nuanced communication cues of intonation and body motion.

Author Keywords

Kinetic typography; Instant messaging; Animation; Intonation; Body Motion

ACM Classification Keywords

H.5.2. [Information interfaces and presentation]: Miscellaneous

INTRODUCTION

As a text-based medium, instant messaging suffers from a lack of nonverbal cues. Face-to-face communication is rich with vocal nonverbal cues such as inflection, tone, pitch, volume, and rate of speech, as well as non-vocal, nonverbal cues such as posture, facial expression, gestures, personal space, and touch [2]. The digital medium opens up possibilities for novel text-based communication, including the use of kinetic effects. ATIM uses kinetic animation in order to better express nonverbal cues like intonation (pitch and timing) and body motion. To be effective, the sender's animated cues must be perceived and understood by the receiver [2].

ATIM is a messaging system that enables users to send and receive animated text that is integrated into the chat log. Animations are provided for three trigger keywords: "okay," "yes," and "no." This paper presents the three design

UIST '15 Adjunct, November 08-11, 2015, Charlotte, NC, USA
ACM 978-1-4503-3780-9/15/11.
http://dx.doi.org/10.1145/2815585.2815741

principles from which we created the system: legibility, simplicity, and visibility. We also discuss the usefulness of ATIM using preliminary study results.

Past research has shown that kinetic typography can consistently convey emotion, while some animations are more strongly tied to specific emotions [1][4]. Past efforts to incorporate kinetic effects into instant messaging focused on motion typography of entire statements, with emphasis on changing the location of the word [1][1]. Because the animated words are translated significantly in a 2D space, these systems require playback windows separate from the plaintext chat logs [1][1]. ATIM presents a chat system with integrated inline animations, using kinetic effects which transform and distort single words.

SYSTEM DESIGN

Three principles inform the interface design (see Figure 1):

Legibility: Instant messaging requires rapid interpretation of received messages. In contrast to static text, the length of an animation dictates the time a recipient spends reading a word. ATIM is designed to make accurate interpretation of texts faster than previous instant messengers using animation. Previous interfaces typically had two windows: one for the plaintext chat log and another for playing a animation sequence one at a time [1][1]. ATIM integrates animations into the existing chat log and loops them automatically instead of requiring user effort. ATIM's animations were designed to occur inline without significant translation or expansion outside of the bounds of regular text lines.

Simplicity: Users sending messages need to quickly and easily select animations. ATIM suggests predefined animations: the user is restricted to picking an available option rather than customizing or creating their own.

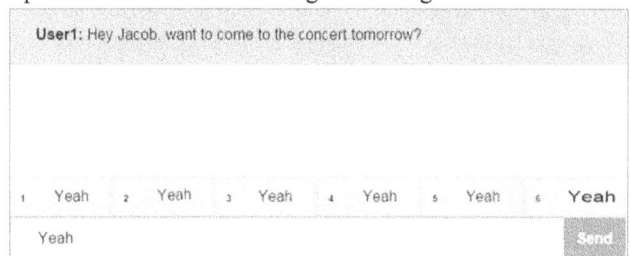

Figure 1. ATIM interface showing animation options for "Yeah." Users can type a number to select and send a message with the specified animation or click the animation. A video of ATIM is at: http://bit.ly/1Ge7Hsq

Visibility: In most messaging interfaces, emoticons are accessible through a button which brings up the emoticon library. Occasionally, emoticons will also automatically replace typed character emoticon equivalents, such as :) becoming a smiley-face emoticon. ATIM uses regular expressions to trigger the animation suggestions every time an equivalent of "okay," "yes," or "no" is typed. When animation suggestions are present, the user can easily type a number corresponding to one of six animations to send the message with the appropriate animation.

We focused on the trigger keywords "okay," "yes," and "no" because these are among the most common sentence words used in chat communication, and they often lack nuance.

Each of the trigger keywords can be animated with one of six suggestions pulled from a library of nine unique animations. The animations were designed to occur inline in accordance with the legibility design principle. The basic instant messenger functionality of ATIM is developed using Socket.io and Node.js. CSS is used for animating the text.

PRELIMINARY RESULTS AND DISCUSSION

To evaluate the effectiveness of ATIM as a system for conveying intonation and body motion, we recruited 20 users for a two-part study:

First, the transcript testing evaluated how users inferred emotional meaning from animated text. Users read three animated or non-animated chat transcripts with the intonation they believed was appropriate while we recorded, verbally labeled each of the keywords with an emotion, and explained their reasoning. Users who read transcripts with animated text were consistently more nuanced and expressive in their readings. A lightly bouncing "okay" in one transcript was described by various users as "enthusiastic acknowledgment," "accepting in a positive way," "lighthearted," "eager" and "casually affirmative" while the control users described the plaintext "okay" as "unexcited" and "just acknowledgment."

When asked to read example chat transcripts, users interpreted many animations to have specific intonation, and sometimes body motion. A "No" moving back and forth from left to right was perceived as someone shaking their head while saying "No" and some users shook their heads and mimicked the animation while reading the word. A horizontal stretching "NOO" was loudly vocalized with exaggerated dramatics. The evaluations of our control group, who read the plaintext transcripts, had less emotional variation in their descriptions of emotionally ambiguous answers. One user described the plaintext transcripts as being very "transactional." Plaintext words were frequently perceived to be said without excitement.

Animated transcript tagging resulted in fewer "neutral" classifications than the control group, suggesting that ATIM

successfully provides emotional context to previously ambiguous messages.

We can also draw a conclusion about the helpfulness of gestural vs. inflectional animations. Overall, half of the animations represented emotion through visualization of vocal inflection, and the other half represented emotion through visualization of bodily gestures like bouncing, trembling, or head-shaking. In the experimental transcript-tagging, the animations which received the most consensus were those that were gestural, representing emotion through visualization of bodily gestures like bouncing, trembling, or head-shaking. Users also reported clearer understanding of the gestural animations. This is likely because gestural animations translate a visual gesture into a visual movement, whereas inflectional animations translate auditory qualities into visual movement, which is a fundamentally more subjective translation.

Second, the scenario testing evaluated how users chose animations to communicate different emotions. Users were given six hypothetical chat scenarios and asked to choose the animation they would use to reply with. Results indicate that selecting an appropriate animation is more subjective than interpreting provided animations because there was less agreement among users in scenario testing than transcript testing.

Text animations provide an opportunity to communicate with more visible nuance than static text, but comprehension of messages is dependent on sender and recipient having a mutual understanding of the other's written style. In this way, incorporating text animations into your digital text communications is akin to expanding messaging vocabulary-- new words are only helpful if the recipient also understands their definitions.

This paper demonstrates the value of animated text in adding intonation and body motion cues in instant messaging. Future work should define a set of animations optimized to maximize range of expressivity and minimize ambiguity of meaning, perhaps by focusing on gestural rather than inflectional animation.

REFERENCES
1. Bodine, K., & Pignol, M. (2003). Kinetic Typography-Based Instant Messaging. *CHI 2003*.
2. Ford, S., Forlizzi, J., & Ishizaki, S. (1997). Kinetic Typography: Issues in time-based presentation of text. *CHI 97*, 22-27.
3. Lee, J., Jun, S., Jodi, F., & Hudson, S. (2006). Using Kinetic Typography to Convey Emotion in Text-Based Interpersonal Communication. *CHI 2006*.
4. Malik, S., Aitken, J., & Kelly, J. (2009). Communicating emotion with animated text. *Visual Communication, 8*(4), 469-479.
5. Tubbs, S., & Moss, S. (2006). *Human communication: Principles and contexts*. New York, NY: McGraw Hill.

Author Index

www.ingramcontent.com/pod-product-compliance
Lightning Source LLC
Chambersburg PA
CBHW081546220326

41598CB00036B/6584